The Kidney
and the Cane

CRITICAL GLOBAL HEALTH: Evidence, Efficacy, Ethnography
A series edited by Vincanne Adams and João Biehl

The Kidney
and the Cane

*Planetary Health and
Plantation Labor in Nicaragua*

ALEX M. NADING

Duke University Press   *Durham and London*   2025

Project Editor: Michael Trudeau
Designed by Courtney Leigh Richardson
Typeset in Garamond Premier Pro by Westchester Publishing Services

Library of Congress Cataloging-in-Publication Data
Names: Nading, Alexander M., III, 1979– author.
Title: The kidney and the cane : planetary health and plantation labor in
Nicaragua / Alex M. Nading.
Other titles: Critical global health.
Description: Durham : Duke University Press, 2025. | Series: Critical
global health | Includes bibliographical references and index. Identifiers:
LCCN 2024041594 (print)
LCCN 2024041595 (ebook)
ISBN 9781478031871 (paperback)
ISBN 9781478028666 (hardcover)
ISBN 9781478060864 (ebook)
ISBN 9781478094302 (ebook other)
Subjects: LCSH: Sugarcane industry—Environmental aspects—
Nicaragua. | Sugar workers—Health and hygiene—Nicaragua. |
Kidneys—Diseases—Risk factors—Nicaragua. | Chronic diseases—Risk
factors—Nicaragua. | Sugarcane—Climatic factors—Nicaragua.
Classification: LCC HD9114.N52 N35 2025 (print)
LCC HD9114. N52 (ebook)
DDC 331.25/6097285—dc23/eng/20250217
LC record available at https://lccn.loc.gov/2024041594
LC ebook record available at https://lccn.loc.gov/2024041595

Cover art: Sugar mill workers, Chichigalpa, Nicaragua. 2012. AP Photo/
Esteban Felix.

Publication of this open monograph was the result of Cornell University's
participation in TOME (Toward an Open Monograph Ecosystem), a collaboration of the Association of American Universities, the Association
of University Presses, and the Association of Research Libraries. TOME
aims to expand the reach of long-form humanities and social science
scholarship including digital scholarship. Additionally, the program looks
to ensure the sustainability of university press monograph publishing by
supporting the highest quality scholarship and promoting a new ecology
of scholarly publishing in which authors' institutions bear the publication
costs.

Funding from Cornell University made it possible to open this publication
to the world.

Contents

Note on Words, Names, and Places

This book, like all ethnographic works, is about real people and places, and events that happened not too long ago. One common convention in such works is to give pseudonyms to the people, and sometimes the places, described. Some of the reasons for this are ethical. Almost no one ever asks to be the subject of an anthropological study; the issues at play remain politically fraught; and revealing precise identities and locations could put innocent people at unnecessary risk. Other reasons are intellectual. In anthropological scholarship, as opposed to journalism or historiography, what matters are the things that can be generalized from specific contexts, which means that often, the specifics can be less important than the big takeaways.

With the exception of public officeholders or scientists who are regularly quoted or publicly profiled in the press, I have chosen to provide pseudonyms or otherwise obscure the identities of the individuals whose stories constitute this book. And although the names I give to villages and communities in the book are drawn from those of actual places in Nicaragua and within the environs of the Montelimar plantation, I have altered them to protect the identities of the people I describe. The majority of the direct quotations drawn from interviews or conversations were either recorded with participants' informed oral consent or reproduced from written notes I took at the time, also with the oral consent of those present. When I attended public events, I recorded when permission was granted by the organizers but otherwise took handwritten notes. Since nearly all these events, conversations, and interviews were originally in Spanish, and since I was the only person with access to the notes and recordings, any errors in translation or transcription are mine.

The names of Nicaraguan sugarcane plantations, and of the community organizations that raised questions about environmental and labor conditions on them, are real. One reason for this is that when it comes to the social movements I describe in the book, many of the facts, names, and even points of dispute were already part of publicly accessible records, news accounts, or peer-reviewed scientific articles before I began my research. Another is that the corporations themselves have, since the start of my research, embraced an industry-wide move toward transparency in addressing the uncertain health effects of sugarcane production. In the case of the Montelimar Corporation, whose workers and former workers are the main subjects of this book, managers were informed of my presence on company land and in meetings of community organizations about the conditions there. I am grateful for the corporation's willingness to be so accommodating, and even though I know that some readers may not agree with every conclusion I make, I have tried to represent both the company and the people in the surrounding community fairly and accurately in these pages. Again, any factual errors are my own.

From the beginning of this project, I felt I had no choice but to position myself alongside rural Nicaraguans living in the sugarcane zone as an engaged observer, rather than as a detached or neutral one. The stories I tell in this book, then, come with a definite point of view. Even though this is primarily a book about the community that surrounds a sugarcane operation and not any particular sugar corporation's managerial or organizational structure, I believe there are lessons in what follows not just for anthropologists or health scholars but also for those, including the corporations named herein, who are interested in ensuring the welfare of those who continue to make a living in and through the sugarcane industry.

Prologue

LIVES WORTH SUPPORTING

In 2015, two statements were published about environmental health crises. One was written by a group of twenty-two experts from global power centers including London, New York, New Delhi, and Beijing. The other was written by the representatives of a fledgling grassroots community movement in rural Nicaragua. One uses the crisp technical languages of economics, public health, and ecology. The other oscillates between the stilted prose of international law and the morally charged poetry of social suffering. One contains page after page, footnote after footnote, and graph after graph, illustrating the planetary-scale dangers posed by climate change. The other contains modest testimony to environmental and bodily harm in one particular place. Both statements contain lots of bullet points. One list of bullet points outlines a comprehensive strategy for sustaining life on a planet soon to be home to nine billion people. Another list outlines a set of politely worded suggestions about how those in corporate and political power might begin to consider the lives of a few hundred people.

The first of these statements was a blockbuster, at least in global public health terms. Published in November 2015, "Safeguarding Human Health in the Anthropocene Epoch," the report of the Rockefeller Foundation–*Lancet* Commission on Planetary Health, has been cited more than two thousand times. The Rockefeller-*Lancet* report is the result of a painstaking meta-analysis of environmental and epidemiological research. Among other things, it blames unchecked agricultural intensification for the loss of human and animal habitats, the erosion of soils, toxic chemical exposure, and (even though agricultural intensification was meant to produce more food) a rise in food insecurity worldwide.[1] Action must be taken, the report's coauthors suggest, to reimagine global health as *planetary health*, an approach premised on "the understanding that human health and human civilization depend on flourishing natural systems and the wise stewardship of those systems." Though it is written in the sober and apolitical language of sustainability and economics, the Rockefeller-*Lancet* report acknowledges that poverty and inequality remain serious impediments to both human and environmental flourishing. It advocates policies that create a "safe and just operating space for humanity."[2]

The other statement is decidedly more obscure. Its title, "Complaint of CFI Project 32253," doesn't help. It was published in August 2015, just three months prior to the release of the Rockefeller-*Lancet* report, on the website of a little-known office of the World Bank called the Compliance Advisor Ombudsman (CAO). The complaint was filed in the name of a group of around seven hundred rural Nicaraguan people who identified as "workers, former works [*sic*], residents and members of the communities belonging to the Montelimar Sugar Mill." Project 32253 was the title of a loan given to the Montelimar Corporation by the International Finance Corporation (IFC), the private lending arm of the World Bank Group.[3]

The Montelimar complaint is not a sprawling document. It runs to just seven pages, but it specifies how the unchecked push for agriculturally fueled economic growth damages lives and landscapes, causing a loss of water and forest resources, deterioration of soils, and chronic exposure to toxic chemical pesticides. For the Nicaraguan people who filed the complaint, the most distressing consequence of sugarcane production was the onset of an epidemic of chronic kidney disease. While chronic kidney disease is normally associated with diabetes or hypertension, by 2015, thousands of workers and residents living around the Montelimar sugar mill had become sick or died of what became known as chronic kidney disease of nontraditional causes (CKDnt). They were neither diabetic nor hypertensive. They suspected that the CKDnt epidemic was a result of their proximity to the industrial sugarcane industry. Based on this suspicion, residents formed a community association "to respond to the crisis of health and environment, and to develop viable measures to restrict it." "All of us," the complaint states, "have the right to a dignified life in a healthy environment."[4]

To me, that last turn of phrase is more satisfying than the Rockefeller-*Lancet* report's call for "a safe and just operating space for humanity," but whichever you prefer, I hope you can see the overlap in sentiments. Divergent as they are in length, audience, and style, the Rockefeller-*Lancet* report and the Montelimar complaint each ask their audiences to consider which lives are worthy of economic, political, legal, and technical support.

On Nicaragua's Pacific coast, one particular form of life has been supremely well supported over the past twenty-five years: industrial sugarcane. Nicaragua is a small country, and while its sugar production accounts for just a fraction of global supply, the country's sugar businesses began expanding at an unprecedented rate around the turn of the twenty-first century. According to an estimate by the Nicaraguan Investment Promotion Agency, by 2013–14, sugarcane exports were growing faster than those of any other agricultural product. Those in political power during the first two decades of the twenty-first century, whether they hailed from the left or the right of the political spectrum, had come to view supporting the life of sugarcane as a means of supporting human life. And, significantly, climate crisis was on their minds. For the Nicaraguan government and its supporters at the IFC and the World Bank, more investment in sugarcane might not only perpetuate the country's gains in food export but also develop its capacity to produce biofuels, including ethanol and energy generated from sugarcane pulp, or bagasse. This alternative energy strategy has been a key policy tenet of Nicaragua's current government, which, since the 2007 accession of Daniel Ortega and the left-leaning Sandinista National Liberation Front to power, has touted its commitment to reducing fossil fuel consumption.[5]

Since 2005, the country's two largest sugarcane firms, Nicaragua Sugar Estates Limited, a privately held Nicaraguan company, and Monte Rosa, a subsidiary of Central America's largest sugar producer, the Guatemalan corporation Pantaleon, have received over US$100 million in loans from the IFC to develop cogeneration facilities that burn bagasse to power sugar mills and the national electrical grid, and to expand ethanol production. The IFC's $15 million loan to Montelimar, the country's smallest sugarcane firm, would help the company launch a third biofuel plant. The Montelimar project also promised to increase the company's annual sugar production from thirty-three kilotons to sixty-seven kilotons, to increase its landholdings by some 25 percent, and to divert more water toward irrigation.[6]

Though the spike in investment in industrial sugarcane in places like Nicaragua is somewhat recent, it is best understood as part of a longer history. Efforts to make improvements in commercial agriculture that would simultaneously improve human well-being are the calling card of what Raj Patel calls "The Long Green Revolution."[7] During the Green Revolution's first phase in the 1960s, its proponents—including the Rockefeller Foundation—justified the consolidation of smallholdings for commercial crop production with an appeal to global health. They argued that increased agro-export capacity was the only way to provide abundant food and thus stave off famine.[8] The World Bank's more recent turn to investment in energy indicates a continued belief in the linkage between agro-industrial growth and human health. One argument in favor of biofuel, in fact, is that a reduction of dependence on fossil fuels could lower fuel prices and thus reduce overall food costs.[9]

What transpired after the IFC made its loans to Nicaraguan sugarcane plantations highlights the weakness of such arguments. For a start, the expansion of sugarcane has intensified an already steady deterioration of Nicaraguan forests. Starting in the 1950s, the World Bank, the US government, and a variety of agricultural corporations, including US-based pesticide firms, supported the conversion of Nicaragua's Pacific region into a cotton-producing belt. The result was the destruction of thousands of hectares of old-growth forest.[10] Even after the cotton boom faded, the damage continued. According to the environmental watchdog World Rainforests, between 1990 and 2010, Nicaragua lost 31 percent of its remaining forest cover, as sugarcane operations started to expand, alongside peanut farming and cattle ranching.[11] There is now nearly no forest left on the country's Pacific coast. Loss of forests means increased carbon in the atmosphere and increased annual temperatures. Instead of creating more salubrious environments, investments by private capital, states, and supranational organizations in cotton and sugarcane monoculture in Nicaragua and elsewhere have created even more extreme environments, marked by decreased biodiversity, increased presence of toxic agrochemicals in air and water, and more intense heat. These points are all highlighted in the 2015 report of the Rockefeller-*Lancet* Commission on Planetary Health, and they are echoed in climate modeling studies that place Central America among the regions at highest risk for catastrophic heat waves.[12]

Though the stories to come all take place in the context of the Long Green Revolution, this book is not an indictment of the IFC's policy regarding Nicaraguan sugarcane. The IFC's repeated investment in Nicaragua's sugarcane zone did not, by itself, cause deforestation, the overuse of agrochemicals, or steadily increasing mean annual temperatures. Nor did the IFC's investment cause the CKDnt epidemic that was the primary concern of the group that filed the 2015 complaint to the CAO. What the conversion of the sugarcane zone into an investment hot spot did do was make an ecological and medical disaster more visible.[13] The recent wave of investor interest in Nicaraguan sugar underscores how the global drive for agro-export-driven growth has reached what one group of CKDnt researchers calls "a physiological limit . . . at which acclimatization and behavioral modifications can no longer overcome the biologic stressors of unsafe working conditions and environmental exposures."[14]

What happens socially and politically when bodies and places reach these kinds of limits? This is the central question for the anthropology of planetary health, and late industrial disaster more broadly. As this abbreviated history of Nicaragua's sugarcane boom shows, supporting the life of sugarcane requires extreme measures, and it requires sacrificing the viability of some species and some ecological systems for the viability of others. Supporting compromised bodies (like, say, supporting the bodies of people with kidney failure through dialysis) and supporting artificial monocultures (like, say, maintaining hundreds of thousands of hectares of sugarcane) is a matter of working along the edges of life and death.[15]

For all its bullet-pointed policy recommendations, the Rockefeller-*Lancet* report is not particularly inspirational reading. My favorite part is panel 14, on page 2014, an inset box titled "Why the grassroots matter." It tells the story of how the movement for HIV treatment access led by African, Asian, and Latin American HIV patients and allies took on pharmaceutical corporations and governments to demand lifesaving drugs. In doing so, panel 14 tells us, these grassroots activists turned the tide of the AIDS pandemic. This is a story I tell my medical anthropology undergraduates every year. It is a story that finds a group of disenfranchised and marginalized people, many of them very sick, asking those with more power and influence if their lives were worth supporting.

As much as I was heartened as a medical anthropologist that panel 14 made it into the Rockefeller-*Lancet* report, it remains troubling that a scholarly paper with 432 references and twenty-two named authors contains no example of a grassroots effort to actually address what the report's executive summary calls "the degradation of nature's life support systems."[16] Instead, panel 14 says, "Better evidence is needed for the importance of planetary health than exists at present." There are plenty of possible ways to provide such evidence, but none of them, including the one in this book, has the satisfying narrative arc of the HIV treatment access story.[17] Attempting to foreground such stories in the context of an emerging epidemic remains risky, since so much of contemporary science, including climate change science, agricultural sustainability science, and global health science, depends not on the telling of relatable, human stories but on the collection of replicable, hard data.[18]

While the term *planetary health* is never used in the Montelimar complaint, that obscure document opens a window onto what planetary health might look like in practice, and why it is important. This book approaches the question of planetary health—for planetary health is still a question, rather than a paradigm—from the vantage point of a particular group of people in a specific place, over a relatively short time. Like many stories told by anthropologists, it works from the edges. It recounts lives lived and lost not just on the margins of the global health industry represented by the Rockefeller Foundation and top-flight journals like the *Lancet*, but on the margins of the global sugarcane industry.

To take a cue from the wording of the Rockefeller-*Lancet* report, the stories in this book are about "life support systems." In colloquial medical English, the term *life support* indexes a technological achievement (think of respirators and breathing tubes). Used more broadly, the term reminds us that to be alive is to be in relation to things and beings that cooperate with us, like technologies and drugs and foods and caregivers, and even to things that do not do such a good job cooperating, such as sugarcane and the tools large companies use to cultivate it, from water to harvesting equipment to toxic pesticides. But the thing about life support is that it is always temporary. In every individual case, life support will eventually fail. At some point, agrochemicals stop helping produce crops and start damaging soil and water to such a degree that industries are no longer viable (just google "Nicaraguan cotton" and find out). At some point, hemodialysis stops keeping end-stage kidney disease patients alive. Life support is what happens when the possibility of a full resolution is no longer available. An appropriate term to describe a variety of projects aimed at addressing the crisis of the Anthropocene, life support is the project of ensuring collective endurance amid the certainty of individual loss.[19]

This book is about how people grapple with life support systems, from legal frameworks like the CAO, to irrigation works, to pesticide application regimes, to state-sponsored social security programs, to occupational health measures, to dialysis treatment itself. It explores how these systems are stabilized and destabilized by one another. It suggests that a close look at what happens along the unstable edges where life support systems meet might provide insights into the possibilities and limitations of planetary health.

Introduction

Saúl Bermudez was around thirty-five years old and just about to start his third
year of law school when he was diagnosed with type 2 diabetes. He took his
law courses at night and on Saturdays so he could keep his paying job, driving
a taxi in his hometown of León, Nicaragua. One day, about a year after his
diagnosis, Saúl helped organize a wake for his uncle, who had died from com-
plications related to diabetes. Wakes in Nicaragua are big events, and in the
León neighborhood where Saúl grew up, it sometimes seemed like everyone
was related to everyone else in some way. There were so many people coming
to pay their respects that the family had rented a plastic tent and pitched it
over the sidewalk and curb, with plastic chairs set up underneath. As Saúl sat
in the shade wiping the July afternoon sweat from his face, he was accosted by
a mildly drunk distant cousin.

"Your aunt tells me you're working in the sugar mill," the cousin said, with
a slap of Saúl's back.

Saúl was startled. Even though León was surrounded by thousands of hectares of sugarcane fields, Saúl hadn't ever worked in them. But the phrase "working in the sugar mill" (*trabajando en el ingenio*) had another, more metaphorical meaning. It meant "diabetic." In Nicaragua, as in other parts of the Americas, diabetes is often euphemized as "sugar" (*azúcar*). "Working in the sugar mill" is gallows humor. Keeping track of your blood sugar in a place where glucometers are prohibitively expensive, and trying to eat well in a place where the cheapest available food is high in sugar, high in carbs, and high in fat, is a lot of work.

So is cutting sugarcane, Saúl thought to himself. Though he had never actually worked in a sugarcane plantation, he knew what they were like. In fact, his recent interest in studying the law was directly connected to his work as a taxi driver, which had been how he had come to know more than most people about the sugarcane industry. Around 2005, Saúl was hired as a driver for a team of international lawyers who came to Nicaragua to assist a group of people that had been diagnosed with a previously unknown condition: chronic kidney disease of nontraditional causes (CKDnt).[1] While "traditional" chronic kidney disease is associated with diabetes, CKDnt is not. As its name indicates, there is no scientific consensus about what triggers it. In Nicaragua, CKDnt has sickened or killed thousands of people. Unlike "traditional" chronic kidney disease, CKDnt tends to strike people at a relatively young age. Many of the Nicaraguans with CKDnt are in their thirties and forties, and diagnosis as young as twenty-five is not unheard of.

Aside from their age, most of those who became sick with kidney disease had another thing in common. They once worked as field laborers on sugarcane plantations. Most believed that the sugarcane company that had employed them bore responsibility for their illness. They were convinced that exposure to something in the plantation landscape—probably poisoned water or polluted air—was causing their kidneys to fail. This conviction led them to contact the lawyers, who hired Saúl. By the time Saúl got involved, CKDnt was already reaching epidemic levels. But people wanted to know why, after years of service, sick workers were being sent home to die. The lawyers and the ex-workers were in the midst of a tense debate with the owners of the sugar company over how (and whether) the company should help affected workers in the later stages of disease get access to dialysis, and how (and whether) research should be done on how occupational conditions in the fields might have contributed to the epidemic. First, though, they had to work out how (and whether) the company should acknowledge the epidemic's very existence.

Formal negotiations between that company, Nicaragua Sugar Estates Limited (NSEL), and the workers' organization went on for nearly six years, and the movement that began there gave rise in 2015 to a second movement, which called itself the Asociación Montelimar Bendición de Dios (AMBED). AMBED was composed of former workers at the Montelimar sugar plantation, located about one hundred kilometers to the south of the NSEL plantation. By the time of AMBED's founding, Saúl had decided to enter law school. As AMBED was forming, he again acted as driver and fixer for the international lawyers on the case, but he also took on an advisory role. He organized meetings and an executive board, and he helped communicate AMBED's concerns to the Montelimar Corporation. As at NSEL, the work with AMBED was stressful and sometimes dangerous. In the early days of the movements at both plantations, Saúl, his international counterparts, and the former sugarcane workers who had organized themselves were alternately physically threatened and tempted with bribes and gifts in exchange for their silence. The Nicaraguan police either jailed those who spoke out about the epidemic or threatened to do so. Money for running meetings and filing legal papers was in chronically short supply, and the sugar industry, one of Nicaragua's oldest and most powerful, mounted a sustained legal and public relations counteroffensive to deflect blame and sow uncertainty.

Saúl's diabetes diagnosis came during AMBED's early days. If the cause of CKDnt remained a mystery, the cause of his diabetes seemed anything but. Saúl's family, like many in Nicaragua, was full of diabetics, and he was not eating well. He had spent hundreds of hours in a car driving across the Montelimar plantation and back and forth from León. When he was diagnosed, Saúl's older brother, a doctor, told him that to protect his kidneys, he needed to change his diet, keep his stress level low, and try to get some exercise. Knowing how quickly diabetes could progress, Saúl's brother counseled him either to take a leave of absence from the work at Montelimar or to quit law school. His brother figured that Saúl would choose to stay in law school. After all, a qualified lawyer could make good money doing lots of uncontroversial, low-stress, safe tasks: notarizing documents, handling divorces, settling property claims. Instead, Saúl chose to continue at Montelimar, where I joined him and began following his work with AMBED in 2017.

The Work of Planetary Health

Within the corridors of global policy and science, a call to reimagine global health as "planetary health" was sounded in the middle of the 2010s. Planetary health has its roots in the ecological and land health movements of the mid-twentieth century, but at its core is the alarming idea that the contemporary medical and public health sciences are simply not equipped to address the health consequences of climate change, from increasing heat to air pollution to water scarcity to land degradation.[2] One reason is that the health sciences have historically been put in the service of furthering the very economic projects that caused climate change in the first place: aggressive resource extraction, fossil fuel–driven development, and the expansion of pesticide-driven industrial monocrop agriculture, including that of sugarcane. For too long, planetary health advocates claim, care for the environment and care for human health have been treated as separate domains. The challenge is to think of care for what they call "Earth's life support systems" not just as environmental work but as work for human health.[3]

But planetary health is work in another sense. Many of the health problems now associated with climate change, including respiratory disease, reproductive abnormalities, metabolic diseases, and CKDnt, can also be understood as consequences of inequitable labor relations. It is safe to say that those whose working lives are the least valued, in terms of pay and on-the-job treatment, are most at risk of climate change–induced illnesses. There is a growing recognition that climate change is a major contributor to health inequities worldwide. To date, however, relatively little attention has been given to the role that might be played in addressing those inequities by the people most directly affected by global warming, the saturation of ecosystems with toxic substances, the loss of forest cover, the extinction of species, and the depletion of water resources— that is to say, the role played by the people for whom planetary health is at root a question of working conditions. One problem is that even those interventions designed to protect workers from climate-related diseases ignore the simple fact that workers are also people—people for whom the question of health in the workplace is inseparable from the question of health at home.[4] This book, then, treats the category of "plantation labor" broadly, giving analysis of the work of making and maintaining houses, gardens, and communities an equal footing with analysis of the work of growing sugarcane.

To do so, I draw on ethnographic research conducted between 2017 and 2020 with AMBED and others living in the environs of the Montelimar sugar plantation. I adopt a critical approach to planetary health. By "critical," I do not mean "dismissive." Rather, following an approach taken to health and disease in the context of sugarcane plantation production by other anthropologists, I explore how actions taken in small, seemingly out-of-the-way places, such as the villages that dot the Nicaraguan sugarcane zone, reverberate across the globally dispersed spaces of capitalism and global health. The literary scholar Elizabeth DeLoughrey defines climate change as a "world-changing rupture in a social and ecological system."[5] For people in the sugarcane zone, the mass onset of a novel kidney disease was just such a rupture. My interest is in what planetary health might look like if their understanding of that rupture were treated as just as valuable as the knowledge produced by ecologists, epidemiologists, and medical doctors.[6] Doing so, I offer a glimpse of what the goings-on in individual bodies might tell us about planetary-scale change.[7]

Put another way, this book takes planetary health's central conceit—that Earth's life support systems are human systems—to its logical conclusion. It considers what happens when we think of human bodies not as existing *in* a planetary environment but, through work, as constitutive elements *of* that environment.[8] The book's six chapters explore how people living in the sugarcane zone worked across six systems designed to support life—both human life and that of the sugarcane crop. These included legal systems like the ones that brought Saúl into the story of CKDnt; occupational health systems; agricultural systems of irrigation and pesticide application that may have contributed to environmental and bodily harm; state and corporate social security systems; and systems of biomedical care. Making sense of CKDnt, and of the limits and possibilities of planetary health, entails understanding how such life support systems "are animated and interrelate."[9]

Planetary health is relatively new. Plantation labor is not. But the relationship between the two is far from incidental. The formation of sugar plantations in the Caribbean, and later in Central America, began with a violent clearing of forests, which led to extensive soil erosion and the choking of essential waterways. Across the Americas, this landscape transformation depended on the forcible conscription of human labor through enslavement and, later, through the seasonal coercion of poor and disenfranchised rural peasant populations with promises of food, money, or medicine.[10] Over more than four centuries, deforestation, water contamination, and mass displacement at the hands of the plantation complex became key contributors to what we now call "climate change." Thanks to sugarcane cultivation, landscapes like that of Nicaragua's Pacific coast were permanently, irrevocably altered well before any of the principal figures in this book drew their first breath. The change in the landscape continues. Some of the elements have been subtracted or added. Enslaved people no longer predominate in the sugarcane industry, but that is still a relatively new development. In addition to radical deforestation and rerouting of waterways, agrochemicals are now central to sugarcane cultivation.

This centuries-long effort to support the life of one crop, sugarcane, has caused what the geographer Julie Guthman, drawing on the language of medical philosophy, calls "iatrogenic harm" to the plantation complex and the people who work in it.[11] In other words, the continued effort by plantation companies to find new ways of sustaining the life of this valuable crop causes damage to human lives, and to the lives of other animals and plants. This is not to suggest that plantation agriculture is a zero-sum proposition, or some sort of trade-off between one form of life and another. Plantations that produce sugar, as well as tea, coffee, or soy, are not stable enough systems for that.[12] As Alex Blanchette has argued in his writing on industrial pig farms, industrial agriculture is best seen as an unruly, uncertain experiment in the admixture of human and nonhuman life with machinery, pesticides, fertilizers, pharmaceuticals, air, and water.[13] Industrial agriculture is not a singular thing but an "assemblage," an unstable arrangement of capital, labor, land, and technology.[14] It is this instability that causes iatrogenic harm. As monocrop production comes to economically and socially envelop the surrounding spaces of social reproduction like rural villages and towns, and as it comes to rely on more intensive and more dangerous mechanical, chemical, and human inputs, efforts to keep the agricultural system running begin to threaten the system itself. The nature of the threat ranges from antibiotic resistance to the deepening of racial, ethnic, and gendered disparities in economic and political power to novel human diseases like CKDnt.

As its name indicates, the cause of CKDnt is still debated. There is a swirl of theories about the connection of the disease to the accreted bodily burden of decades of agrochemical application, to the sheer bodily exhaustion of sugarcane labor, to genetic predisposition, and even to the overuse of over-the-counter anti-inflammatory drugs by sugarcane workers. Today, the most widely circulated theory has to do with rising temperatures. As a leading CKDnt researcher told the *Guardian* newspaper on the eve of the 2021 COP26 conference in Glasgow, Scotland, the kidneys are "the immediate interface between [humans] and the climate crisis—because when it starts getting hot, we lose a lot of water and salt through sweat."[15] People with CKDnt are now being portrayed as bellwethers for a global climate crisis.[16]

The continued uncertainty around which of the possible "nontraditional" causes is to blame for CKDnt is instructive for a critical understanding of planetary health. Many of the factors associated with CKDnt—including chemical toxicity, diminished water tables, food insecurity, and rising annual temperature—have become associated with climate change. It would be misleading, however, to claim that new diseases like CKDnt are caused by climate change. The flaw in the claim that climate change causes human disease is that it externalizes the planetary climate from the bodily one. This flies in the face of decades of historical and social research on allergies, immunity, environmental epigenetics, the human microbiome, and chemical exposure.[17] This research shows that bodies become healthy or diseased not because chemicals, heat, microbes, or allergens invade previously sealed bodily systems but because human biologies are, as the anthropologist Margaret Lock puts it, always already "situated" within fundamentally unstable ecologies.[18] What is happening to the kidneys of sugarcane workers is not a result of climate change. It *is* climate change.[19]

This may sound hyperbolic, but it has some grounding in the history of kidney science. For some time, the kidney has been viewed by doctors as what the twentieth-century American physician and philosopher Homer William Smith, in a rather strange book called *From Fish to Philosopher*, called the "master chemists" of the body's "internal environment."[20] The kidneys absorb and break down toxins that enter the body through ingestion, respiration, and exertion, which means they are the organs that are most actively involved in adapting bodies to their surroundings. Smith believed that humanity itself was the result of a biological and evolutionary struggle to adapt to a violently changing planet. Human bodies are, he suggested, "a product of Earth's troubled history."[21] Were it not for the evolution of the kidney, with its unique capacity to filter external toxins and wastes from the body's internal environment, Smith argued, livers, lungs, and brains would not have evolved as they did. By doing this, our kidneys "constitute the major foundation of our physiological freedom," as well as freedom of thought and will. The kidneys, he wrote, "make the stuff of philosophy itself."[22]

I agree with Smith, up to a point. Where I quibble with him is on his insistence that bodies and environments are insides and outsides to one another. In recent years, thanks to the rise of planetary health, kidneys and their function have stirred a great deal of philosophizing about humanity's place in the world, but that body-environment binary tends to get reproduced in bold pronouncements such as *Time* magazine's 2023 declaration that kidney disease is "the black lung of climate change."[23] In this book, I call attention to less stark and less declarative speculations about what kidneys and their struggle to function might mean. To do so, I turn to the concerns that first emerged among ex-workers in the Nicaraguan sugarcane zone back at the start of the twenty-first century.[24]

It is thanks in large part to the willingness of those ex-workers and their allies to ask questions about what was harming them that CKDnt is now recognized as a global epidemic, affecting rural people, primarily industrial farmworkers, in Central America, Mexico, Sri Lanka, India, Egypt, and even, evidence suggests, the United States.[25] In what follows, I recount some of the controversial and dangerous work they did in the early days of the epidemic, but my main emphasis is on the everyday task of forging collective existence in irrevocably damaged bodies, in an irrevocably damaged place. While the question of exactly what causes CKDnt has not yet been answered, my goal is neither to develop a forensic argument about why so many thousands of sugarcane workers have died nor to indict any particular sugarcane company or government agency for malfeasance. Instead, I am setting out to examine how people take meaningful action amid what I see as the central conundrum of planetary health: while the generalized damage to the Earth is undeniable, uncertainty abounds about how to think and take action in the face of that damage. Rather than search for root causes, I ask what becomes of environmental health in a world beset by what the geographer Kathryn Yusoff calls "excessive causality."[26] In this book, there is no "big reveal." No magic gene. No toxic chemical turned smoking gun. This is a story about planetary health, not as an encompassing condition but as an ongoing, messy, and paradoxically very local process.

Helicopter in the Hot Sun

The Nicaraguan sugarcane zone is haunted by helicopters. It seems odd, but most of the time we didn't really hear them overhead. Maybe this was because Saúl's Hyundai Accent sedan made such a racket as it slogged through the sometimes muddy, sometimes rocky plantation roads. The road that took us out to the village of El Zapote was actually one of the better ones. When I first visited El Zapote, an old man who lived there assured us with great confidence that that road might as well be an *autopista*, a highway, compared with the other routes in and out of the village.

I'm not sure I'd go so far as to compare it to a highway, but this road, which wound for several miles at sea level through acres of cane that formed a green-to-golden wall on either side, was certainly easier on Hyundais than some others in the zone. Lowland dirt roads like this one eventually connected to the yet-to-be-completed asphalt autopista that would take you to a string of always-under-construction beach resorts that awaited Nicaragua's always-about-to-happen tourist boom. The few motorcycle taxis and trucks that passed for public transportation in and out of El Zapote tended to take the shorter, steeper, and decidedly more treacherous road: the one that led straight up the ridge from sea level to the only paved highway in the area, which ran from the outskirts of Managua to the town of San Rafael del Sur. Men like the one who promised us a smooth highway-like ride at sea level knew that bumpy ascent well. It was the route they took, three times a week, to meet the bus that would take them to one of the few hemodialysis clinics in Managua, about two hours away. The dialysis patients were all former sugarcane plantation workers, and they all had CKDnt. During the four days each week when they were not traveling to or from dialysis, some of them theorized together about the cause of their disease. The helicopter figured prominently in those theories.

But like I said, it sometimes took extra work to even notice the helicopter. Spotting the little black aircraft overhead was a bit like spotting a *guardabarranco* (*Eumomota superciliosa*), the stunning multicolored bird that is Nicaragua's official national ambassador to the tropical skies. One minute we would be putting along, avoiding the deep ruts made by the giant cane-collecting trucks and just trying to keep our heads still, and the next minute, a blue and red and orange flutter in the cane would snag one of our eyes and draw it back to the section of green wall we had just passed. Birds visited now and again as if to remind us that our monotone surroundings were actually alive, metabolizing the all-too-abundant sunlight, the adequate if not abundant nutrients in the Pacific coastal soil, and the precious water from the rivers and creeks that fell down from the tropical uplands, only to be sucked into the stalks of cane before they reached the sea.

The helicopter, on the other hand, reminded the men recovering from the dialysis journey that death—their own and that of the cane—was not far off. From the helicopter's belly, clouds of odorless chemicals, aimed with varying degrees of precision, would cascade in the direction of the monoculture below. If my research on the global sugarcane industry provides any guide (agricultural companies in Nicaragua are not required to disclose their precise cultivation methods), that chemical was probably the massively successful commercial herbicide glyphosate. Whatever it was, it worked. It turned the green cane to brown, bringing the oversize grass one step closer to becoming that most unavoidable, irresistible, and terrible of global commodities: refined sugar. Modern sugar production, like the production of most any modern agricultural product, really begins with mass slaughter.[27]

When you ask people with CKDnt, as I did over and over again between 2017 and 2020, what might be causing it, they still frequently gesture with their hands, or more often with that unique jerk of the chin that Nicaraguans sometimes provide in lieu of words, to the air. By the time I started doing research in the sugarcane zone, the helicopter and the chemical, which cane plantation managers and workers call a "ripener" (in Spanish, *madurante*), were relative newcomers to the local agricultural complex. Many of the former workers who depended on hemodialysis to stay alive could remember when the only way to "mature" the cane—to get rid of the unwanted leaves of grass and condense the sugars in the hardy stalks those leaves protected—was to wait for it to ripen on its own time, and then set it on fire. Mass cane burning had not disappeared by the time I started visiting the sugarcane zone, but many could reckon the origins of the CKDnt epidemic back to when the helicopters and chemical ripeners first came on the scene, sometime around the late 1990s.

Their logic went like this: the chemicals the helicopters unleashed, whatever they were, did tend to drift past the borders of the cane fields, through the slots in the narrow curtain of trees that guarded workers' villages, into their gardens, and onto their heads. While ideas about the deadly effects of agrochemicals and the wave of human death in the sugarcane zone have made their way into some epidemiological theories, more than a decade and a half of research on the disease has not found a clear and unambiguous connection between toxic exposure and CKDnt on sugarcane plantations.[28] This is not to say there *is* no connection, or that the people who look skyward when trying to explain the thousands of deaths in their communities are deluded. When the helicopter misses its target and chemicals fall onto plantation villages, residents feel some reasonable sense of entitlement to speak out about the acute damage that chemicals do to crops, and about the less certain long-term toll they take on humans, animals, waters, and soils. In that sense, the haunting helicopter gives these residents an opening to begin questioning not just the specific harm done by the chemical but the more general fate of life in the sugarcane zone.[29]

Those residents know that what is uncertain in Nicaragua's sugarcane zone is not simply the cause of CKDnt. While it is easy to think of disease as the central source of uncertainty in the region, what is actually uncertain—indeed, deeply fragile—is the region's dominant environmental form, the sugarcane plantation itself. Journalists, food justice advocates, and even many CKDnt scientists frequently depict the sugar industry as an enormous behemoth, ruthlessly exploiting people and land for short-term profits. The truth is less stark. Sugarcane plantations are ecologically fragile in ways that are certainly different from, if not entirely unrelated to, the fragility of the bodies of those who work them.[30] It is the fragility of a plantation, rather than its strength and coherence, that makes it so destructive, but that same fragility also provides room for people to develop what Katherine McKittrick calls "creative space to challenge" the plantation system.[31]

Plantations are not the same everywhere, but one important way of separating a plantation from other kinds of industrial monocultures is that a plantation depends for its existence on the reproduction not just of crops but of racialized and gendered difference. Since its inception, the Nicaraguan sugar business has explicitly operated on a racial and class hierarchy in which white landowners or well-connected ladinos exploited the labor of Indigenous people and campesinos whom they considered fundamentally inferior.[32] An equally important feature of plantations is that those who own and manage them consistently find ways to disavow their culpability in racial and gendered violence through paternalistic gestures to care for laborers. Such gestures—from patronage systems in which access to work comes with access to limited food, medicine, or housing, to contemporary corporate social responsibility schemes—keep workers and other plantation residents minimally alive. Plantations may promise care, but what they offer both crops and the people who do the work of planting and harvesting them is a rudimentary and time-limited form of life support, one that is premised on the continued productivity of both.[33]

Such a minimalist approach to life support was essential to the global success of sugarcane. Since cane is not native to the Americas, colonial plantation owners and field laborers experimented to find those varieties that would grow best in vast monocultures.[34] The harvest required a violent intensity of labor, and it rewarded economies of scale. The seeding, burning, and cutting process lent itself to the expansion of a chattel slavery model premised on the fungibility and interchangeability of bodies.[35] Sugarcane's potential for ecological and bodily violence was rooted in its potential for scalable expansion: more and more of the same crop system, adjusted for climate and geography. The suffering of field laborers multiplied in parallel, reverberating across time in stories and images about the inhumanity of both past colonialism and contemporary capitalism. An eighteenth- or nineteenth-century painting of cane production in Louisiana, or Haiti, or Cuba, or Brazil tends to look remarkably similar to a twenty-first-century photograph: Black and brown (mostly male) bodies, machetes in hand, skin glistening in the hot sun, swinging, killing, dying.[36] One era's imagery haunts another's.

Nicaraguan sugar complexes, though relatively new by world-historical standards, are haunted by the legacy of the system of chattel slavery that developed elsewhere in Latin America and the Caribbean. Working in Puerto Rico in the middle of the last century, the anthropologists Eric Wolf and Sidney Mintz illustrated how, as sugar production industrialized, companies discarded the "old style" obligation to provide land and housing to workers, an obligation that began when the sugar barons' ancestors were slaveholders. "New style" plantations attempted to banish the ghosts of the premodern slave plantation by severing economic operations from other aspects of rural life. For example, they replaced direct provision of land and food with indirect economic and political investments. Such investments were often couched as promoting modernity and development.[37] In places like Nicaragua, where sugarcane operations did not begin in earnest until after the formal end of the transatlantic slave trade, the "new style" form at first seems dominant. Today, large operations like Montelimar have achieved economies of scale by controlling massive tracts of land and hiring workers on a seasonal basis, limiting their obligations to provide the care that previous generations of plantation owners might have offered.[38]

Yet even in Nicaragua, vestiges of the "old style" remain. One sign of the overlap between the old and the new appears in language. People around Montelimar rarely used terms like *plantación* or *hacienda*. In this book, *plantation* is by and large an analytical term that I adopt. Instead, Montelimar's residents interchangeably portrayed the sugar complex as an externality, *el ingenio* (literally, "the mill"), and as a murkier space of interdependency, *la zona* (the sugarcane zone). Well before the helicopters started appearing overhead, people who worked in the sugarcane zone understood their pasts and futures as inextricably entangled with the surrounding monoculture. Many of their villages were constructed on land ceded to their ancestors by large landowners (*patrones*). Access to land would have been given in exchange for labor power, but just as important, a *patrón* could, potentially at least, be a source of support in times of need. As in other parts of Latin America, a loose "moral economy" driven by senses of obligation and debt operated in parallel to an agricultural economy shaped by labor-management relations.[39]

This moral economy is another haunting presence on contemporary plantations. As Jeffrey Gould recounts in his historical study of the Ingenio San Antonio, a sugar plantation to the north of Montelimar, a myth once circulated among the workers, which said that "the company had signed a pact with the devil in order to further accumulate wealth.... The devil pact specifically allowed the company to convert dead laborers and their families into cattle."[40] The company would then sell these cattle to a hacienda. "The death of [a laborer] did not mean the end of his service to the company," Gould writes. "Rather...the worker continued to produce wealth for the company... either as oxen or as food for the work force."[41] Dead workers haunted the living ones. This is an old tale, a variation of stories about the devil and capitalism that recur across Latin America.[42] Those I met at Montelimar talked frequently about bodily sacrifice, and some could even remember when the patrón who controlled Montelimar's land was none other than Nicaragua's dictator, Anastasio Somoza, whose vacation home sat just down the ridge from the sugar mill, until his ouster by the popular Sandinista revolution in 1979. Former workers framed their relationship to sugarcane as one that was defined by a donation not just of time and energy but of bodily substances, particularly sweat and blood, to the commodity crop.[43] In the moral economy, such sacrifices were supposed to be rewarded by patrones with a modicum of care and concern, but as we will see in this book, that sense of mutual obligation was as much a haunting collective memory as a reality.

Haunting matters to this narrative in one final way. Plantations are not just systems for producing crops and keeping workers minimally alive and healthy. They are also, fundamentally, systems for sustaining the transfer of wealth and power through channels of white, elite privilege. This is true in Nicaragua, as it was in the American South, where my own ancestors were slaveholders. My great-great-great grandfather Benjamin Rush Jones was the brother of Eliza Theresa Jones Sims, the wife of J. Marion Sims. Sims was a Montgomery, Alabama, doctor whose research on vaginal fistula involved exploitative experimentation on the bodies of at least sixteen enslaved Black women, including painful repeated surgeries and involuntary administration of opium.[44] Sims's niece, my great-great grandmother Susie Theresa Jones Waller, lived at a plantation located near Mt. Meigs, where Sims had his first clinic. I am thus a descendant of the very same slaveholders who enabled Sims's work in Montgomery during that period, and I am related to Sims by marriage.[45] In a fairly direct way, I am an economic and social beneficiary of the medical exploitation Sims enacted through the Alabama plantation economy. My grandfather, Susie Theresa Jones Waller's grandson, helped pay for my education with wealth accrued from a plantation. For me, this connection is an example of how antiblackness haunts the field of medicine but also the field of medical anthropology.[46] There is no redemptive way for me to write about the plantation ethnographically, because I too am haunted by it.

Six Life Support Systems

AMBED was one of several advocacy organizations that sprang up in Nicaragua's sugarcane zone after CKDnt became a recognized problem there. It was neither the largest nor the most well-known. Its most enthusiastic participants over the years included a part-time taxi driver with two-thirds of a law degree, a couple of American lawyers, three former sugarcane cutters, and a former sugarcane company clerical secretary. As an anthropologist, I was an adjunct of sorts to AMBED's activities between 2017 and 2020.

For AMBED, the terms and tactics of environmental advocacy that might have been borrowed from other environmental or health activist groups were never sufficient for maintaining momentum. Over the past two decades, anxieties about CKDnt and its possible relationship to sugarcane plantation production have drastically rearranged social and political relationships among former workers, their families, international aid workers, university scientists, doctors, and sugarcane companies in Pacific coastal Nicaragua. These individuals and institutional players do not constitute a collection of "stakeholders." Instead, they meet one another in an ongoing process of trying to give name and form to a bundled set of economic, medical, environmental, and political problems.[47] During the time we worked together, AMBED struggled to maintain a steady base of members who fit the conventional definition of "active." The dozens of general assembly meetings I observed were often sparsely attended. Many of AMBED's international supporters (including me) drifted in and out of the picture due to funding constraints, family obligations, changes in employment, and communication breakdowns. Saúl Bermudez himself would eventually leave AMBED under a cloud of suspicion about his loyalties, but this book is not a story about the messy intrigue of a struggling social movement.

Even if it included almost no public protests, boycotts, or voting drives, the group's work was political, if politics means, as Tania Murray Li puts it, "the expression, in word or deed, of a critical situation."[48] Yet AMBED's story reflects a version of politics that is at odds with the one that tends to dominate both liberal political theory and many studies of environmental health. This dominant version of politics imagines what the Chilean scholar Manuel Tironi has described as "well-organized, outspoken and articulated individuals ... mobilizing cognitive (and economic) resources in the face of an externality."[49] Polluting industries make easily objectifiable externalities, yet even when groups of people are deeply affected by industrial actions, ethnographic work reveals again and again that those groups frequently choose not to externalize industry in an agonistic or directly confrontational way, but to work with and against it in a more creative, heterogeneous, and open-ended way. One reason they do this is that histories of labor—in factories, in plantations, in mines—put them in a double bind. These histories give them a sense of connection to the very polluters that harm them.[50] The people whose stories make up this book worked to trouble the sharp distinction between field and village, worker and caregiver. They refused to operate within the fixed categorical slots of medicine, environment, or labor. The effect of this refusal was to keep the questions surrounding CKDnt open to scrutiny and, by extension, to establish what many saw as the central fact of life in the sugarcane zone: that people who resided there, even if they did not work directly in the cane, were entangled with the industry—biologically, economically, and ethically. Thus, AMBED is less a subject of this book than an example of how contemporary environmental advocacy traps its participants in multiple double binds: both calling on them to join together with corporate, state, and supranational organizations to repair the world, and to acknowledge that that very process of joining is a reductive one that can drive people apart. As Kim Fortun puts it, advocacy is not the antidote to disaster; it is part of disaster itself.[51]

Each of the six chapters of this book explores how people grappled with a system designed to support plantation life—both the human life of laborers and residents in the zone and the life of the sugarcane monoculture itself. These are all "open" systems, and they all traverse scales from the bodily to the regional to the global. Each has imperfections and gaps, which means, as Fortun has argued, that no person's role in them is ever fixed. Furthermore, each system has pressure points where they are subject to change.[52] As each chapter shows, it was at such pressure points that problems like CKDnt, toxicity, the economic and social rights of workers, and planetary health itself became workable and thinkable, but also where the scope of the slow-moving disaster of plantation capitalism became apparent.

In chapter 1, the system in question is a quasi-legal transnational corporate grievance mechanism underwritten by the World Bank's Compliance Advisor Ombudsman (CAO). When the lawyers who hired Saúl first came to Nicaragua, they were preparing to file a petition to the CAO on behalf of sugarcane workers at NSEL affected by CKDnt. Later, AMBED filed its own CAO grievance, in hopes of convincing the Montelimar Corporation to address community concerns about environmental health. It is easy to be cynical about the capacity of an unwieldy supranational body like the CAO to effectively deliver social and environmental justice, but chapter 1 describes how AMBED cautiously embraced the CAO's logic of grievance-making. The CAO grievance mechanism encourages mediation over litigation. It invites companies to meet community members in a dialogue about specific, tangible demands, and to seek trade-offs between the needs of both parties, as if they were equals. The chapter shows how AMBED creatively blended the equalizing, universalizing logic of the legal grievance with place-based knowledge, or "knowledge of the ground." Along the way, it elaborates on the group's ethical orientation. As the group's name ("Blessing from God Association") implies, AMBED took a nonsecular approach to collective organizing and accountability, one that offers a counterpoint to the dominant liberal, technocratic approach to climate justice emblemized by the CAO.

One of the most visible outcomes of the CAO mediation process was the onset of occupational studies of CKDnt in Nicaragua and elsewhere.

Chapter 2 thus turns from legal systems to systems of occupational health. The leader of one of the first groups of international scientists to study the CKDnt epidemic told me that when his team initially came to the Nicaraguan cane fields in 2008, sick workers approached them demanding that they test the soil, the water, and then their blood for the presence of the poison chemicals they were sure would be there. Such tests are notoriously difficult under the best of circumstances, and no link between toxic substances and CKDnt was found. Instead, the scientists started to notice another possible trigger. Perhaps, they hypothesized, CKDnt was the result of something as essential to the production of sugar as water, chemicals, and soil: heat. What has become known as the "heat stress nephropathy" hypothesis now appears in nearly every reputable scholarly paper on CKDnt. More than any other causal theory, the heat stress hypothesis has helped make CKDnt emblematic of the need for a new science of planetary health. A desire to test that hypothesis has drawn international occupational health researchers to the sugarcane zone. While the coming of such research offers some hope to workers, chapter 2 shows how the recent scientific and corporate focus on mitigating heat elides the fact that rising heat is enabled by national policies and transnational industry norms that permit the expanded use of agrochemicals. The systematic push to find ways of continuing to profitably produce sugarcane under conditions of extreme heat was paralleled by the efforts of nonworkers, particularly women, to make knowledge claims about the slower and more accretive changes in climate wrought by chemically driven cane production.

I delve more deeply into how those changes were embodied in chapter 3, where the life support system in question is the vast irrigation network that fed Montelimar's expanding cane fields. For AMBED, waterways were a means of both dividing and connecting plantation and nonplantation space, work and home, and human and nonhuman life. The embankments of irrigation canals, dams, and pipes, as well as beaches and riverbeds, turned out to be effective places not just for producing evidence of the impact of sugar production on bodies but also for flipping the terms on which CKDnt could be understood—from a disease of agricultural production to a disease of social reproduction. Questions about the distribution of water, as well as its quality, highlighted how the work of supporting the life of sugarcane became problematically at odds with that of supporting the lives of others who called the sugarcane zone home. Ethnographically, I show how AMBED and the communities it represented linked the kidney's primary biological function, cleansing the body of wastes, to the social acts of cleaning that took place along these embankments, conjuring a "renal environment" out of the plantation landscape.

Chapter 4 turns to the system of pesticide application and regulation. Chemical toxicity was perhaps the most pressing concern for residents of the sugarcane zone, but because toxic damage here, as in other places where chemical exposure occurs, was sometimes slow and sometimes acute, sometimes painfully obvious and other times merely possible, residents had to develop creative ways to keep attention on the problem. Rather than see toxicity as simply a question of material interactions between bodies and chemicals, the chapter illustrates how people in the sugarcane zone worked to make toxicity legible through a variety of media, including the oral sharing of stories and the exchange of videos and photographs on platforms like Facebook and WhatsApp. By rethinking toxic worlds as mediated worlds, people in the sugarcane zone found a method for questioning the premises of both pesticide regulation and toxicology. If toxicity is made in the circulation of narratives, and not just in the circulation of molecules, then the media of telecommunication, digital photography, and storytelling become essential tools in environmental politics.

Even those life support systems that appeared to be designed explicitly to provide aid to people affected by CKDnt often served in practice to support sugarcane production—to rescue the industry from itself. Chapter 5 discusses former Montelimar workers' engagements with Nicaragua's national social security system. Those affected by CKDnt had to work through the corporation to wrest benefits from the social security agency. Social security systems may seem less "open" than legal or regulatory or irrigation systems, but historical evidence about the place of sugar production in the development of the Nicaraguan welfare state shows how conditions like CKDnt challenge the structural integrity of social safety nets. Social security systems are premised on the idea that to receive insurance from the state, one must be identifiable as a productive worker. Since social security provides aid to injured workers, such systems also depend on an ability to clearly define what counts as a workplace injury. What the CKDnt epidemic has exposed is that the categories of both the worker and the working environment turn out to be fluid and contestable. The chapter uncovers the messy negotiations that go into establishing which bodily and ecological conditions count as "working conditions."

Moving from social safety nets to systems of care for the sick, chapter 6 examines what was perhaps the most significant outcome of AMBED's mediated settlement with the Montelimar Corporation: access to hemodialysis for dozens of former workers with late-stage kidney disease. The chapter charts the journeys of hemodialysis patients back and forth from the sugarcane zone to the hemodialysis wards of Nicaragua's capital, Managua. To be honest, it may be unfair to call the kidney disease treatment approach in Nicaragua a "system." Not all those who are offered the opportunity to receive dialysis treatment accept it, and not everyone who does accept it sees it as an unambiguous good. Moreover, those who qualify for this benefit constitute a decided minority of all those affected by the epidemic. Through stories about the ambivalence of patients toward treatment, I argue that corporate social responsibility, a key element of most designs for planetary health, has the effect of reinforcing a view of labor that is as old as the plantation itself, namely, that working bodies are fungible and interchangeable.

Against Problem Closure

An impulse to identify discrete and measurable determinants of disease continues to animate many of us who are concerned about planetary health. This book is intended as a check on that impulse. Along with other critical anthropologists, I agree that it is appropriate to push back against the distributive hope that is lodged in many policy and institutional approaches to health (planetary or otherwise), namely, that with enough of the right kind of expertise, we might restore nature and normalcy.[53] Across this book, many of the actors are the same: Saúl, AMBED's leaders, the people who tended to small houses and gardens in villages dotted across Montelimar's vast sugar-growing complex. The actors are the same, but the problem, how to work at the intersection of the multiple systems that have been designed to support plantation life, is reconfigured. This makes closure a challenge. One of the lessons this reconfiguration provides for a critical approach to planetary health is that there is no way of returning to a "before," when life support systems worked better, when the drive to expand human health could be reconciled with the drive to expand economic growth.

Each chapter finds people eschewing an approach to social action that is based on the presumption that a return to a prediseased condition is possible, or even desirable. Instead, they approach CKDnt in a noninnocent register, one that over time has come to suppress the search for root causes and cures. The search for root causes, as the disability studies scholar Eli Clare writes, "requires damage, locating the harm entirely within human body-minds, operating as if each person were their own ecosystem." The notion of restorative cure, Clare continues, relies "on a belief that what existed before is superior to what exists currently." These beliefs about cause and cure, in turn, are rooted in dominant definitions of what counts as "*normal* and *natural*."[54] While the people whose work and lives I discuss in this book certainly see failing kidneys as a form of damage, they refuse to locate that damage solely within their bodies. Furthermore—and this is not surprising if you think about it—they refuse to believe that what existed before the CKDnt epidemic began, a destructive plantation system that thrived on the exploitation of poor and marginalized rural people, is either superior to what exists today, or is normal, or is natural. While CKDnt has been devastating, it has also created an opening for multiple ways of imagining health.[55]

There is a temptation, perhaps especially among critically minded medical anthropologists, to approach stories about contested or neglected diseases with a particular kind of cause in mind: cause as end point or goal. Think social justice or human rights. We anthropologists tell ourselves that through in-depth, long-term, place-based research, we can arrive at a previously hidden empirical vantage point that will unlock the mystery. This makes sense. Scholars committed to the marginal, the disempowered, the unfree, or the afflicted have a stake in the clinical project of alleviating suffering. But such scholars (and I include myself here) might do well to hold in abeyance that temptation to unlock, to solve, to provide problem closure.

What if instead we worked toward a way of knowing that, in the words of John Jackson, refused to "simply treat mystery as its mortal enemy, as nothing more than a land to be conquered"?[56] That is a good summary of what many of the Nicaraguan CKDnt patients and their allies have tried to do. Today, they still point anxiously to the helicopter, but they don't all agree that the helicopter is some sort of smoking gun. They acknowledge the heat, and they even buy into the narratives that link CKDnt to global warming. But—and I admit this has been frustrating—people in Nicaragua's sugarcane zone experiencing the CKDnt epidemic have never galvanized around a single cause. Instead, they find themselves on edge.

For that reason, the chapters that follow take place not in the sugarcane fields themselves but in the rivers, villages, and roadways that run along their edges. It is along these edges, I suggest, that we might come to a more convincing understanding of how the unraveling of planetary ecology manifests in local biology. The villages in which sugarcane zone residents live and die are physically located on the ecological and economic edges of monocrop production systems. Residents' day-to-day lives entail work (only some of it remunerated and recognized as such) in the forest edges and irrigation embankments that separate homes from cane. As the sugarcane zone heats up, and as the chemical regimes of crop management become more intense, they find themselves enveloped in the anxieties of corporations and states navigating uncertain profit margins and varying degrees of financial solvency. All the while, they find themselves on the edge of inclusion in economic and political orders, as they struggle to extend the reach of private and public systems of medical care.[57] As a global reconfiguration of the norms and practices of medical and environmental science, planetary health still remains something of an aspiration. But as a grassroots project, it has already begun, in an unlikely place: on the edge of the sugarcane zone.

I

———

Grievance, Ground, and Grace

"This way. Take a right," Don Alvaro Guerrero said from the back seat.

"Are you sure it's not straight ahead?" asked Don Alvaro Torres, who was sitting next to Don Alvaro Guerrero.

"No, hombre," Don Alvaro Guerrero insisted. "What do you know? Saúl, take a right here. The road's nice and dry."

Saúl looked suspiciously into the rearview mirror of the Hyundai Accent that carried the four of us into the southern sector of the zona. The two Don Alvaros were the longest-serving and most active members of AMBED's board of directors, and Don Alvaro Guerrero, our self-appointed navigator, had grown up and spent much of his life working in the section of the Montelimar plantation where we now found ourselves. Earlier in the drive, when we were still more certain about our bearings, we had passed the small plot, or *parcela*, where he grew corn. The parcela sat adjacent to a large stand of cane and across the road from a beachfront property rumored to belong to the family of President Daniel Ortega.

It was November, still the rainy season. The plantation roads were rutty and rough in the best of conditions, and we were trying to make our way to the village of Loma Alegre, an isolated hamlet on the edge of a river at the outer limits of Montelimar-controlled land. If we could get there, our plan was to meet a group of residents to alert them to their rights under a recently signed agreement between AMBED and the Montelimar Corporation. Part of that agreement permitted AMBED to "publicize [the] existence and function" of the corporation's internal grievance mechanism, or *mecanismo de quejas*.[1]

With a sigh, Saúl took Don Alvaro Guerrero's suggestion and popped the vehicle into gear, swerving back and forth to stay on the dry red patches of the road. Saúl often told me that he loved to drive, but right now, I wasn't so sure. The Hyundai was registered as a taxi, which meant that using it for trips to the zona took a toll on Saúl's other means of making a living. In order to keep in good standing with his taxi cooperative, he had to have it washed on return and, as he was likely remembering now, repair any damage done. As we rounded the first bend on Don Alvaro Guerrero's chosen route, a massive mud puddle revealed itself in the middle distance.

"Guerrero . . ." Saúl groaned suspiciously, his voice rising.

"It's good, it's shallow," Don Alvaro Guerrero assured him.

"*Guerrero . . .*"

Don Alvaro Torres and I laughed. We had been in similar spots with the Hyundai before. Over the course of the previous few months, the mud and rocks had choked the exhaust, ripped off a rear bumper, and punctured tires, and the heat had fried the air-conditioning. As a result, more than a few of my research dollars ended up going to local repair shops, but out here, we were on our own.

Saúl approached the puddle with caution. The Hyundai's bald tires were already slipping and sliding on its banks. Saúl couldn't slow down too much, I reasoned silently to myself, lest we get mired before we even made it to the water. There was a dryish patch of grass and dirt to the left of the puddle. Perhaps it was just firm enough to carry us around.

"Guerrero . . ." Saúl moaned again as he gunned the engine to enter the sneak route. After a few seconds of revving and swerving, the right front tire dipped into the puddle bank on the right, and we came to a halt.

More laughter ensued, none of it louder than that which came from Don Alvaro Guerrero and Don Alvaro Torres as both men slithered out of the left rear door. I followed Saúl out of the driver's side door, my shoe immediately covered in the molasses-colored muck.

After we looked things over for a while, I was appointed to take the wheel, while the other three pushed from behind. We made it out, and I remember thinking as I lay in bed that night what an adventure this had turned out to be. The comical and unheroic struggle of a couple of paunchy, cautious, fortysomething men from elsewhere (Saúl and me) and a couple of jocular, unfazed fiftysomething locals (the two Don Alvaros) to get from point A to point B made for a good fieldwork anecdote, but I figured it would not be much more than that.

Years later, I realize that moments like this underscore something that was too obvious to the two Don Alvaros to state directly. As lifelong residents of the zona, Don Alvaro Torres and Don Alvaro Guerrero knew something that even Saúl, who had been driving these roads for years now, had trouble fully grasping. They knew what it really meant to be stuck, and we were not really stuck. Hence, the laughter. Our struggle was a parody of the much more serious situation that AMBED was trying to address.

There are dozens of villages located in or around the Montelimar plantation, and many of them are difficult to access. Because these villages are nearly all enveloped in sugarcane, they can seem, and have been depicted, as "islands" in the monoculture. The unforgiving plantation roads are the only transportation corridors available, which means that the prospect of getting stuck can have all kinds of consequences, especially for those who are sick. The material quality of roads matters to the experience of health and disease here, as it does everywhere.[2] We made repeated visits to Loma Alegre, for instance, because the two Don Alvaros were concerned that people with CKDnt who lived there would be less likely to seek treatment if someone did not check in on them now and then.

One thing the two Don Alvaros had in common was a sense of place honed over years working in sugarcane production, and over lifetimes that included stints participating in the popular Sandinista revolution. In the 1970s and 1980s, rural campesinos, urban working-class people, and a disaffected middle class rose up to topple the dictatorship of the Somoza family and remake Nicaragua as a social democracy, only to be thwarted by the anticommunist zeal of the United States, which funded a counterrevolutionary war. As combatants in that war, the two Don Alvaros had developed what the Argentinean doctor and Cuban revolutionary Ernesto "Che" Guevara called in his writings on guerrilla warfare "knowledge of the ground."[3] Guevara's conceptualization of guerrilla tactics emerged in part from his study of the Nicaraguan nationalist Augusto César Sandino, the namesake of the Sandinista movement. Sandino, in turn, had been a student of Nicaraguan and broader global histories of peasant struggle. In the 1920s and 1930s, Sandino led a small rural militia that spearheaded the ouster of occupying US military forces from Nicaragua. The country's history, particularly in the agricultural corridor of the Pacific coast, can be understood as a series of violent clashes between landed elites, many of them supported by the United States, and Indigenous and peasant groups.[4]

Monique Allewaert, a literary critic and scholar of eighteenth-century plantation life, adapts Guevara's idea of knowledge of the ground to explain how maroon communities and others who escaped colonial bondage survived in the swamps and mires that surrounded rice and sugar plantations. This kind of knowledge was essential to Black Caribbean resistance to the logics of the plantation.[5] Colonial writers saw the plantation zone as a force that pulled bodies apart, one that undermined the colonial and capitalist project of "[turning] bodies into singular yet abstract corpuses."[6] That the plantation had a capacity to pull bodies apart was, of course, fundamental to the colonial economy. Black and brown bodies were not imagined to need to be singular or abstractable in the Enlightenment liberal worldview that was emerging in parallel to the Atlantic plantation economy. As unfree labor, they could be treated, to use the term deployed by Hortense Spillers, as fungible, interchangeable "flesh."[7] Plantation zones, as ecological forms, are the outgrowth of the assumption that the integrity of some bodies matters less than the integrity of others, that liberal citizenship must be protected for some but not for others.

Another thing the two Don Alvaros had in common was a belief that despite the destruction and violence of the plantation, blessings from God could still be witnessed there. The context for this chapter, and for much of my fieldwork, was a multiyear mediated dialogue between AMBED and Montelimar's management. Starting in 2017, I regularly accompanied Saúl and AMBED's leaders on journeys around the zona as they worked to collect various kinds of documents from residents living in its roughly forty villages. I joined them as they filtered these documents through the company's mecanismo de quejas, as well as the circuits of the Nicaraguan legal system and the World Bank's system for ensuring corporate accountability. These documents included official papers such as work and pay records, clinical reports, and land titles. As we will see in later chapters, they also included photographs and videos, recorded on mobile phones, depicting what AMBED understood as the contamination of waterways by the sugarcane mill, aerial spraying of chemical pesticides, and large-scale deforestation. I took some of these photographs and videos, recorded many of the conversations we had, and helped collect the documents. I also used grant money to pay for gasoline, car repairs, food, and equipment. In this way, for a time, my ethnographic project helped give shape to AMBED's advocacy work, and vice versa.[8]

Mediation systems like those that were enacted at Montelimar offer an alternative to a civil court, where a person or group might seek compensation from a company for injuries caused by its activities. Mediations are designed to end, and to end with definitive results. But even as AMBED pushed the corporation to pay more attention to the epidemic, the group was animated by something less definitive than the kinds of concessions and trade-offs one might expect from mediation. As I show in this chapter, AMBED worked betwixt and between the norms of liberal legal accountability and the decidedly less mathematical kind of accountability promoted by another authority, that of the Christian God invoked in the organization's name, the Montelimar Blessing from God Association (Asociación Montelimar Bendición de Dios). The guerrilla generation of knowledge of the ground and the seemingly conservative appeal to blessings from God might at first seem incompatible. But Nicaraguan class and revolutionary politics are entangled with religiosity in ways that are difficult to explain using either Marxist gestures to "false consciousness" or romantic idealizations of the theology of liberation.[9]

On its face, AMBED's origin story, which I recount in this chapter, is one in which plantation residents *were* being treated as people whose integrity—bodily and political—mattered. One version of the story finds a small group of relatively poor rural people gaining a voice before the World Bank, the largest economic development organization on the planet. It can read very much like a tale of marginal people finally being invited as full members into the community of global citizens. Such an invitation came at the cost of illness and injury. It is doubtful that the invitation would have been extended had CKDnt not existed.[10]

Over just a few years, AMBED amassed an array of legal, scholarly, and bureaucratic documents, including clinical records, work records, land titles, corporate complaint forms, and epidemiological surveys. In the clinical and research spaces of global health, documentary practices often double as means of governance, helping render the variable perspectives and experiences of patients, caregivers, and laborers into uniform, legible, translatable data. But documentation is never only a device for extending the legal, bureaucratic, or medical gaze.[11] AMBED's approach to documentation combined a fidelity to the demand that community groups seeking recognition keep paper records with an acknowledgment that social change depended upon knowledge of the ground.[12] Together, documentation and knowledge of the ground formed the basis for a nonsecular approach to environmental and social accountability, in which blessings played a central role.

Assembling Grievances

In 2003, an American undergraduate student I'll call Jane Bernstein came to live with a group of Indigenous Sutiaba farmers in an area called Goyena, located a few miles north of the city of León and adjacent to the sugarcane plantation owned by Nicaragua Sugar Estates Limited (NSEL). Few of the residents of Goyena were directly employed by NSEL. Instead, they operated small farms on land held by the Indigenous council. When Jane first came to Goyena as part of a study abroad and service-learning experience, she befriended Don Silvio, a farmer and local leader who was helping his neighbors amass a documentary archive.

I met Don Silvio years later, in mid-2017. When I visited his house, he showed me a pile of decaying documents, dating back as far as his first meetings with Jane. "I tried to keep everything we collected over the years," he said apologetically, "but the rain and the bugs have taken most of them." Most of the documents that remained were one-page community claim forms, part of NSEL's internal grievance system. None of the claims in Don Silvio's archive mentioned kidney disease. Rather, in varying degrees of detail, they described how farmers' crops—peppers, squash, cucumbers, and plantains—had been damaged or destroyed as a result of NSEL's application of aerial pesticides (figure 1.1). Each claimant put a monetary value on the loss and delineated the precise area of land under cultivation.

The information on these forms was collated into a spreadsheet, with each page stamped and signed by the company's representative, along with representatives from the Nicaraguan Ministry of Agriculture and Forestry and the León departmental authorities. The forms are classic examples of the kind of documentation that, whether in corporate or state contexts, is almost always the pretext for recognition and legitimacy.[13] To create this archive, Don Silvio and other leaders gathered their neighbors in a local community center and, one by one, helped them fill in the claim forms. In a context of stark inequality, in which limits to literacy made it difficult for individuals to lodge complaints that would stick to states or corporations, the act of filling in the grievance documents in a collective, public fashion made a powerful statement. Don Silvio saved the papers not only to preserve a record of each individual case but also to commemorate a moment of Indigenous solidarity. This archive of quasi-bureaucratic forms was, paradoxically, evidence of the decidedly nonliberal ties that his community had to this land.[14]

Around the same time that the Goyena farmers started documenting their problems, a few miles to the north, a small group of men from the town of

FIGURE 1.1 Community claim form created in Goyena in 2003. Photo by the author.

Chichigalpa had begun to hold a regular vigil outside the gates to NSEL's sugar mill. These men were former cane cutters who were in varying stages of what later became known as CKDnt. Don Silvio encouraged Jane to make the short journey to meet them. The ex-workers told her a story in which key documents were conspicuously absent. Sugarcane plantation labor makes incredible demands on the body. It is so physically demanding, in fact, that even before the CKDnt epidemic started, a yearly medical exam was a prerequisite for plantation employment (see chapters 3 and 5). During these exams, tests on the men's blood turned up biomarkers for early-stage chronic kidney disease. Over the course of the late 1990s and early aughts, hundreds of would-be workers with such biomarkers were dismissed.

When they were dismissed, the workers were not given access to their medical records. Instead, they were advised to go to public or private clinics, get a diagnosis, and then gather the pay stubs and work records they had accumulated over the years so that they could petition the National Institute of Social Security for benefits. But clinical exams were costly, and the visits to the social security office to verify work records revealed a high level of underreporting on the part of

NSEL and its many subcontractors. Many former workers had trouble documenting that they had ever been employed in the sugarcane plantation at all.

The kidney disease was becoming a well-known scourge. Jane spent much of the rest of her first visit to Nicaragua, as she told me later, "just going to funerals." Young people (overwhelmingly men), in the prime of their lives, in their twenties and thirties, were wasting away. Jane's accompaniment of the Goyena farmers and the workers' group to funerals, community meetings, and informal venting sessions continued in subsequent years, as she began work on a graduate degree in environmental studies, and as the workers' organization evolved into an advocacy group, the Chichigalpa Association for Life (ASOCHIVIDA). By 2005, Don Silvio and his neighbors had decided that NSEL's internal mecanismo de quejas was a dead end. Even when they were compiled and submitted en masse, the community complaint forms, in which the word of small farmers was set against that of the company, were proving ineffective. The Ministry of Agriculture and Forestry seemed unwilling or unable to follow up, and the company's response was laconic at best. For their part, ASOCHIVIDA's members had begun to believe that plantation working conditions—pesticides, excessive heat, long hours—were responsible for making them sick.

Both groups felt that they needed more documentation.

Over the next few years, Jane started collecting samples of well water and soil and testing them for the presence of known pesticides. Everyone was convinced that agrochemicals would be the link between the destroyed crops and the destroyed kidneys. But Jane and her collaborators could find no definitive evidence of dangerous levels of either chemical or heavy metal residue. In parallel to the environmental sampling, Jane undertook another kind of documentation. She collected first dozens, then hundreds, of stories about farmers losing a year's worth of crops, about their fear of drinking well water, and about former sugarcane cutters being sent home by their employers to die. Even though the toxicological studies failed to turn up any solid evidence, Jane managed to collect a mass of qualitative material, in the form of testimonials, photos, and films. But it would take the intervention of the world's largest development organization, and the momentum of a global financial push to expand sugarcane production, for that evidence to gain traction.

Transparency Comes to the Sugarcane Zone

While sugarcane has been cultivated at an industrial scale in Nicaragua for well over a century, the industry has expanded at an unprecedented rate in the past two decades, thanks in part to more than $100 million in investment by the World Bank through the International Finance Corporation (IFC), part of a broader resurgence of international investment in monocrops in the early twenty-first century.[15] As it began this push for investment in monocrops, the World Bank also started to recognize a need to increase the transparency of its activities. The overwhelmingly poor and marginalized people whose lives were being targeted for "development" interventions like the expansion of industrial agriculture needed to have faith that the Bank's loans would actually improve their lives. Such people needed a way to hold the Bank and its corporate partners to account. They needed a way to be recognized as legitimate sources of critique and complaint. To that end, in 1999, the Bank created an entity called the Compliance Advisor Ombudsman (CAO), a body that would respond to "environmental and social concerns and complaints of people directly impacted by IFC . . . projects."[16] Like other corporate or organizational ombudsman offices, the CAO is independent of the IFC, and it reports directly to the World Bank's president. The CAO is also independent of local government authorities.

The CAO refers to itself as "a fair, trusted, and effective independent resource *mechanism*."[17] The term *mechanism* connotes a functional relationship.[18] In both sociology and epidemiology, *mechanism* is a synonym for *cause*. A sociologist might ask what brings a group of sugarcane workers together to sign their names to a grievance directed to an office of the World Bank. For the sociologist, the mechanism might be a shared sense of liberal personhood. An epidemiologist might ask what causes otherwise healthy kidneys to fail. For the epidemiologist, the mechanism might be a chemical or other environmental trigger. Both sociological and epidemiological mechanisms gain their legitimacy through documentation: the compiling of voting records, datasets, randomized controlled trials, toxicological measurements, and clinical reports.[19] But it is notoriously difficult to identify causal mechanisms in environmental health. The effects of toxins can often take years to manifest, and studies of environmental diseases are costly, time-consuming, and frequently contrary to the interests of corporations and the states that support them.[20] There is also ample evidence to suggest that an abstract notion of liberal personhood means less in the actual lives of the rural poor and Indigenous people of Latin America than sociologists and lawyers might assume.[21]

Around the time that the CAO was formed, the Spanish cognate of *mechanism* (*mecanismo*) was becoming a familiar industry term. As corporations like Montelimar and NSEL expanded, they began to embrace corporate social responsibility principles. The presence of community claim forms and mecanismos de quejas on sugarcane plantations reflects a broader sense that an image of transparency and magnanimity would be good for business.[22] These corporate mecanismos operated only when workers or community members activated them—when they turned their knowledge of the ground into written complaints. As the story of Goyena illustrates, however, mecanismo was not an abstract sociological or epidemiological idea in Nicaragua. It existed not just in written documents themselves but in the process of documentation.

In 2005, as Jane and her US and Nicaraguan colleagues were struggling to draw attention to the kidney disease crisis in the NSEL environs, they contacted the Washington, DC–based Center for International Environmental Law (CIEL). CIEL informed them that the IFC was planning to make a $55 million loan to NSEL. The infusion of cash would allow NSEL to expand its plantations and construct an ethanol plant near Chichigalpa. CIEL saw an opening. The environmental assessments that NSEL carried out for its application to the IFC had examined only the impact of the ethanol plant itself, not health, labor, or environmental conditions in the surrounding villages. Due diligence had not been done to communities like Goyena, and no acknowledgment had been made of the growing kidney disease crisis, even though NSEL's own company doctors had been seeing it spread firsthand. This seemed to CIEL like something the CAO would want to know about.

In 2008, CIEL submitted a grievance to the CAO on behalf of the residents of Goyena and ASOCHIVIDA. The grievance made a disparate set of claims, alleging violations of people's "right to freedom of association, right to safe and healthy working conditions, right to health, and right to water."[23] It accused the IFC of failure "to assure itself that NSEL's community engagement led to broad community support for the project"; failure "to ensure local disclosure of NSEL's social and environmental assessment"; and failure "to conduct the necessary due diligence of NSEL's environmental and social track record."[24] The grievance told about the deaths of farmers' cattle due to contaminated groundwater; about a blockage of paths and roadways connecting villages that limited freedom of association; about poor flood control; about damage to small farms and gardens; about air pollution from pesticides and burning sugar; *and* about suspected kidney disease. It is not clear either from the wording of this document or my subsequent discussions with those involved that the complainants were interested in using the CAO grievance mechanism only to address kidney disease. The section of the grievance that lists "desired remedies" separates the demands of "all complainants" from those of "former NSEL workers." The one conviction that all parties shared was an intimate, historically informed knowledge of the ground: a sense that the damage wrought by sugarcane plantation agriculture had become intolerable.

From Complaints to Complaint

The 2008 grievance resulted in a CAO-sponsored mediation between the complainants and the company. By the time the mediation began, the people of Goyena, most of whom had never been employed by NSEL but who did claim that their cattle and soil and crops had been damaged by the company's activities, were no longer involved in the process. The circumstances surrounding this are still hotly debated. Some residents I interviewed alleged that bribery and intimidation by the state and NSEL played a role, but I have no concrete evidence of that. What the eventual exclusion of the Goyena complainants does illustrate is a point highlighted elsewhere in anthropological scholarship on agrarian struggles for social recognition, namely, that any nominal citizenship rights that might come with modern democratic statehood are tenuous for groups, particularly Afro-Latinx or Indigenous groups, whose very presence presents a challenge to national narratives of modernity.[25]

By late 2008, ASOCHIVIDA and NSEL had negotiated a plan to appoint a US-based research team to study the kidney disease problem.[26] Both sides scored this a success. The disease eventually known as CKDnt started making national and international headlines. Parallel research in neighboring El Salvador and Costa Rica, as well as India and Sri Lanka, turned up similarly alarming rates of illness. Almost without fail, journalists reported the story as a case of occupational injury. Nonworkers tended to be depicted as grieving widows or children. Reading these stories, it is difficult to discern that the landscape also included groups like the people of Goyena, with deep ancestral ties to this land.

After the mediation process began, ASOCHIVIDA's membership swelled from just a few dozen to over two thousand, thanks in large part to the group's ability to be a convincing producer of documents. ASOCHIVIDA helped potential members gather evidence of employment by NSEL or one of its subcontractors and obtain written evidence of CKDnt diagnosis. Benefits for members include access to subsidized medicine, clothing, and microcredit. By developing a savvy understanding of company, state, and epidemiological documentary practices, ASOCHIVIDA has succeeded beyond most everyone's expectations. That said, ASOCHIVIDA remains a community formed around a narrowly defined pathology, which allows it to make limited claims on the corporation. Nearly all its activities continue to be routed through the figure of the CKDnt patient and ex-worker.

Since 2008, NSEL has helped to fund and promote ASOCHIVIDA's efforts to help CKDnt patients and their families. While it initially disavowed a connection between labor and CKDnt, the company has now made the protection of workers central to its corporate social responsibility platform. This has paid dividends. During the period of my fieldwork, NSEL received more than $18 million from Proparco, the private lending arm of the French international development agency, partly because of the company's commitment to "responsible" sugar production.[27] The CAO grievance process seems to have empowered actors like the members of ASOCHIVIDA, even as it has allowed NSEL to establish its bona fides as a good corporate citizen. NSEL portrays its participation in the mediation process as a sign of its commitment to worker welfare. In 2018, the company was certified fair trade.[28] If you buy the fair trade version of its signature product, Flor de Caña rum, in your local shop, you can thank the members of ASOCHIVIDA (and the people of Goyena) for the privilege.

Mechanisms and Blessings

In 2013, the IFC was preparing a second multimillion-dollar loan, this time for the Montelimar Corporation, the smallest of Nicaragua's four sugar companies. The Montelimar loan was announced shortly after the mediation between ASOCHIVIDA and NSEL concluded.[29] Remarkably, given what had happened at NSEL, the section of the IFC's environmental and social review document that deals with the question of "community health, safety and security" states that "Montelimar's operations have limited potential impacts on a sparsely populated area in the vicinity of cane growing and the Montelimar mill." The initial Montelimar loan documents make no mention of community concerns about agrochemical usage, about access to clean and abundant water, or about CKDnt—even though the epidemic had been underway for nearly a decade leading up to the loan's approval, and the loss of these natural resources had been underway for much longer. In fact, in the IFC's initial disclosures regarding its Montelimar loan, the section on broad community support states that "Broad Community Support is not applicable for this project."[30]

When she learned of the IFC's plans, Jane Bernstein traveled to Montelimar. Along with Saúl and the two Don Alvaros, she accompanied workers and community members in meetings and conducted interviews, replicating the work she had done in Goyena and Chichigalpa. After about six months, residents decided to form their own organization, which they called AMBED. AMBED filed its CAO grievance in 2015. As in the 2008 NSEL grievance, this one demanded assistance from the company for CKDnt-affected workers seeking social security benefits and work records, but the grievance went well beyond working conditions. It mentioned damage to soil, air, and water due to pesticide application and poor management. It demanded that independent water quality studies be conducted. In addition, it requested documentation of ancestral land tenure. Since many residents had lived for generations on land owned by the company or its antecedents (the entity now known as the Montelimar Corporation has only owned the plantation since 2000), they risked summary evictions as the plantation expanded its holdings. Finally, the complaint demanded that the company "recognize that all of us have the right to live a dignified life in a healthy environment."[31]

When I first met her over Skype in 2017, Jane was quick to tell me that "*they* [Jane's Nicaraguan collaborators from AMBED] chose the name." She assured me that even though the name invoked the blessing of a Christian God, AMBED was not church affiliated in any way. She implied with her tone that it was fine with her if I wasn't church affiliated either. I knew what she meant. She was speaking to me in a particular kind of gringa-to-gringo code: a gestural language often adopted by North Americans of a secular humanist stripe who come to places like Nicaragua with aid and solidarity in mind. We had to acknowledge the Christian valence of AMBED's name, it seemed, but we did not need to account for it, much less espouse it, even if we wanted to work with those who united under it. The members of AMBED were not out to convert anyone, least of all the wealthy, white *internacionalistas* who were there to help.[32]

But Nicaragua is what the southern American author Flannery O'Connor would call a "Christ-haunted" country.[33] In everyday conversations, phrases like "La sangre de Cristo!" (The blood of Christ!) stand in for what in English vernacular might simply appear as "Wow!" O'Connor was not herself an activist or even much of a progressive humanitarian. For a start, her misgivings about the civil rights movement in her home state of Georgia and the derogatory descriptions of Black characters in her fiction make her a somewhat displeasing critical interlocutor. Like me, she inherited the racial privilege that trickled down from a southern plantation society. Still, her observation that "the Southerner, who isn't convinced of it, is very much afraid that he may have been formed in the image and likeness of God" rings true as I think about my internal ambivalence about the status and staying power of blessings from God, or what O'Connor would call "grace," in the sugarcane zone.[34] For O'Connor, God's grace was not mechanical but mysterious. That mystery was not something one could unpack; it was the condition of haunting itself.

CKDnt seems plenty complex, plenty mysterious, without having to bring grace into the picture. The edifice of a certain kind of critically engaged scholarship is constructed of neat, discrete categories of acting and being, including a bifurcation between "traditional," "conservative" religious belief and "progressive" political practices.[35] In describing AMBED, one could craft a believable tale about a poor and injured community rising up against the industry that harmed it, marshaling science and law and the left-wing sympathies of people like Jane and me to its side. The problem is that such a tale would not be the full story. It would not be false per se, but telling it would reinforce a view of the sugarcane industry and the communities that surround it as ecologically and socially separate, and of Christianity as an ethical adjunct to grassroots organization. AMBED's insistence on grounding its grievances in a Christian ethos offers lessons for understanding not just the realities of contemporary sugarcane production but also the planetary crisis in which sugarcane production is implicated.[36] In other words, knowledge of the ground is bound up in the unknowable mysteries of divine blessings, or grace.

The linguistic anthropologist Paul Kockelman offers a useful way of thinking about this in his accounts of landslides in highland Guatemala (where land degradation is being hastened by climate change). He notes that divine agency is present in Q'eqchi' explanations for the causes of environmental degradation, but "grace," including in its Christian valence, is also invoked in Q'eqchi' attempts to mitigate it. For Kockelman, grace is "a kind of ethical and practical caring for those whose lives have been degraded, or who live amongst degradation."[37] The "blessing" in AMBED's name thus points to another side of the story of labor, environment, and health. In the increasingly evangelical Christian-leaning world of the Global South, including Central America, blessings can be material rewards, but they can also be less tangible signs of grace—strengthened family or social ties, opportunities for self-refashioning, or simply moments of recognition.[38]

Assembling AMBED

Javier Cáceres was a devout evangelical Christian and former sugarcane worker. He was, in his own telling, "blessed" to have been rescued by God and brought into the evangelical church, which had helped men like him, Don Alvaro Torres, and Don Alvaro Guerrero give up alcohol and rededicate themselves to their families. Javier was one of dozens of AMBED members whose thoughts kept coming back to the mystery of one particular blessing—the one that came via the World Bank. The World Bank was not an unfamiliar figure in Pacific coastal Nicaragua. Its blue-and-white logo adorned projects that had benefited local communities in many ways. Most anywhere international development programs happened—say, the building of a school or the improvement of a hospital—that name, Banco Mundial, was likely to be invoked on the day that a mayor or national assembly member cut the ribbon.

What reason would the Bank have for giving a loan to the Montelimar Corporation? Javier asked me and the other men seated outside a small tortilla stand in El 54, a scattered group of houses located around kilometer 54 of the road between San Rafael del Sur and Pochomil. The corporation was already rich—rich enough, in fact, to do its own occasional community-minded deed, like when its engineers had installed communal wells in a few villages some years back, or when it paid for the painting of one of the local schools. These and other corporate social responsibility projects were well advertised when they happened, and images of their completion were circulated in the company's public relations materials and in the Nicaraguan trade magazine *Azúcar*, a publication that contained page after page of testimonials about the blessings that accrued to those who kept the faith with the economic and social potential of industrial sugarcane.

The men sitting in the shade eating tortillas with a salty cottage cheese called *cuajada* and drinking watery, sugary coffee nodded their heads. The only explanation was that the company was *not* in fact blessed. The company must have seized World Bank money that rightly should have gone to the people affected by the CKDnt epidemic. As they waited for that Sunday's AMBED general assembly meeting to begin, Javier and his friends continued to speculate on the nature of international development finance. At the assembly, they would be reminded by AMBED leaders and CAO representatives, not for the first time, that the loan was not ever meant for the community. It was always meant for the company.

AMBED's general assemblies were always held on Sundays. During the planting and harvesting season, Sunday was the one day of the week that sugarcane plantation workers did not go to the fields. It was also the one day each week when people with late-stage CKDnt did not go to Managua to receive hemodialysis treatments. So two Sundays a month, members would pile into the beds of rented pickup trucks and head for El 54. Early in the morning, before the sun and humidity got overwhelming, the setting felt pastoral. The ridge afforded a distant view of the sugarcane fields, stretching on a clear blue morning to the Pacific Ocean.

Assemblies were scheduled to begin at 8:00 a.m., but in typical Nicaraguan fashion, most attendees didn't start arriving until at least half past that hour. Business would not really begin until Doña Iris arrived. Doña Iris was AMBED's elected secretary, and her position made her responsible for taking attendance and collecting (or attempting to collect) the twenty córdobas each member was asked to contribute to defray the costs of the collective transport and other group activities. When AMBED was founded, twenty córdobas equated to a little over fifty US cents, but even though the figure seemed nominal, more than a few members declined to pay, citing financial hardship. As with the World Bank loan, many others questioned how that money was being spent, and on whom. These financial questions would dog AMBED for the duration of its existence and would lead to the fracture of its leadership on multiple occasions.[39]

When AMBED entered into the grievance process, the group agreed to certain constitutive rules, devised in consultation with representatives of the CAO. Regular meetings were central to establishing AMBED as a bona fide community organization. By October 2015, some seven hundred people had joined, electing a six-member board of directors, including the two Don Alvaros and Doña Iris. Within the space of just over a year, AMBED had become a player in the workings of supranational development finance. After more than a year of assessment and preliminary meetings, in January 2017, the CAO initiated a formal process of mediation between AMBED and the Montelimar Corporation. This mediation, or *mesa de dialogo* (literally, "dialogue table"), would be chaired by an independent international lawyer hired by the CAO, and it would feature a series of regular, closed-door meetings between AMBED's representatives and Montelimar plantation management. In the weeks between official mediation sessions, AMBED was expected to continue holding its biweekly general assemblies (figure 1.2).

This was what made Doña Iris's careful register of attendance so important. Once the dialogue began, AMBED had to repeatedly attest to the CAO, to the Montelimar Corporation, and to itself that its membership was robust, active, and faithful to the mediation process. According to AMBED's bylaws, any person who failed to show up for more than two consecutive meetings would forfeit their membership and, as the leaders consistently reminded those who attended each meeting, they would forfeit their opportunity to reap any benefits wrought from the mediation.

I began my research at Montelimar roughly six months after the mediation began. Though I asked to be allowed to observe the mediation sessions, I was not particularly surprised when my requests were quietly ignored by the CAO and the legal representatives of both AMBED and the Montelimar Corporation. For the duration of my time studying CKDnt in Nicaragua, I would be observing the process from a distance, and after all, the general assembly meetings seemed like a fruitful and appropriate venue for ethnography. What could

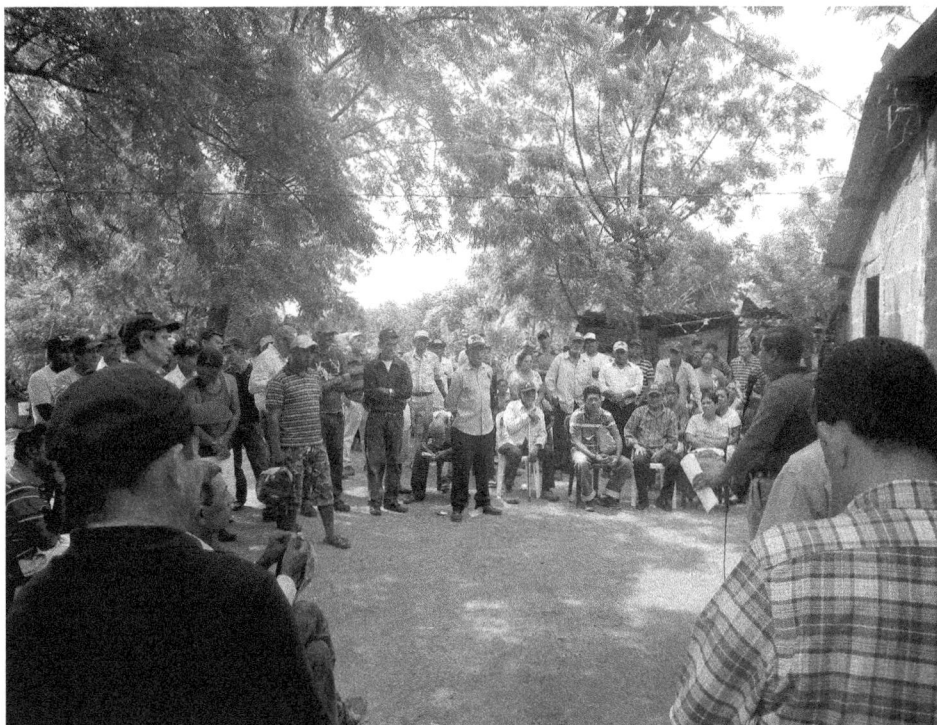

FIGURE 1.2 An AMBED general assembly, 2017. Photo by the author.

be more attractive to an anthropologist interested in health and environmental activism than a meeting? At the general assemblies, I could observe what anthropologists call "biological citizenship" emerge in nearly real time, watching as a group of individuals coalesced around a common medical condition![40] Grassroots environmental health activism and robust democratic deliberation seemed right there. Though my hopes were high, they were misguided.

The AMBED general assemblies didn't just start late. They weren't plagued only with the problem of members refusing to pay their twenty-córdoba contribution. While meetings were potentially spaces for integrating poor, marginalized, and chronically ill individuals into the future-oriented, liberal posture of development finance and corporate social responsibility, those same individuals—people like Javier Cáceres and his friends—dealt daily with what Zoë Wool and Julie Livingston call the "unproductive dead ends of a toxic or melancholic present."[41] To be asked to pay even a nominal membership fee in order to reap some small portion of the millions in World Bank loan money seemed to be too much for many. AMBED's leaders spent much of their time looking for ways to keep members faithful to the idea that a closed-door mediation process orchestrated by a foreign lawyer might lead to more meaningful and lasting blessings, if not for the members, then for their families and communities. Those who attended the assemblies were constantly asking themselves whether it was possible, or desirable, to collectively organize for a better future in a context in which most of the people involved—including nearly every person in the organization's principal leadership—were facing a premature death.

It became apparent over the course of the general assembly meetings I attended that AMBED was anything but a thriving organ of liberal democratic action. Attendance at the assemblies peaked early in the dialogue process, when over three hundred people had gathered to be counted among those affected by the epidemic. In early 2017, AMBED and Montelimar signed an agreement that achieved some important goals. The company agreed to provide funding for some 120 CKDnt-affected former workers to open a textile cooperative. The company also agreed to provide food aid, transportation, and a small stipend to workers with CKDnt who needed dialysis, and logistical and clinical support to those who were awaiting approval for pensions from the national social security scheme. Only patients who had worked for at least two years in the plantation since the Montelimar Corporation purchased it in 2002 were qualified for these benefits.[42] The words *pesticide, water, land, fumigation,* and *dignity* are absent in that 2017 agreement, though it does state that the Montelimar Corporation's corporate social responsibility strategy includes "the Environment" as a "central pillar."[43]

Saúl, Don Alvaro Torres, and Don Alvaro Guerrero were all too aware that even if they attended the assemblies, men like Javier Cáceres still had their doubts about the whole business. AMBED's leaders would take turns at the microphone begging for patience, commitment, and sacrifice from those who had showed up. Much of the assembly's biweekly program involved a litany of AMBED's achievements in the CAO-brokered mediation sessions, but after coming to a few, even I grew weary of recording the same list of benefits and concessions, and I started to sympathize with those who wondered whether this amount of paperwork, registration, and just plain waiting around was worth it.

There is an easy critique of the bureaucratic formalities to which AMBED's leadership subjected itself and its members. In the eyes of a large corporation and of the World Bank, social collectives do not exist without the evidence documented in attendance registers, account books, and minutes. The "social" in "corporate social responsibility" had to be constantly performed and verified, much as faithful commitment in Christian communities must be performed, if only to preemptively justify the blessings that might later accrue to the sanctified.[44] None of the things that preexisted AMBED—people's deep ties to the land on which they lived, the bonds of kinship that connected individuals across villages, a decades-long history of labor, not to mention shared recognition of the impact of a mass epidemic—seemed to be enough to establish that there was a collective desire for dialogue, or change, or even recognition. The formality of general assemblies was necessary for turning a dispersed array of individuals into a recognizably social entity, an outside to which the corporation could turn its responsible attention. But even if AMBED often acted as a vehicle for funneling development dollars to deserving hands, it faced the greater challenge of constantly demonstrating to its own wavering membership that it was more than just a formalized stakeholder group.

Returning Documents to the Ground

In the work that took place outside the general assemblies, AMBED's leaders used their knowledge of the ground to do something both more ambitious and less legible to the CAO and the international legal watchers who would verify the group's legitimacy. A final element of the 2017 agreement included the invitation to AMBED to "publicize [the] existence and function" of the Montelimar Corporation's internal grievance mechanism.[45] The medium of this grievance mechanism was a standard form that bore an eerie resemblance to those filled out years before by the Sutiaba farmers in Goyena. Each month, Don Alvaro Torres would present these forms to the company, whose representatives would give updates on their efforts at finding resolutions through mediation.

To be clear, the 2017 agreement did not create the internal grievance mechanism. Rather, in the agreement, AMBED committed to making its members aware of the grievance mechanism's existence. For the corporation, this likely meant that AMBED would be testifying to its members that Montelimar was a responsible partner dedicated to resolving community problems. For AMBED, this section of the agreement opened space to expand the range of issues to which the company might respond. It allowed AMBED to work as something more than a conduit for channeling transnational loans into corporate social responsibility projects. That clause, rather innocuous on the page, became an invitation to the two Don Alvaros and Saúl and me to get in the Hyundai and do some fieldwork.

That fieldwork is the basis for most of the next five chapters, but here is an early example of how a visit might proceed. We came to the village of El Popol in July 2017 to meet a man with a known case of CKDnt. Though the man we sought was not at home, we were invited into the house of one of his neighbors, Doña Patricia, a woman of about thirty who informed us that she had an uncle and a cousin who were also affected. By the end of the day, one CKDnt case had turned into four others. In these visits, Don Alvaro Torres usually was the one who took it upon himself to inform those we met about the internal grievance mechanism. Sure enough, Doña Patricia had her own grievance. She had been visited some months back by a surveyor from the company, who had provided her with a map of her house lot. Everyone in El Popol got one of these. They were told that these documents would allow them to formalize their land tenure.

El Popol, like many other villages we visited, is inhabited by people whose ancestors were initially given land by the company as part of their compensation for plantation work. Their land had never been legally distinguished from plantation land. But when people in El Popol took their new land surveys to the municipal authority, their documents were not recognized. Doña Patricia was told she would have to pay to have a state cadastral surveyor confirm the findings. On the day of our visit, Don Alvaro helped her fill out the small grievance form and arranged a community meeting for the following weekend to document other similar cases. Over the course of several visits to El Popol, AMBED's leaders collected other grievances, about a lack of steady domestic water supply due to the company's extensive well and dam system, field supervisors who withheld wages without cause, and, of course, the abiding problem of aerial pesticide application.

Montelimar's internal grievance mechanism provides space for testimonies and allegations. It does not promise transparent resolutions in all cases. Indeed, the 2017 agreement states that while AMBED may collect complaints from any member of any plantation community, "With regard to the content of the response provided, the [Montelimar Corporation] is only required to provide such information to AMBED for complaints coming from former workers who are members of AMBED, not when complaints are submitted by active workers or members of the community who are not former workers."[46] The internal grievance mechanism is framed here as open to anyone, while transparent resolution of grievances is only guaranteed to those recognized as workers.

Despite this limitation, AMBED continued collecting and submitting complaints from anyone. It seemed to be both abiding by the terms of the agreement (to publicize the grievance mechanism) and pushing beyond its strict, binary labor-management configuration. AMBED did this with good reason. While the company alone was asked to answer for some of the grievances—specifically the pesticide issue—many of them had ramifications beyond the remit of corporate social responsibility, implicating local and state government agencies from the water utility to the land office to the Ministry of Health and the National Institute of Social Security. For AMBED, the corporate grievance mechanism became a way of asserting rights and demanding accountability from other powerful actors (government deputies, municipal authorities, and, it seems, sympathetic anthropologists), and even of discovering other documentary mechanisms (the cadastral survey, the clinical record, the letter of complaint to an elected representative). The mechanism converted knowledge of the ground into transferable paper form, making it legible but not reducible to the language of bureaucracy. In this way, AMBED's work became a version of what Kregg Hetherington calls "guerrilla auditing." The group actively blurred lines of accountability and expanded the scope and number of problems that might come into public view.[47]

What is noteworthy about this kind of bureaucratic mobilization is the way in which it uses a kind of associative logic to highlight links between problems (and people) that the company, the CAO, and the state might see as categorically different. For example, while Montelimar owned or controlled nearly all the land that surrounded most villages, waterways are public property under Nicaraguan law. One complaint Don Alvaro put in his own name outlines a concern that aerial fumigation was penetrating a municipal reservoir located in the middle of a cane field. This reservoir served the residents of a nearby town center. When AMBED began to investigate, residents in El Popol, which is located between the reservoir and the town center, pointed out that while their houses sat along the route of the potable water pipes, they were not actually served by the municipal water system. Villagers in El Popol instead relied on water from a nearby river, whose quality was the purview of the national environment ministry rather than the municipality. What began as a process of documentation under the corporate grievance process opened up potential avenues of documentation by other routes.

In order to function, the internal grievance mechanism required the kind of groundwork that Jane and her American cohorts, the people of Goyena, and the ASOCHIVIDA members had done years earlier in the NSEL case. The documentation they amassed back then was collected in order to open a case, to jump-start the CAO's more formal global grievance mechanism. For AMBED, the groundwork continued after the CAO mechanism had already been engaged. In a reversal, AMBED was turning local, anecdotal documentary work—work that is supposed to culminate in a global, instrumental, institutional response—into the outcome of that very response. The collection of simple complaint forms permitted AMBED to ask what Nicholas Shapiro,

Nasser Zakariya, and Jody Roberts call "the question before the question," the kind of question that precedes the scientific study or legal adjudication of things like the role of toxic chemicals or other working conditions in causing injury. AMBED was just as dedicated to keeping alive concerns about land tenure and water access and household garden diversity as it was about accounting for people stricken by CKDnt.[48]

There was another reason why AMBED insisted on taking its work beyond the strict labor-management framework and including other community members. Like most evangelical-leaning organizations in Nicaragua, AMBED's leaders believed that grace and blessings from God could come to anyone, regardless of their work history or their connection to a particular corporation. Through a combination of faith and groundwork, they showed how the ostensibly controlled and closed system of CAO-sponsored grievance-making and mediation could actually be treated as an open system. For AMBED, that system had potential for reconfiguration, and for the inclusion of people who might otherwise look like outsiders to the plantation economy.[49]

Nonsecular Accountability

Moving between knowledge of the ground and the documentation demanded in liberal models of grievance and mediated resolution, AMBED developed its own method of what Fortun calls "looping," working back and forth between scales and epistemic forms.[50] Its leaders recognized that these scales and forms only partially include one another. Documentation does not necessarily lead to accountability, and knowledge of the ground does not always need to be codified into documents. Even though they kept adding to the list of things the corporation and the World Bank should recognize, and even though CKDnt remained the galvanizing issue, AMBED's leaders insisted on pulling the conversation away from clean causal explanations and into the murky waters where biofuel, land grabs, pesticides, and water quality mingled with biomarkers, clinics, and pharmaceuticals, all cloaked in the possibility of blessings from God.

The agreements brokered by the CAO between groups like AMBED and corporations like Montelimar reflect what Yusoff calls the "recuperative logic" of growth-oriented development, in which actions for redress are precisely calculated to counterbalance harm. Such logic runs headlong into the altogether less reductive economy of blessings—those favors whose value is indeterminate and difficult to reciprocate. AMBED's name, Bendición de Dios, is not simply an invocation of a higher power but a recognition that some gifts cannot be repaid through the recuperative mechanisms of law or corporate social responsibility.

For Yusoff, these include the perverse gifts of late capitalism: "[ocean] acidifi-cation ... extinction, sterility ... and toxicity."[51] Figuring out what is owed in return for such gifts required AMBED to take the tools of liberal citizenship and fuse them with knowledge of the ground, moving with a pinch of grace.

The invocation of God's blessing in AMBED's name might be a claim to a kind of self-awareness, a sort of ready-made package for the group, an ethos and a telos rolled into one. But when I went back and started over again to think about it, the name AMBED started to appear more like a question the group posed to itself. The organization started to seem less a community of stakeholders dedi-cated to pushing discrete shared interests than an unsettled assembly of people who genuinely wondered both what had happened in the past that led them to the CKDnt epidemic and what the future might hold. The thing about bless-ings and divine grace is that they are mysterious, haunting. It is never certain who will be blessed, or why.[52]

Instead of thinking of AMBED as a group of issue-oriented activists who passively accepted the mechanical logic of liberal accountability, I came to think of it as representing a nonsecular approach to accountability. Nonsecular accountability assumes that what links powerful groups like corporations to marginalized and exploited ones like those who reside in Montelimar's villages are grounded social relationships, rather than the abstract structural positions described in legal documents. Frustratingly for those (including self-appointed solidarity figures like Jane Bernstein and myself) who would have wanted to see a clear, class-based, anticorporate movement spring up in the wake of the CKDnt epidemic, it did not. Rather than accept the sharp distinction between corporation and "community" now so prominent in both ideal imaginaries of the rural peasant activist and corporate social responsibility initiatives, nonsec-ular accountability works on the assumption that a simple transfer of wealth is not enough to ensure mutual recognition.[53] Any mutual recognition between exploiter and exploited must come along with a recognition of the irrevocable damage to the ground on which they both stand. AMBED's appeal to the possi-bility of a blessing is thus a quiet refusal of the possibility of a liberal settling of accounts. Like evangelical Christianity itself, nonsecular accountability takes the toxicity of the present as its starting point.[54]

Nonsecular accountability depends on the deliberate effort to establish con-nections, in AMBED's case, between events like pesticide poisoning and kidney epidemics, and between the productive work of growing sugarcane and the re-productive work of making persons. Nonsecular accountability, then, means not just reliable and loyal attendance at meetings, though it is that. It is not just confidence that with enough documentation, recognition of harm will follow, though it is that. Nonsecular accountability is a form of pragmatic action in which evidence is always accreting and eroding, materially represented in something like the piles of community claim forms I glimpsed at Don Silvio's house back in Goyena. Nonsecular accountability is also aware of its own fleetingness. AMBED itself was far from stable. Its registered membership steadily eroded, dues were constantly in short supply, and its leadership became mired, both materially and socially, as it attempted to keep the work alive. In point of fact, AMBED never was legally registered as a nongovernmental organization in Nicaragua. The paperwork kept getting bogged down in the offices of National Assembly members and notaries.[55]

Nonsecular accountability is not a model for how to restore life after catastrophe but an invitation to work together to face the uncertainty that persists. It provides a counterpoint to the individualistic and transactional logics of twenty-first-century corporate plantation capitalism; to the narrowly medical versions of therapeutic or biological citizenship elaborated in the anthropology of global health; and, it must be added, to the romantic visions of popular anticapitalist mobilization lauded in much critical scholarship on rural social movements and environmental politics.

2
———

Atmospheric Fixes

The one-room house Doña Iris shared with her *marido*, Don Pachi, was almost always exposed to the sun. It sat atop a knoll on the outskirts of Villa El Carmen, on a grassy swath of land that gave them enough room to run a few chickens. The sunlight seared away the moisture in the soil, making it easier for the chickens to forage for insects. When I first sat down for an interview with Doña Iris and Don Pachi, the three of us constantly had to adjust the location of our plastic chairs to keep them under the shade of one of the two trees that stood inside the barbed wire surrounding their property. Together, we formed a kind of human-plastic sundial.

Doña Iris, who had once worked at Montelimar as a clerical secretary and now served as AMBED's secretary-treasurer, was fond of what she called her *pedacito de casa* (her "little piece of home"). She and Don Pachi could raise the chickens alongside a few plants, and it was just a short walk to the town, where they could get other basic foodstuffs or catch the bus to Managua for larger shopping trips. But Doña Iris and Don Pachi were also somewhat captive to the plot on which they lived because both had been weakened by kidney disease. Doña Iris was diabetic, and Don Pachi, a former cane cutter at Montelimar, had CKDnt. Excessive heat exposure is always dangerous, but for people with compromised kidney function, it is especially risky.[1]

Doña Iris and Don Pachi were in what I have come to think of as an "atmospheric fix." Their daily movements around the yard, keyed to the drift of the tree's shadow, illustrate that shade and sunlight, cool and heat, are social relations rendered into air qualities. The atmosphere that surrounded Doña Iris and Don Pachi was the outcome of human labor, what the geographer Mike Hulme calls "atmospheric cultivation," those "intentional, but not always sagacious, projects of improvement through which . . . the atmosphere bears the imprint of considered human thought, design and action."[2] The cultivation of monocrops has always entailed atmospheric cultivation. The effects of that cultivation are violent and uneven. As industrial farms grow, pesticides drift, dust storms become more frequent, and new forms of damage emerge, from antibiotic-resistant bacteria to cancer clusters.[3] Agricultural workers continue to bear the brunt of these negative feedback loops. In recognition of their atmospheric impacts, agribusinesses around the world have begun developing methods for cultivating more tolerable working conditions. These methods tend to focus on discrete atmospheric elements: offsetting greenhouse gases by planting trees, using sensors to monitor ozone and dust, or promoting the use of air filtration for homes and factories and personal protective equipment for workers.

These technical fixes are examples of what Joseph Masco calls "normalizing extremes," mobilizing technology and science to make long-established global capitalist projects fit within a changing planetary ecology.[4] The question is not how to make the planet reasonably safe for *every* body but to make it reasonably safe for *laboring* bodies, that is, those that produce value by doing legibly productive work.[5] In the sugarcane zone, even as these deliberate attempts at protection enabled work to continue, they perpetuated the kinds of environmental conditions that made it harder and harder for smallholders like Doña Iris and Don Pachi to protect themselves, and more and more dangerous for them to spend time outside. The World Bank estimates that average annual temperatures on Nicaragua's Pacific coast have risen by over one degree Celsius since the 1960s. Rainfall has decreased by 5 to 6 percent per decade over the same period.[6] There are simply not enough trees in the sugarcane zone to provide shade, to maintain an inhabitable hydrologic cycle, or to absorb the damage of unregulated aerial pesticide application.

But normalizing extremes is not the only means of cultivating atmospheres. There is another, which I call "atmospheric homework." Atmospheric homework is a form of both labor and collective study. It entails questioning how ecological damage creates dangerous atmospheric conditions that do not manifest as extreme. Such dangers are invisible to the industrial logics of environmental or health science. Through atmospheric homework, people make accretive environmental harm legible. Atmospheric homework entails everyday efforts to question what dominant systems, including those of industrial agriculture, treat as normal. To do atmospheric homework is to do things like cultivate shade in a rapidly deforesting landscape, to share worries about the smell and taste of air and water, to try to make life livable on terms that are not necessarily premised on productivity. Atmospheric homework is a form of intervention that centers bodies that work but also bodies that care, bodies that smell, bodies that tremble with anxiety. Atmospheric homework is still about *work*, but its politics emerge from those forms of reproductive labor, often coded as "women's work," that are excluded from the calculations of agribusiness, even though agribusiness has been dependent on them since the inception of the plantation. Doing atmospheric homework means asking modest questions and taking small, sometimes seemingly insignificant steps to improve local surroundings, despite the uncertain impact of agrochemicals, extreme heat, and a diminished water table.[7]

To explore the tension between normalizing extremes and atmospheric homework, and between macroscale planetary change and microscale survival practices, this chapter begins with a short history of atmospheric cultivation in the sugarcane zone.[8] I show how two key components of that atmosphere, agrochemicals and heat, came to prominence as social and environmental matters of concern long before the advent of the CKDnt epidemic. I then delve more deeply into the processes of normalizing extremes and atmospheric homework, following efforts to fix the atmosphere of the sugarcane zone in the wake of the epidemic. As heat mitigation has become the most prominent form of addressing CKDnt, what look like proactive steps by transnational scientists and corporations to protect a vulnerable workforce have ended up deepening the spatial and social bifurcations between plantation and nonplantation, work and nonwork.

Making a Toxic Desert

The presence of toxic agrochemicals in Nicaragua's atmosphere is firmly embedded in the national imaginary. In "Lights," a 1979 poem that is sometimes quoted by scholars of Nicaraguan agriculture, the radical priest and poet

Ernesto Cardenal describes the "smell of insecticide" as the "smell of Nicaragua."[9] Cardenal's poem tells of his return from exile to witness the final push to overthrow the Somoza dictatorship. The poem is narrated from aboard an airplane that takes a circuitous route along the Pacific coast to avoid the Nicaraguan army's antiaircraft guns. From the window of the plane, the poet recognizes the lights of major cities—Rivas, Granada, Masaya, Managua—and the pilot points out the lights of Montelimar, the luxurious seaside redoubt of the dictator himself, Anastasio Somoza Debayle. By that point in the revolutionary struggle, Somoza was already on his way out of the country, fleeing the hand of Sandinista justice, but Montelimar remained, surrounded by sugarcane and cotton farms owned by the Somozas and their allies. It is likely that Cardenal could have seen, just behind the beachside estate, the lights of the sugarcane mill.

If you were to fly above the area today, as Cardenal did in 1979, you would be able to identify the villages amid the stands of cane by the telltale sign of defiant old trees. These forest islands stand out against the expanding monoculture. When Somoza Debayle's father, Anastasio Somoza García, took de facto control over the country in the late 1930s, small farmers and Indigenous people could still make a living by carving out modest subsistence plots, but today's home gardens provide a supplement, at best, to store-bought food. Though it is still listed in most guidebooks as a "tropical dry forest," most of Nicaragua's Pacific littoral today is something more like a man-made desert. The forests are nearly all gone. They were victims of a Green Revolution–inspired push to turn a "backward" economy of haciendas and small peasant farms into a modern, efficient industrial agricultural export engine.

The Somoza dynasty spearheaded this dramatic transformation. Between 1912 and 1933, Nicaragua was occupied by the US Marines, who were there, at least initially, to deter other global powers from attempting to build a transoceanic shipping canal in the country. The US-backed Panama Canal project had been preceded by several attempts to build canals across southern Nicaragua, whose lake and river systems offered a potentially more welcoming passage between the Atlantic and Pacific Oceans than those of Panama. During the occupation, the United States showed little appetite for economic development initiatives, even the colonial-style commodity crop plantations US interests had established elsewhere in Central America. Nicaragua's agricultural sector languished by comparison to those of its neighbors.[10]

The marines were finally driven out in 1933 after being worn down by the innovative guerrilla tactics of Augusto César Sandino's campesino army. Although Sandino was a deeply committed agrarian socialist, he entered an alliance of convenience with the Liberal wing of the Nicaraguan landed elite, including Somoza, in order to ensure the ouster of the occupiers. The Americans left Somoza in charge of a US-trained military force, the National Guard. Not long after the US retreat, Somoza orchestrated Sandino's assassination and quickly mobilized the National Guard to consolidate his political power.

Though he was a slippery figure, Somoza gained a foothold in the wake of the US departure by positioning himself as a Liberal, which in the Nicaraguan political alignment of the time meant that he envisioned modern export-oriented commerce as the key to Nicaragua's future. The opposition Conservative Party was dominated by established descendants of the Creole gentry who preferred to keep farms as the semifeudal haciendas that they had inherited from their ancestors.[11] Somoza began putting his Liberal economic vision into place by first ensuring Nicaragua's support for the Allies in World War II. After the war, he oversaw an agricultural boom, underwritten by US capital.[12] The historian Hilary Francis describes the early years of this boom as a "fever" that temporarily ushered in a détente between Somoza and his critics within the Conservative Party.[13] Somoza successfully sold political leaders across the Liberal-Conservative spectrum on "a belief in the almost magical power of foreign, particularly US, technology" to realize his long-held vision of the country as "the granary of Central America."[14]

What Nicaragua's Conservatives shared with Somoza was a fervent anti-communist politics, one that identified campesinos like those that Sandino had organized in the anti-occupation struggle as potential threats.[15] Between 1951 and 1958, under the banner of the Nicaraguan Technical Agricultural Service, US and Nicaraguan agronomists rapidly built a modern agrarian-industrial complex, centered initially on cotton production. The National Guard used force to evict small farmers from their homes and to speed the process of cutting down trees to make way for cotton.[16] This dramatic transformation of the landscape accelerated in the 1960s with the help of the Alliance for Progress, the Kennedy administration's attempt to counter the rise of left-wing political groups in Latin America through a combination of development aid and support for militaries and governments sympathetic to the US position in the Cold War, including the Somoza regime.[17] As the environmental sociologist Daniel Faber explains, "Along Nicaragua's entire Pacific plain, cotton land expanded 400% between 1952 and 1967, while peasant lands devoted to corn, beans, sorghum, and other food grains dropped over 50%."[18] Small farmers and Indigenous groups were evicted from their traditional lands, old-growth forests and mangroves were destroyed, and numerous species of tropical animals were rendered nearly extinct.[19]

The cotton boom was a Cold War project through and through. In crude terms, fewer forests meant fewer small farms. Fewer small farms meant that formerly self-sufficient farmers had to seek employment in the cotton fields to survive.[20] For Somoza, this made campesinos into a much more legible and pliable constituency, one perhaps less likely to respond to the form of agrarian populism espoused by the intellectual and political descendants of Sandino. Early in his rise to power, Somoza worked to cultivate the loyalty of this emerging rural working class through the institutionalization of revised labor codes and workplace protections, including social security (see chapter 5).[21]

Somoza's regime enthusiastically embraced the new wave of commercial petrochemical pesticides introduced to the market after World War II.[22] Per capita, Somoza-era Nicaragua was among Latin America's biggest spenders on imported agrochemicals during the middle of the twentieth century. Even after Bayer Chemical's 1951 tests of methyl parathion (a derivative of a nerve gas developed by the Nazis during World War II) killed and sickened thousands of people around the city of León, Somoza, urged on by his cotton-growing cronies, opted to continue the use of the pesticide against boll weevils.[23] During this period, Nicaragua became a case study in the phenomenon of the "pesticide treadmill," in which insect and weed resistance leads to the progressive search for newer and harsher chemicals.[24] The residues of these substances persisted in soils, plants, and bodies. A 1991 study estimated that "the 700,000 people living in Central America's cotton region [had] more DDT in their body fat than any other population of human beings in the world."[25]

Ernesto Cardenal's observation that the smell of insecticide was the smell of Nicaragua may have been a bit of ironic nostalgia, but on the eve of the Sandinista revolution, heat and toxicity had become the defining features of the agrarian atmosphere, particularly on the Pacific coastal plain. Thanks to the loss of forest cover, residues that fell from crop dusters would swirl out of the friable soil, back into the air, and through lungs and cracked doorways. There was no escape.

When the Somoza dynasty was toppled by the popular Sandinista revolution in 1979, the atmospheric ravages of the previous three decades were plain to see.[26] By 1979, the cotton boom had been receding for some time, and Sandinista economic planners blamed the largely US-based petrochemical industry, which had insinuated itself into the fabric of the Somoza state, for the decline.[27] Even as they fought militarily against a US-backed counterrevolutionary force, the government of the Frente Sandinista de Liberación Nacional (FSLN) took on the project of undoing the ecological harms perpetrated under Somoza. Pesticides that had been legal to use under the old regime were finally banned in the early 1980s, in keeping with international norms, and it was in this period that Nicaragua became an incubator of new forms of eco-friendly agriculture, perhaps most famously shade-grown, organic, and fair trade coffee.[28]

While the cotton plantations withered, sugar remained resilient. Sugarcane had been grown commercially in the Pacific plains for more than one hundred years, but by the 1980s, its prominence in the export economy had drastically increased. Under the FSLN, all the country's major sugarcane processing and growing operations were nationalized, including the Montelimar mill, which had been under Somoza's direct control. The choice to keep these large export operations intact as industrial monocultures was largely a practical one. Larger farms could provide preferential employment to combatants in the revolutionary and counterrevolutionary wars, many of whom were born as peasants but had entered the workforce as seasonal plantation workers. Even though the Sandinistas did actively work to restore access to quality farmland so that these workers and their families could make a living during the offseason, the long-term effects of deforestation and pesticide-driven agriculture had hollowed out the promise of subsistence or smallholder food production. In 1991, one year after the Sandinistas were voted out of power, marking the end of the revolution, Miguel Caseres, an adviser to the country's Institute for Natural Resources and the Environment, estimated that the soils of the Pacific plains were eroding at a rate of more than twenty tons per acre, which was more than four times the acceptable rate.[29]

Energizing the Sugarcane Boom

Sugarcane operations expanded only modestly during the postrevolutionary period of the 1990s, as the state farms were sold back to private investors. By the turn of the twenty-first century, however, the political and policy winds were again blowing strongly in favor of monocrop expansion. In Nicaragua, this push was spearheaded in part by Enrique Bolaños, a politician who had made his fortune during the cotton boom and who was elected vice president in 1996 and president in 2001 on the Liberal Party ticket. Bolaños's administration was bookended by two key events. First was a protracted struggle by banana plantation workers to hold US fruit companies to account for the long-term health effects of workplace exposure to dibromochloropropane (DBCP), a carcinogenic soil fumigant that had been banned in the United States in 1977 but was used in Nicaragua by the Dole corporation until at least 1980.[30] In his first year as president, Bolaños presided over the passage of Special Law 364, which would allow workers who believed they had been injured or rendered sterile due to exposure to DBCP to sue Dole, Dow Chemical, and the Shell Corporation for damages. Bolaños did this despite his deep ties to the agricultural and pesticide industries, and despite smear campaigns by his political enemies, who accused him of being in the pocket of the chemical industry (Bolaños's son did, in fact, work for the Monsanto Corporation).[31] Bolaños's willingness to take on the pesticide industry was part of his broader strategy to revive Nicaragua's flagging economy through a return to Liberal Party principles of free trade and export-driven development. Near the end of his term, he presided over Nicaragua's accession to the Central America–Dominican Republic Free Trade Agreement.

Less well publicized, though no less significant, was Bolaños's enthusiastic embrace of agricultural intensification for bioenergy development. In 2006, his last year in office, he signed Executive Decree 42, which was issued in response to "the need for global production of renewable, clean fuels."[32] Calling for increased investment in the sugarcane and oil palm sectors, the decree stated that, compounded with Nicaragua's existing resources, further investment in biofuels "put us at the forefront of the new paradigm for agriculture in the 21st century: Bioenergy."[33] Bolaños's decree was released around the time that the World Bank and the IFC were starting to invest in the global biofuel sector, including through loans to Nicaraguan sugar companies. The IFC's $55 million loan to Nicaragua Sugar Estates Limited (NSEL), which eventually led to global recognition of the CKDnt epidemic, was approved mere weeks after Executive Decree 42 was published.

Here, then, was a new atmospheric fix. At the time of the IFC loan and the executive decree, petroleum prices were steadily climbing, and in countries like Nicaragua, the accumulated effects of climate change were keenly felt, even by business-friendly leaders like Enrique Bolaños. For the IFC and the World Bank, more investment in sugarcane might not only perpetuate the country's gains in food export but also develop its capacity to produce homegrown sources of "clean" energy, including ethanol and biomass fuel generated from sugarcane pulp, or bagasse. The World Bank's report *Rising Global Interest in Farmland: Can It Yield Sustainable and Equitable Benefits?* (2011) proposed that the acquisition of land for energy-generating monocultures would yield both environmental gains, by reducing dependence on fossil fuel, and development gains, by giving rural people living and working in "inefficient" farm systems better-paying jobs.[34] In the name of closing what development policymakers had long seen as a "yield gap" or "productivity gap" between Euro-Atlantic and Latin American agriculture, the IFC supplied already-large Nicaraguan sugarcane firms with loans to acquire even more land.[35] These concerns about efficiency, yield, and productivity are consistent themes of

Nicaraguan agrarian history, dating back to the Somoza dynasty's anticommunist drive to industrialize in the 1940s, 1950s, and 1960s. Along with the decades-long process of pesticide-driven landscape transformation in the Somoza years, these concerns set the scene for the eventual medical and corporate response to CKDnt.

Normalizing Extremes: The Spaceship in the Cane

As we saw in chapter 1, when Nicaraguan sugarcane workers first mobilized to address CKDnt, they were met with resistance from plantation companies. Company officials steadfastly denied that labor conditions were to blame for the epidemic. They asserted that some combination of behavioral and genetic factors must be the cause. An early victory of the patient advocacy movements that filed the CAO grievances at NSEL in 2008 and at Montelimar in 2015 was an agreement by sugarcane companies to allow epidemiological research on CDKnt to take place on plantations. The workers' expectation was that these studies would reveal a connection between the disease and pesticide exposure. They did not. Comparative, population-based epidemiology explored several potential causes of CKDnt, from behavioral choices (e.g., alcohol consumption, self-medication with nonsteroidal anti-inflammatory drugs) to genetic predisposition to pesticide exposure to heavy metal intoxication.

Among all the possible causes, heat stress has consistently been identified as the factor most amenable to systematic experimental scrutiny. Studies of the relationship between heat and CKDnt are now dominant in the pages of the scientific journals where CKDnt researchers share their work. In 2020, one prominent CKDnt scientist put it this way: "As in all chronic diseases, multiple conditions over the course of a lifetime will ultimately contribute to the risk of getting a disease, including low-dose exposures to toxic agents. However, regarding a driver of an epidemic, it is common sense to focus on the obvious rather than speculating that unknown agents, unidentified after decades of an epidemic, are persistently killing tens of thousands of people, mainly workers."[36] What is noteworthy about this statement, which appears in an article that makes a vigorous argument in favor of focusing CKDnt research on heat stress rather than "unknown" pesticides, is that it couches heat as "the obvious" factor at play.

What makes extreme heat exposure, and the dehydration and compromised kidney function that result from it, appear "obvious"?

One answer emerges from the long historical entanglement between normative ideas about work and scientific ideas about heat and energy. As the political theorist Cara Daggett explains, beginning in the nineteenth century, a European quest for dominance over the extraction and control of petrochemical and biological energy sources in colonized areas was wedded to a quest to corral and manage the energetic inputs and outputs of industrial working bodies in the metropole.[37] The plantations of the American tropics and the coal-fired factories of North America and Europe were, from the start, thermodynamically connected to one another. The drive to replace fossil fuels with biofuels has done little to change this. During the early days of industrial capitalism, the capture of heat in steam engines helped push the limits of mechanical production, even as it reaffirmed those of biological reproduction. The bodies of factory workers in industrializing England, and later America, were fueled by plantation sugar.[38] As the historian Anson Rabinbach notes, the very concept of "fatigue" as a dissipation of labor power emerged in the nineteenth century through the coupled sciences of economics, social medicine, and mechanics. Early industrial machinery released tremendous, unprecedented amounts of heat not just into turbines or pistons but also onto the surrounding factory floor, into the atmosphere, and into the bodies of laborers. The confluence of medical and economic concern extended to a planetary scale. Industrial age social reformers expressed anxiety about the exhaustion not just of bodies and machines but of life itself. Citing the second law of thermodynamics, they were worried about "the heat death of the universe": the slow dissipation of natural *and* mechanical heat that would spell the end of all life.[39] Thermodynamics created "a new image of nature whose topos was 'conflagration'—a cosmos of fire, heat, and work."[40]

A more specific answer, however, emerges after a closer look at the environmental history of the sugarcane zone that I sketched earlier. Progressive (and near-total) deforestation, the draining of water resources, the enclosure of farmland for the production of pesticide-intensive crops, and the construction of an agricultural economy in which intense, low-paid work was often the only viable option for many campesinos all contributed to creating the "obvious" problem of heat exposure. Since the middle of the twentieth century, pesticides have been essential tools for converting the heat of the Nicaraguan sun into food and energy. The medium for this conversion was, and continues to be, the bodies of those who work and live in monocrop landscapes.[41] The landscape is hotter, in other words, *because* of pesticide-driven monoculture.

Heat is an obvious factor for a third reason. Heat stress is a known problem in occupational health, something that experts in the field are accustomed to studying, and as recognition of climate change has grown, heat has seemed even more like the "natural" place to begin intervening.[42] The idea that CKDnt might be a *climate*-induced illness may have actually helped convince Nicaraguan sugar companies to acknowledge the epidemic. In mid-2017, NSEL's website reprinted an article by a *Vice News* journalist who had earlier helped to publicize a movement to boycott the company's signature product, Flor de Caña rum, in the wake of several damning press accounts of the CKDnt epidemic.[43] In the article, the journalist partly repudiates that boycott, pointing to studies of an association between heat exposure, rising global temperatures, and CKDnt in Central America, Sri Lanka, and India to argue that the disease was not a problem of Nicaraguan sugarcane production per se but of global climate change.[44] In these kinds of accounts, climate change becomes an externality, and rising temperatures emerge as an "obvious" threat not just to working bodies but to sugarcane production itself. What disappears is any notion that heat has a history—that the atmosphere now seen as dangerous for workers and companies alike was deliberately cultivated. Paradoxically, climate change emerged as a new atmospheric fix for a sugarcane industry beleaguered by accusations that its labor practices and use of pesticides had caused CKDnt.

In climate summits, grant proposals, and meetings among sugarcane industry insiders, the planetary health crisis consistently comes to look like a crisis of productivity. As an illustration of this point, a meta-analysis of heat-related disease published in the *Annual Review of Public Health* in 2016 found that "heat exposure . . . affects workers' capability to undertake physical activities without harm; in hot conditions, work capacity falls, leading to a decrease of labor productivity."[45] In 2015, management consultants at Verisk Maplecroft warned that rising temperatures could cut productivity in Southeast Asia by as much as 25 percent in the next thirty years.[46] States, insurance companies, and labor unions from California to Texas are rewriting occupational health rules to deal with the threat of heat to both health and productivity. The problem, as Sarah Horton explains in her anthropological account of heat-related death and illness in California's agricultural sector, is that there is scant evidence that such narrow policy prescriptions, which treat the "occupational" as a discrete category amenable to intervention and manipulation, actually save lives. The managerial imperative to maintain worker productivity, rather than occupational heat itself, is just as likely to be a source of morbidity.[47]

Based on the emerging scientific consensus about the heat stress hypothesis for CKDnt, a vocal group of occupational health specialists has begun working to mitigate the onset of the disease in workers. Around 2018, they convinced the owners of sugarcane plantations in several Central American countries, including Nicaragua, to permit a new round of epidemiological experiments. Unlike the earlier CKDnt studies, which were largely observational, the purpose of this newer round was to test the hypothesis that an active intervention, in the form of the regular provision of water, rest, and shade to laborers throughout the workday, could stave off acute kidney injury caused by heat stress in the short term and prevent the onset of CKDnt in the longer term.[48] A corollary hypothesis is that the provision of water, rest, and shade would constitute a worthwhile (i.e., remunerative) investment on the part of sugarcane companies.[49] These experiments explicitly sought to close what policymakers had long seen as a "productivity gap" that kept agricultural economies in countries like Nicaragua lagging behind those of more developed nation-states.

In coordination with the multistakeholder trade organization Bonsucro, near the end of the 2010s, the CKDnt-focused nongovernmental organization La Isla Network launched the Adelante Initiative, an effort to test the theory that the provision of electrolyte-enhanced water and mandated rest periods in a shaded space could stem the onset of kidney injury.[50] The key experimental apparatus in the Adelante Initiative is the shade tent. One Adelante project report describes how, over a series of cane harvests, researchers iteratively adjusted the location of tents, their color, the angle of their orientation relative to the sun, and the number of workers who could occupy them at any one time.[51] The goal was to define the capacity of the tent and the electrolyte-enhanced water solution to provide relief.[52] In the absence of definitive knowledge about what causes CKDnt, Adelante patterned its work on the template of other "evidence-based" global health projects, "[proceeding] in such a way that project implementation becomes a form of experimental variable testing."[53] If the water-rest-shade experiments proved successful, project leaders believed that lessons learned could be translated to any sugarcane plantation that is accredited by Bonsucro's system for certifying "responsible" sugar producers and promoting their products to socially conscious consumers.

What was *not* under scrutiny in this experiment was the plantation itself; nor was the role of pesticides in creating the kinds of economies of scale that almost inevitably lead workers to become dangerously exposed to extreme heat. The experiment presumed that the plantation environment was and would remain extreme. The construction of a microclimate in the form of the tented refuge would make that extremity marginally more tolerable, or so went the Adelante hypothesis. Since 2018, the water-rest-shade protocol has been taken up across the industry, including at Montelimar.[54]

The shade tent is a space of exception. Like the microenvironment of a spacecraft, the microenvironment of the tent, in Valerie Olson's words, "simultaneously normalizes . . . bodies and the outer spatial milieus that they inhabit."[55] At the same time, it manages workers' bodies "not just as living bodies but as at-risk living systems seamlessly integrated with mechanical and environmental systems."[56] The creation of what we might call, following the anthropologist Göçke Günel, a "spaceship in the cane," amounts to a "technical adjustment" to the plantation, a means of making sugarcane production viable "without interrogating existing social, political, and economic relations," including the embodied inequalities on which cane production depends.[57] The water-rest-shade intervention acknowledges the reality of climate change and the human cost of sugarcane production while deferring direct action on the root causes of either.

To be sure, there is much to admire in a project like Adelante, which has become a pillar of Bonsucro's global certification standards for responsible sugar production. Through a technical adjustment to management practices, it aims to adapt the particular conditions of sugarcane fields to the presumably universal condition of global warming. The next step, according to Adelante, is "to provide an incubator from which the standard for effective occupational safety and health can be . . . scaled to other industries and geographies."[58] As Gabrielle Hecht has argued, these kinds of international standards "aspire to . . . coevalness. . . . In principle, they [offer] ways of comparing procedures in distant places . . . against a benchmark. . . . In principle, they deny the legitimacy of displacing harm to spaces inhabited by marginalized people, asserting that all places should adhere to the same environmental and labor norms."[59] Hecht warns that while "international standards . . . can be devices for seeking remediation . . . they can also serve as permits to pollute."[60]

With this in mind, it is worth zooming out to see what this well-meaning shift in management practice might be an alibi for. What kind of planetary health is this? The introduction of this atmospheric fix extends the Green Revolution–inflected dream of closing the productivity gap between the Global South and the Global North. Implementation of the water-rest-shade protocol works on the principle of vertical transfer, from managers to field workers. In the words of a field manager interviewed by Adelante researchers, "Supervisory staff must be made aware first so they accept it first, so that they can pass it on to the fieldworker. Because if we, the supervisors, cannot first absorb the benefit that the program has, we will not be able to transfer it."[61] According to one economic analysis of the Adelante project, "For every dollar spent on Adelante, [a plantation] receives a return of approximately 22%."[62] Like other recent small-scale health care and development initiatives, Adelante introduces a new, low-cost device for keeping human bodies alive that is also a device for accumulating capital.[63] The paternalism of plantation production is fully preserved in this model. In a peer-reviewed qualitative study carried out by the Adelante Initiative, field managers at one plantation discussed the challenges of implementing heat stress–aversion policies. For the managers, as the authors of this study explained, "the cutters appeared to be viewed like children who disregard their health and, hence, need to be reminded repetitively to become aware that their health is important."[64]

"Technoscience," as M. Murphy has written, "dreams the world it makes sense in."[65] Adelante's atmospheric fix reifies the familiar trope of the simple worker in the cane, the man-child who might even work too hard if not for managerial oversight. This protected cane cutter is an example of what Sylvia Wynter calls the "honorary human."[66] Ever since the era of the transatlantic slave trade, the humanity of racialized plantation workers has consistently been predicated on their status *as workers*.[67] Other possible forms of humanity (caregiver, thinker, kin) have been less readily available to them. At the root of the experiment are investment strategies championed by the World Bank, the US government, a range of pesticide companies, and successive Nicaraguan regimes, from Somoza to Bolaños to Ortega, that saw the expansion of monoculture as a pathway to human flourishing.

The problem is that while kidney disease is rife in the sugarcane zone, which makes bodies at risk available for occupational health experimentation, the number of actual sugarcane workers in Nicaragua is getting smaller every year. This reduction in the laboring population is deliberate. Paradoxically, thanks to tools like machine harvesters and aerial crop dusters, the geographic footprint of the cane industry is larger than it has ever been, even though just a fraction of the residents of the communities on the edges of the sugarcane zone will ever work directly in the industry, and only a few hundred of these people will work full-time. The disappearance of formal, recognized labor is very much by design. It limits liability and increases profits. The embrace of the heat stress solution by the ethically minded members of Bonsucro's expanding network of responsible sugar producers, then, creates what Hannah Appel calls a "spatial and phenomenological distance" between sugarcane plantations and the communities that are right next to them.[68]

Atmospheric Homework and the "Rehydration Thesis"

Remarkably, very little of the scientific literature on CKDnt mentions Nicaragua's long history of pesticide-intensive agriculture. The latent toxicity and unavoidable dryness of the landscape have become accepted by those who set industrial standards at the national and international levels as part of life, as quotidian, as noise.[69] That said, not all scientists accept the premise that heat should be the "obvious" focal point for CKDnt research. The thesis that heat stress causes dehydration, leading to compromised kidney function, has been countered by the suggestion that the problem is not dehydration but *re*hydration with potentially tainted water.[70] The problem is that given Nicaragua's toxic history, in which the residues of 2,4-D, paraquat, glyphosate, methyl parathion, DDT, and dozens of other chemicals mingle in the soil and groundwater, there is simply no scientific method for testing this hypothesis. A version of this "rehydration thesis" was kept alive, however, in villages like Valle Rojo, one of the dozens that sit amid the Montelimar cane fields. People kept this thesis alive through an alternative practice of atmospheric cultivation, which I am calling "atmospheric homework."

Doña Claudia lived in the center of the village, directly across from the community's main water source, a tube well that was installed by the Montelimar Corporation in the mid-2010s. Behind her house was a small river, which originated in the upland forest dozens of kilometers away and was interrupted at several points near Valle Rojo by low-head irrigation dams, built during the 1960s and 1970s. Those dams diverted much of the river's flow into open concrete irrigation canals, one of which flowed right through Valle Rojo, just on the other side of the tube well.

When we first met, Doña Claudia quickly told me two things. First, she said that while she had never worked in the Montelimar sugarcane fields, she had CKDnt, as did her uncle and her father, both of whom were former workers. That claim, like the claims of many women to be stricken with CKDnt, remains unverified, but as we will see later, that does not mean it was insignificant. Second, Doña Claudia explained that while it might look like Valle Rojo was surrounded by water, finding water was harder and harder. "The problem here," she said, "with the kidneys, with everything, it's in the water." Doña Claudia's second point reflects a common trope in environmental writing about Nicaragua, that it is "a thirsty country with lots of water."[71] In this country that contains Central America's two largest freshwater lakes and hundreds of rivers and rainforests, poor rural people are constantly looking for a safe way to hydrate.

Doña Claudia was a keen political ecologist. In one of our early meetings, she took Saúl, Don Alvaro Torres, and me to the riverbed behind her house and showed us several spots where people had dug wells over the years to access water for cleaning, crops, and animals. Few of these artisanal wells were serviceable now, and besides, in the dry season between January and May, the river would become nearly empty. In El Niño years (there were three straight between 2014 and 2016, another in 2019, and yet another in 2023), the problem got even worse.

Around the time of the string of El Niños in 2014 to 2016, residents in Valle Rojo convinced a local television station to come to the area to illustrate how the dry conditions were affecting them. The El Niños, combined with decades of deforestation and an expansion of industrial agriculture along Nicaragua's Pacific basin, made it easy for the journalists to link the plantation's appropriation of river water to women's struggles to keep up with their own washing and gardening. Nicaraguan media have been tracking this phenomenon for some time. In 2014, Ruth Selma Herrera, a former director of the country's national water utility, reported that 70 percent of the nation's water was consumed by large agricultural landholders, with just 6 percent going to human consumption.[72]

As we will explore further in chapter 3, the wells installed at Valle Rojo and other villages were the Montelimar Corporation's response to residents' anxieties about water access. They were a tidy piece of corporate social responsibility: an attempt to normalize the extremes caused by the confluence of El Niños, land consolidation, water appropriation, and deforestation. The story of this community's small protest over water access, bound up as it is in the problem of increasingly intense El Niños and long-standing environmental destruction due to industrial agriculture, is an example of what Eli Elinoff and Tyson Vaughan call "troubling the quotidian," the process of denaturalizing climate change by calling attention to the way in which climate disaster becomes an everyday experience for poor and marginalized people.[73] What was at stake for Doña Claudia and her neighbors was not an acute disaster—not exactly. Rather, it was the steadily increasing time and energy it took to carry out basic, everyday reproductive tasks—to forge a nonplantation living in the middle of the monoculture.[74] This human energy drain, linked to the evaporation of local water supply, was connected to a long history of deforestation and water theft.

Even though the installation of the wells happened at the height of the CKDnt epidemic, concern about kidney disease was not a significant element in the protest that was staged around the drying up of the riverbed. By that time, most people already assumed that the cane workers were getting sick because of agrochemical exposure. The coming of the well brought anxieties about chemicals together with anxieties about hydration. As it was in so many others, the Montelimar Corporation's crop-dusting helicopter, laden with the "ripener" that was almost certainly glyphosate, was a prominent figure in Claudia's narrative. Glyphosate is both a key reason why the sugarcane industry in Nicaragua has been able to cheaply expand and a key reason why the industry employs fewer and fewer workers. In many ways, the chemical—and the difficulty of discerning what effect it might have on human health—has been an effective tool for widening the social and economic distance between the plantations and the villages in their midst.[75]

But pesticides don't tend to stay in place.

In one focus group of village women I organized, Doña Esther, one of Claudia's neighbors, explained, "We all drink from wells." She pointed to the one in the center of the village. "But when you draw water from that well, you notice that it has a smell, an odor. . . . They say it's from the fumigation." That smell did not have a specific chemical referent, but as Doña Esther implied, healthy water should not have a smell, or a color, or a taste. A sense of smell is a sort of sentinel function: smoke, putrefaction, and other odors signal, in a small and inconclusive way, a rupture to an ecological system. Seen in the right way, they could even signal something larger—maybe a change in climate.[76] To smell a chemical is a different way of finding oneself within a larger system, one that has affordances distinct from those of something like an international occupational labor standard. Smelling is a form of atmospheric homework, a physical act of letting something troubling in and contemplating it.

And while building shade tents and drinking electrolyte-enhanced water are means of preparing, talking about smells is a means of remembering. When we discussed the smell of the water, neither Doña Esther, nor Claudia, nor anyone else mentioned glyphosate specifically. I would bring it up, and though the villagers could name lots of poisons, what was difficult for them—what they in fact had trouble thinking of as their responsibility—was figuring out which chemical caused which problem, or carried which odor. Much as the movements around water scarcity knowingly referenced a deep history of deforestation and corporate appropriation by the sugar industry and its antecedents, the allusions to smell invoked a shared, layered history of toxic exposure, the kind of history referenced in Ernesto Cardenal's poem about the "smell of Nicaragua."

Later in our focus group conversation, Doña Esther described how, before offering water to her grandchildren, she would put a few drops of chlorine bleach into it. Chlorine is a standard treatment for water in places around Nicaragua where formal municipal gridded water service is available.[77] In Valle Rojo, where there was no municipal supply, she and her neighbors used bleach to, as she put it, "correct" the smell of the water that came out of the well that the corporation had donated after the riverbed protests. There were other methods. A neighbor down the road said that she would place buckets of water in the sun for several hours before drinking them, explaining that the smell would dissipate, even if much of the liquid would also evaporate.

CKDnt beyond the Fields

A reasonable response to Doña Esther's account of improvised water correction might be that there is no causal relationship between the presence of chlorine, which neutralizes bacteria, and protection from agrochemical exposure. There is also no clear connection between the smell of water and the presence of agrochemicals. Glyphosate, after all, is virtually odorless. Suspending the impulse to do this kind of counterforensics, I want to suggest that what Doña Esther was describing was a method for developing awareness, a practiced tinkering with her atmospheric and hydrologic surroundings.[78] The bleach, whose familiar aseptic smell covered over the unsettling smell of whatever else might be lurking in the water, established Doña Esther's "awareness of the political ecology driving industrial harm."[79] She insisted on acting, however ineffectively, to mitigate an injury that the Montelimar Corporation would likely disavow.

Like Claudia, Doña Esther insisted that she, too, had CKDnt. As with the improvised application of bleach, this autodiagnosis meant little on its own, so I wonder why it was so common to hear women, who are frequently portrayed as less likely to contract CKDnt, linking their anxieties about water's availability and quality to the epidemic. One explanation is that CKDnt was an available and legible category, one that could draw attention to the enduring problem of water quality. An anthropologist, a corporate social responsibility officer, or an epidemiologist might have their interest piqued if vernacular reckonings of health were routed through an already known epidemic. But I don't know if I am convinced that these repeated claims to kidney disease are only about medicalization. They may also be about labor, specifically, the labor of managing all the excesses—the multiple forms of pollution, from the bacterial to the chemical—that are obscured by standardized medical approaches to late industrial problems, including the corporate embrace of workplace heat stress mitigation. This is the kind of labor that the next two chapters will discuss in detail.

Women's insistence that they, too, were affected by the disease was a means of claiming that that which lies beyond the plantation fields, that which is definitionally not productive, is also planetary, even if it does not read as extreme. Aside from dialysis, which is available to a limited number of Nicaraguan CKDnt patients, care for those who are diagnosed with CKDnt is provided almost exclusively by family members, mostly women. Women's roles as providers of care for the thousands of people who have the disease are, like Nicaragua's long history of pesticide-driven environmental violence, nearly unacknowledged in the medical literature on the disease.

Men tend to dominate the ranks of sugarcane farmworkers, who are already overrepresented in CKDnt studies. When they do work in the sugarcane fields, most men who live in villages like Valle Rojo find work only seasonally, during the five- to six-month harvest period. In the remainder of the year, they make a living tending to small subsistence plots. When men fall sick with CKDnt, this subsistence labor becomes the responsibility of their wives, sisters, and mothers, in addition to cooking, cleaning, and bathing. What I think the women of Valle Rojo were trying to do with their atmospheric homework was to "bring trouble" to this idea of quotidian, routinized, feminized care, the kind of care that is presumed to just exist in villages like theirs.[80]

So even as CKDnt debilitates and kills more men, and even as the overall size of the workforce in the Nicaraguan cane industry continues to get smaller, the disease has come to stoke a need for more work from women in places like Valle Rojo. Women who may never have set foot in the cane fields find themselves dedicating more and more time to looking for water to give to their family members, to feed plants and animals, to clean, and to bathe. Water is the tool that they need but cannot access to clean up the human and environmental mess caused by sugar production.

To suggest that CKDnt is both a problem of plantation work and a problem of "homework" on the outside of the plantation is not to dismiss the role of field labor conditions in the spread of the disease. When I asked, most women and men in the villages of the sugarcane zone welcomed international research projects like Adelante. Doing atmospheric homework means asking what else might be possible. Attention to how people pose such questions can help us find ways to include things that do not normally count as "extreme" in the stories we tell about planetary health. Atmospheric homework is a start. It is not a direct refusal or refutation of the premises of experiments like Adelante, but a refusal to treat everything that lies outside that experimental space as natural, as given, as noise. When village women talk about being affected by chronic kidney disease, when they speculate about what might be in the water, and when they perform their own experiments with bleach and sunlight and tell their own histories of dehydration, this is what they are doing. The term *chronic kidney disease* names not just the inability of one kind of body or organ to endure extremes but a breakdown in the capacity of many kinds of bodies (bodies of humans, bodies of plants, bodies of water) in historically particular places—the Pacific Basin of Central America, a nameless, minor river valley in a tropical dry forest—to absorb the atmospheric excesses of industrial agriculture.

CKDnt is a condition in which the vulnerability of the working body seems conjoined with that of the biosphere. It is a condition in which the effects of overfarming and overexertion reverberate and resonate between persons and working environments. Among other things, CKDnt is an atmospheric condition: a dysfunctional relationship between a system and its surrounding context. It is a disease in which working bodies can no longer adapt to their surroundings.

The point of looking at CKDnt beyond the fields, as we will do in the next two chapters, is not simply to critique the hubris of global standards by offering the counterpoint of local contingency. It is rather to acknowledge that the work, however halting and individually failing, of trying to articulate what is troubling about everyday experience is also planetary work. A response to the sugarcane industry's systematic disavowal of responsibility for deforestation, for drought, and for toxicity could of course entail calls for regular water quality testing and redistribution (and it does), but residents of Valle Rojo and other villages have good reason to be suspicious that a straightforward toxicological approach to the health problems they face will get them anywhere. After all, they already know that their bodies have been used as dumping grounds for methyl parathion, DDT, and other chemicals. They make no claim or aspiration to purity; rather, they make a more radical claim: that as much as late industrial science and plantation economics would write them out of the story of modern sugar production, they are inextricably entangled with it. This entanglement is violent and unstable, and attempts to normalize it through conventional methods of environmental health surveillance do not necessarily lead to justice. Claims to save industrial workers from the excesses of global warming do little to answer the question of why, even as the vulnerability of those categorized as formal laborers becomes increasingly associated with a changing climate, that changing climate seems to be demanding that those outside the formal sector do more work.

3

———

Renal Environments

Saúl called it the *baño ecológico*, which translates to something like "nature's bathroom."

The baño ecológico is always available to men in Nicaragua, for whom it is not a particularly egregious etiquette violation to discretely micturate behind a gas station, under a tree, or perhaps a few feet into a stand of sugarcane. For me, the baño ecológico encompassed all these places. Saúl and I spent a lot of time in the Hyundai driving back and forth across the Montelimar landscape, and I did my best to keep myself hydrated, which meant that I peed, a lot. Nothing testifies to white male gringo privilege quite like a crystal-clear stream of urine absorbed without argument by a desiccated tree trunk. In a pinch, public urination seems moderately acceptable because urine is relatively inert. Unlike stool, its brown, putrid neighbor, urine is a modest, if slightly salty, emulsion. Small amounts can always be diluted. Indeed, after a short while, and presuming that the person doing the urination remains out of sight of potential onlookers, a little urine becomes undetectable.

Sort of like the way that toxic pesticides can become undetectable after they leach into the ground. Of all the fluids and solids human mammals produce— blood, semen, milk, stool, even sweat—urine occupies an odd place. Sociologically, consideration of urine tends to come alongside consideration of plumbing, infrastructure, and perhaps the gendered inequality of privacy. Men like me can easily avail ourselves of the baño ecológico. Women assume more personal risk if they venture outdoors to relieve themselves.[1] The idea behind the baño ecológico, that nature—a stand of trees, a creek, a bush—has the capacity to absorb human waste, makes sense in rural Nicaragua and other places where population densities are low (it helps if there are plenty of healthy trees and waterways). But when people urinate at scale, the baño ecológico gets overwhelmed. The trees become weak; the grasses die; the streams can no longer support fish, moss, algae, or other forms of life. But let's not presume that urination is always an act of alienation, or disavowal, or even shame. No one with kidney disease ever takes urination for granted. They recognize urination, and the renal processes that enable it, as a relationship, one that makes persons and environments simultaneously.[2]

Questions about waste and excess in the Anthropocene are, as the term *Anthropocene* implies, often posed in one direction. That is, they are questions about the nonhuman environment's capacity to absorb the excesses of human activity. A planetary health approach attempts to reverse that direction, asking how much excess human bodies can absorb. Urinary health and kidney function are apt places to look for answers to these questions. As filters for wastes both encountered in the environment and produced by the body during physical exertion, kidneys can be seen as the body's internal cleansing service. Lungs, skin, and eyes are points of immediate contact with the environment, but the kidneys' job is to do the actual work of adapting internal chemistry to external conditions. The result of that adaptation is urine.

Indeed, it is not too much to think of the contemporary Nicaraguan sugarcane zone as a renal environment. The flows of toxins, water, urine, and waste through rivers, irrigation systems, and bodies subvert any neat distinction that might be made between the renal system as a domain of bodily waste and water management and the ecosystem as a domain of transcorporeal, more-than-human waste and water management. Kidney disease sets in not just when bodies fail to properly render waste into liquid urine but when the wider flows of waste and water break down, when the fragile system that filters living from nonliving matter, the excessive from the essential, breaks down. In this way, we can think of climate crisis itself as a crisis of renal health on a planetary scale.

Sugarcane companies in Nicaragua have been taking the measure of renal health at the scale of the individual human worker for more than two decades. Urinalysis plays a key part in a common origin story surrounding CKDnt, which says that the disease was discovered in the health clinic at NSEL. In 1996, NSEL's staff physician, Dr. Felix Zelaya, noticed a curious spike in kidney disease in the community surrounding the company's plantation. Zelaya began systematically testing the urine and blood of NSEL workers for abnormal kidney function biomarkers, particularly the presence of the protein creatinine.[3] Under normal conditions, creatinine is filtered out of the body by the kidney via urine, but when kidney function deteriorates, the protein leaks into the blood. Zelaya used creatinine counts and other data to calculate each worker's estimated glomerular filtration rate (eGFR). An eGFR that remains below 60 for a sustained period is an indication of chronic kidney disease. Over the course of the late 1990s, Zelaya and NSEL generated a database of some three thousand suspected kidney disease cases.[4] That work gave rise to both a new diagnostic category, CKDnt, and a new management practice. By 2005, workers at all four Nicaraguan sugarcane companies were undergoing routine urine and blood tests to measure kidney function during every harvest, and companies were refusing to employ anyone who showed signs of CKDnt.

While it was clear by the time my fieldwork began that workers were getting sick, the precise consequences of the complex liquid flows of water and sweat and urine and chemicals through the plantation landscape were difficult to know. Creatinine counts and eGFRs are, like many attempts to discern the inner workings of the body, momentary impressions. These numbers can rise and fall depending on what someone has had to eat, how much they have had to drink, and what they do for a living. They are snapshots that offer a glimpse into a complex, more-than-human metabolic process. But when they manifest as numbers, as they inevitably did on the laboratory reports received and annotated by doctors in that scraggly, stereotypically physicianesque chirography, they carry a great deal of weight. For thousands of people employed in the sugarcane zone, the results of those blood and urine tests meant the difference between a season of relatively well-paid work and a future of joblessness and debility. This kind of corporate collection of medical data extends the alienation of workers from their bodies beyond the space of actual field and factory labor. It also permits corporations to stay ahead of problems before they become matters of public concern. The existence of such data does little to assuage uncertainty and doubt about the causes of disease. In fact, rumors about what kinds of medical knowledge the company possessed amplified latent concerns about the environmental conditions that led to the CKDnt epidemic, leading to the grievances we explored in chapter 1.[5] AMBED filed its grievance against Montelimar knowing that healthy urination depends on healthy kidneys, which depend on a healthy extrabodily environment. Its call for a recognition of the right to "a dignified life in a healthy environment" was thus not just a rhetorical flourish.[6] It was a suggestion that renal health and environmental health were inseparable.

The protein of primary concern at sugarcane mills, creatinine, is the product of the strenuous expenditure of energy, something like an emission in the atmosphere. Through the corporate testing regime at sugarcane mills like NSEL and Montelimar, waste proteins in the urine and the blood became proxies not just for the conditions of workers' bodies but for the quality of the relationship between their bodies and the surrounding environment. From its origins at the dawn of the Industrial Revolution, the science of occupational medicine has been a project of calibrating the human organism's ability to expend energy while absorbing and efficiently excreting waste, both the waste created by working muscles and the waste created by the tools of the trade: the heat emitted by a machine; the dust thrown up by a blade; the smoke pouring out of an exhaust pipe; the invisible, often odorless aerosolized excess of agrochemicals.[7] A body's fitness to work is measured by its ability to withstand exposure to these waste products.

This chapter describes how AMBED worked to reimagine the sugarcane zone as a renal environment. A renal environment is one where the flows of water and waste are regulated and contested. For CKDnt-affected residents, kidney function was always a social function—one that went beyond the body proper. The chapter spends time on the edges between the plantation and its outsides, where nonliving wastes accumulated and mingled and where they were examined for clues about the physiological condition of living organisms and ecosystems, from human communities to sugarcane monocultures. These spaces, what Elizabeth Povinelli calls *embankments*, are key elements of the renal environment. They are sites where forms of life strain against one another. Povinelli uses the term *embankment* to mark out "the sandbags or sand dunes that keep a flood at bay as long as they can keep themselves in place as they are assaulted by pounding and creeping waves; [the] mountains that contain the circulation of winds and trap pollutants until they crumble under their strain . . . the social identities that provide the conduits through which rights are circulated until they are twisted by these circulating rights and take on new identities . . . the skin that protects the inner organs unless a cancer eats it away, having begun from outside contamination."[8] Violence occurs when the people and things positioned along the shifting soils and sands of embankment "are (mis)interpreted as autonomous insides and outsides."[9] The remainder of this chapter moves among various embankments, the edges where land, water, and concrete meet, and where the functionality of kidneys and socioecological systems meet.

Cachaza and Cleaning

Let's start on a familiar sort of embankment, the mouth of the Río Jesús, the largest of the several rivers that course through the Montelimar plantation. The Río Jesús meets the Pacific Ocean in a picturesque mangrove forest that gives way to a wide tan and white beach where fisherfolk in wooden launches punch through the swell each morning, and where faded signs warn less scrupulous would-be seafood harvesters to leave sea turtle nests undisturbed (sea turtle eggs, purported to have aphrodisiac properties, have long been among the local treats that coastal tourists in Nicaragua are invited to sample). The first time I visited the Río Jesús was in July 2017. I went along with Saúl and Don Alvaro Torres. Don Alvaro had brought us there after hearing from acquaintances who lived in villages near the mangroves, folks who made a living from the river and the sea when there was no work in the cane, that the estuary had become choked with a thick, vaguely molasses-smelling sludge. There was no doubt that this was effluent from the Montelimar mill, located just a mile or so upstream. The presence of the sludge was concerning enough for AMBED to file a complaint through the company's internal grievance mechanism. Sludge didn't have anything directly to do with kidney disease, but it signaled to the people living near the estuary that the company was ignoring its responsibility to manage its waste. This much mud was impossible to absorb.

By October of that year, the company had yet to respond, but at the end of that month, Tropical Storm Nate struck the area, flooding every ditch for miles and causing significant damage to houses and roads. I spent much of November 2017 with Don Alvaro, Saúl, and other AMBED members surveying the aftermath. The town of Masachapa, home to a few small hotels and restaurants serving tourists, as well as to a number of staff from both the Ingenio Montelimar and the Barceló Montelimar Beach resort, had sustained significant flood damage, as had many of the upland villages. But Don Alvaro was keen to visit the mouth of the Río Jesús. Getting there required driving the heavily storm-rutted dirt roads out of Masachapa and around the massive and securely fenced-in beachfront property of the Barceló resort, as well as the massive and securely fenced-in compound of the Montelimar mill. Parking at the end of a lonely road on the edge of the mangroves, we walked the half mile down the beach to the river's mouth.

Don Alvaro set himself up on a spit of sand next to the river, with the smokestacks of the sugar mill in the background, and asked Saúl to begin recording a short video on his mobile phone. Within a few minutes, Don Alvaro's assessment of the situation would be posted on Facebook. "Today, we are in this place for the second time to verify its condition," he began, "and we're showing that the river looks clean . . . thanks to Tropical Storm Nate, which did a nice cleanup of this area. Where we're standing now is sand. It's not sludge [*cachaza*], as it was before. . . . So we want to follow up." Don Alvaro used the term *cachaza* advisedly. In Nicaragua, a more common term for "mud" might be *lodo*. *Cachaza* is a less-frequently used alternative, but it is also a reappropriation of a piece of sugarcane vocabulary. Some cocktail connoisseurs will know the Brazilian Portuguese cognate *cachaça*, a rum-like liquor derived from sugarcane. In Spanish, *cachaza* can be a synonym for molasses, or a metaphoric epithet for describing the movement of a person (or maybe a corporation) whose activity is as slow and laconic as the brown syrup that comes from raw sugarcane.

But Don Alvaro was not finished. He concluded by saying, "We're not against the Montelimar mill, but we think of this as a place for people to come to fish, to bathe. And we think that if the mill is contaminating the place, they could take more adequate measures to monitor this contamination, because . . . we can prove that the mill deposits lots of waste in this river." The statement was concise and would have seemed almost impromptu in its informality, but Don Alvaro's choices about vocabulary (*cachaza* instead of *lodo*) and the point he made about not being "against" the Montelimar Corporation showed a level of precision that cut through the amateur camerawork and the occasional stammer in his delivery. He was not there to catch the company in the act of polluting. As he said, he could already prove that they were dumping into the river. Rather, he was there to enlighten the company, to follow up, to monitor its activities. AMBED was mobilizing the corporation's internal grievance mechanism to appeal to it as an ethical ecological actor.

This was not the first time that Don Alvaro and his colleagues had called attention to the condition of waterways in the sugarcane zone. The hydraulic infrastructure of dams, irrigation ditches, rivers, and creeks that characterized the landscape and that kept sugarcane cultivation viable was impressive in its scale. Very little in the area between the Pacific beaches and the foothills of the Central American cordillera was *not* engineered in one way or another to bring water to sugarcane. What Don Alvaro knew was that like a worker's kidney, this kind of complex industrially engineered system was inherently fragile.[10]

In the video, Don Alvaro pointedly gave credit to the tropical storm for "cleaning" an estuary that was being polluted by the sugar mill. In his telling, the storm was a sort of blessing, an unearned gift from above to both the guilty sugar mill and the fisherfolk who were being harmed by its actions. Don Alvaro knew that to clean an estuary was not to return it to some pristine state, but to prepare it to be damaged again. In the years I spent visiting and revisiting the communities of Montelimar with Don Alvaro, he consistently drew my eye to acts of cleaning, whether they were "natural" ones like the flood caused by the storm or "social" ones like the washing of laundry. Though he never said so explicitly, I think I understand why. The compromised quality of these cleaning processes (the river, like the clothes, would be soiled again) was linked to the compromised capacity of kidneys to perform *their* primary function, which is to cleanse blood of impurities. Don Alvaro was situating the kidney as a hydraulic cleaning and irrigation system, nested within a set of larger systems, from regional rainfall and river flows to hyperlocal modes of bodily and household maintenance. He was documenting the cracks that were forming in the material infrastructures that sustained the cane, and in the once-reliable figure of the able-bodied worker in the cane. By bringing attention to the watery worlds on the edge of the cane fields, Don Alvaro and AMBED were working to reframe the disease as a problem not just of economic productivity but of social reproduction.[11]

Economies of Laundry and Irrigation

The village of El Zapote, which we visited in the introduction, sits close to the Pacific coast, next to a river and just downstream from one of Montelimar's major irrigation dams. To get there, you have to drive down one of the deeply rutted plantation roads—roads designed for massive semitrucks rather than the Hyundai that Saúl used to get around the plantation with me and the AMBED leadership. In the dry season, the irrigation dam upstream of the village keeps the water level in the river so low that residents face the challenge of washing clothes in a waterway that is also the only place where cattle, horses, and pigs can bathe, defecate, urinate, and drink. Separating soiled from clean clothing is a matter of degree, rather than of absolutes. Water here is not only scarce but contaminated.

Our visits to El Zapote tended to take place around midday, when the sun was highest, and when, almost without fail, we would find Doña Elba washing clothes in the river. She was always in the same spot, and it was evident as one peered up- and downstream that riverine laundry was a bit of a territorial thing. Each woman on this side of the village had a place, maybe sometimes shared with a daughter or sister, where she returned to do her family's washing. There were obvious advantages to getting a spot where the water was deep, and where the flow was good.

"The river doesn't belong to the company," Doña Elba told Don Alvaro Torres and me in 2017. "It belongs to the community." By common agreement among the users in the village, she had her claim to this slice of the embankment, but that claim stopped where the dry earth stopped. The scarcity and contamination of water occasioned by the presence of irrigation dams, in El Zapote and elsewhere, became the basis for another grievance brought to the mediation table by AMBED. As I explained in the previous chapter, CKDnt tends to be diagnosed more often in men than in women, and it tends to strike early—often when men are in their thirties and forties and in the prime of their working lives. When sugarcane companies tell them that they are too sick to seed, fumigate, or cut cane, these men wind up stuck at home. One outcome of the CAO-sponsored mediation process that AMBED's 2015 complaint initiated is that more and more men have qualified for disability pensions and access to dialysis, but it is often their wives, mothers, and sisters who must figure out how to make do with the resulting reduction in family income.[12]

Here is where washing and cleaning come into the picture. AMBED leaders like Don Alvaro Torres were always impeccably washed and coiffed, and the men who would hitch rides on mototaxis and horses up to the highway to take the bus to the dialysis clinics in Managua also made sure they showed up looking right. This theme has come up over and over again in my research on public health in Nicaragua—the way that aesthetic presentation of the self is much more than vanity or adherence to cultural norms. Dignity, manifested in bodily cleanliness, is constitutive of health itself.[13] In the context of a contested environmental illness like CKDnt, the aesthetic quality of the body cannot be set in opposition to that of the lived environment, especially in a plantation system in which, from the beginning, laboring bodies have been construed as fungible and less than human.[14] Going before the CAO mediators and suggesting that the World Bank had an obligation to defend people's ability to effectively hand-wash clothes might seem like an undignified thing to have to do, but it makes sense if we see kidney function as always dependent on extrabodily forms of life support. AMBED insisted on collecting evidence of how the difficulty of doing socially reproductive labor like cleaning was compounded by an epidemic of kidney disease that, it was confident, would in time be definitively linked to the scarcity and contamination of water. Water thus condensed questions of reproduction, production, and health, but less in the functional sense that phrases like "water is life" might point us to and more in the associative sense in which the metaphysical becomes political.[15]

When AMBED presented the El Zapote villagers' grievance about the state of the river, the Montelimar Corporation's response was that it would of course be willing to "share" water with the community. At the mediation table, company engineers pledged to only irrigate the cane fields at night, leaving more water to flow to the community during the day. At one level, the water "sharing" plan seemed to redistribute a resource in a way that fit the model of corporate transparency we explored in chapter 1. It settled the accounts of villagers and the company. It ratified a belief in the fundamental commensurability of needs that drives the World Bank's mediation-based conflict resolution model, a belief that is echoed in many versions of applied planetary health. Fairer water distribution could act indirectly as an offset for the burden of kidney disease.[16]

But less than a mile away from El Zapote, in broad daylight, it was possible to see the company's irrigation systems in operation. I took pictures of them and proudly showed them around El Zapote on our next visit. The images were surprising to no one, and no one saw them as opportunities to secure more concessions from the company. When Don Alvaro brought evidence to the mediation table that the agreement was not being honored, the company would claim that what we had seen was little more than the result of poor decision-making by local field managers. It took time to change corporate culture, after all.

To me, this seemed like a cynical abuse of power on the company's part. Who, really, could stop it from irrigating? The company controlled the dams; it owned the pipes and pumps and hoses; and everyone depended in some way or other not just on the steady availability of water but on the continued viability of sugar. Certainly, the people of El Zapote had little appetite for direct confrontation. Like the Montelimar Corporation, the residents were in a double bind when it came to water scarcity. Company and residents depended on the very same scarce supply to make ends meet, but of course, they also depended on one another as management and labor. People in El Zapote who were healthy enough to work relied on the jobs that the company provided, including the job of operating and maintaining the irrigation system, even though those same jobs resulted in a situation in which they and their families would be more likely to be exposed to stagnant, contaminated drinking and bathing water.[17] Productive work like the cultivation of cane is frequently couched as dependent on unpaid reproductive work such as that of bathing and cleaning. The "water sharing" deal brokered at the mediation table was in a real sense intended to recognize that dependency. What it failed to recognize was the tendency of monoculture to overwhelm and constrain the possibilities for social reproduction. Even though they knew that they were bound in many ways to the cane, people in villages like El Zapote were not asserting the right to reproduce simply because they needed to do so in order to go to work.

Water may have been a condensing symbol for residents' struggles, but it was not an infinitely divisible, shareable resource. Doña Elba told us quite plainly, more than once, that "the *river* belongs to the community." It was the viability of the embankment, not just the liquid, that mattered to her. With hindsight, I have come to understand her very public act of continuing to launder clothes in the contaminated stream as a form of what Manuel Tironi calls "intimate activism." Filing a grievance premised on the right to launder was a means not of stopping monoculture but of slowing it down.[18]

The complaint about the difficulty of doing laundry provoked consideration not just of how and why so many men were getting sick, but of how they and their families experienced the epidemic in ways that strained the sharp divide between the plantation and its outsides that the water use settlement was supposed to preserve. In her study of communities' relationships with a transnational mining company in Peru, Fabiana Li observed that the effects of mining on the quality of water and soil turned out to be as uncertain as the value mining added to the economy or deducted from nature.[19] She traces how the company attempted to replace polluted water in an irrigation canal used by farmers with water that was "clean" by regulatory standards, but this exchange of two kinds of water (and the assumption that they were "equivalent" in the first place) did not account for the ways in which extractive activity fundamentally altered people's relationship to canals and rivers, relationships that were enveloped in kinship idioms.[20] If life support only happens at the dialysis machine, or if it is only represented in an economic equivalence between different forms of water usage, then something gets missed.

Canals and Community

Riverbeds were far from the only sites of intimate activism. Residents of many plantation villages routinely drew water directly from irrigation canals. The extensive network of gravity irrigation that kept sugarcane nourished is qualitatively and legally distinct from riverbeds, and it would have been difficult for residents to claim the embankments along the canals as community property in the way that the women in El Zapote had claimed the river's embankment.

FIGURE 3.1 Maintaining the embankment on an irrigation canal. Photo by the author.

Irrigation canals were most prominent in upland communities like El Muñeco, a settlement on the far southern end of the Montelimar Corporation's holdings. In these communities, concrete irrigation works are often the only means of doing the reproductive work of washing and cleaning.

But this system, too, is fragile. Canals crumble and decay, and much of the company's capital is dedicated to maintaining them. Villagers who depend on the waters running through irrigation canals end up becoming unpaid participants in that maintenance work: clearing topsoil and brush to prevent erosion, for example. Villagers also fuse the hardware of social reproduction directly to the irrigation system. In the center of figure 3.1 is a pair of concrete slabs, bleached white from repeated use as a surface for laundering clothes.

A few years before my fieldwork began, the Montelimar Corporation heavily publicized its construction of communal water pumps across the district. These pumps were designed to provide villagers with their own supply of washing and drinking water. Drawn directly from the ground rather than routed through the irrigation works, they served to spatially and socially

FIGURE 3.2 A tube well installed by the Montelimar Corporation. Photo by the author.

segregate the water of cane production from the water of social reproduction. Around the same time, rumors began to circulate around villages like the one where the pump depicted in figure 3.2 is located that the concrete irrigation canals would soon be "modernized" and enclosed. The open watercourses would be converted into sealed tubes, protecting the water that the company used from evaporation, as well as what it considered theft. In the name of a constitutional right to water that applies in Nicaragua to both private companies and small landholders, the construction of the communal wells created a new hydraulic boundary between industrial irrigation, geared toward the support of the life of cane plants, and domestic water usage.[21]

This attempt to disentangle productive industrial water use and reproductive domestic use, however, has been persistently undone by the corporation's other major liquid activity: the spraying of agrochemicals from helicopters. While some villagers I met did drink the water from the communal wells, many chose not to for fear of poisoning. One man I interviewed put it plainly: "Our well is in the center of the cane fields. All that poison ends up there in the earth. Then when rain falls, what does it do? [It becomes] the same water that we drink. . . . How could it not? . . . That's why we have so many diseases here."

The potential of pesticides to leak through the water table and into domestic supplies was accepted as fact by nearly everyone who lived in the area. Getting information about the extent of this contamination, however, proved a chronic challenge. One of the renewed promises of the final agreement that AMBED reached in 2023 with the Montelimar Corporation was that the company would finance routine water quality tests across the zone. The company might still contest claims that the CKDnt epidemic had anything to do with its use of agrochemicals, but the tests were seen as a sign of good faith. When these tests began, the company specified that they only be carried out during the dry season, which happened to be when runoff between the fields and villages was least likely. Just as Tropical Storm Nate had "naturally" cleaned out the contamination of the Río Jesús, the company relied on the "natural" cycles of rainy and dry seasons to maintain what villagers saw as the artificial distinction between productive and reproductive life.

The women who lived in lowland communities like El Zapote insisted that what was at stake in their conflict over the scarcity of water was not water itself, but a river. In upland communities like El Muñeco, the situation was different. Irrigation canals were absolutely the property of the company, but the status of the water inside them was ambivalent. As Julie Livingston has written, the "classic critique" of a situation like this—the installation of a communal well of dubious quality to offset access to a private canal—would be to flag "the inadequacy of technocratic approaches to what are ultimately problems of maldistribution." "But," Livingston asks, "what happens when the technology itself is a redistributive one [like a canal, well, or dam]? . . . What happens when the [water] to be redistributed is disappearing? . . . Or if its quality is questionable in the first place?"[22]

Gestures to community responsibility like the communal wells notwithstanding, the equitable distribution of water is not, legally speaking, the purview of corporations like Montelimar. Regulating distribution is the job of Nicaragua's state water authority. Still, for villagers, the obvious source of power was not the government but the sugar company. Ecology and health in this landscape remained in large part moral economic matters, which meant that the corporation's efforts to disentangle itself from responsibility for, or even direct material connection to, the reproductive struggles of local residents were always doomed to fail.[23] The quality of water—both its material contents and its tendency to become laden with multiple meanings, from the economic to the ethical—placed limits on the capacity of the company to use infrastructure to insulate itself from its social surroundings. What was violent here was not that the company was successful in that disentanglement but that its efforts to insulate itself were so easily undone. It is more-than-capitalist relations, rather than just relations of labor to capital, that give form to environmental degradation.[24]

Though they are clearly built rather than natural features of the environment, the miles and miles of irrigation canals are nearly all older than most Montelimar residents. The failure of these old canals and the newer wells to settle abiding concerns about pesticides underscores how embankments are sites of what Povinelli calls "strainings" between forms of life. These strainings produce material and social excesses, the "tailings" of productive and reproductive life.[25] The term *tailings* normally refers to industrial effluents—like pesticide runoff or cachaza—but in Povinelli's reading, tailings can be the material traces left by any attempt to sharply bifurcate forms of life. For people confronting CKDnt, that straining and tailing became palpable in acts like bathing and washing in a concrete stream, replanting a damaged garden, or, indeed, faithfully adhering to hemodialysis treatment.

Dams and Dialysis

If you had a slender enough boat, you could navigate the Montelimar plantation, and just about any other sugar plantation in Nicaragua, by water. At high tide, you could slip through the mouth of a river like the Río Jesús and work your way inland. It would be hard going, especially in the dry season when the sugarcane was being planted. No matter what the water level, though, the big challenge would be the dams. These rivers and creeks are worked over with dams. The dates on their faded concrete cornerstones archive a century of sugarcane cultivation in this area. Some of them were built as far back as the 1960s by Nicaragua's then dictator, Anastasio Somoza Debayle, who owned a part of what is now the Montelimar plantation. When the Somoza dynasty consolidated control over land along Nicaragua's Pacific coast during the middle part of the twentieth century, as we saw in the last chapter, it also normalized the capture of water resources by industrial agricultural interests. (Somoza was so obsessed with irrigation that he is even said to have seeded clouds to make it rain over the arid landscape that is now the sugarcane zone.)

The dams divert the flow of rivers and creeks into the open gravity-irrigation canals. Aided by pumps, these canals provide life support to hectare upon hectare of sugarcane. Once you start to notice it beneath the canopy of trees (the few trees that remain tend to cluster around people, who tend to cluster around rivers and creeks), the sheer scale of this industrial engineering project becomes staggering. The situation in western Nicaragua, a water supply that disproportionately supports commercial crops over people, leaving its outsides denuded and dry, is one that recurs over and over again in the story of sugarcane.[26] While Nicaragua is a relative latecomer to the global sugarcane trade, what has happened in places like Montelimar is resonant with what has happened in other parts of the sugarcane-producing world over the past five hundred years or so. Tracts of food and textile crops have supplanted small farms and forests, causing soil erosion, displacement of people, rises in mean annual temperatures, and new diseases.

The construction and reconstruction of dams at Montelimar are both typical of the *longue durée* of sugarcane cultivation and of what Sarah Vaughn calls the "regional experience" of climate change. Dams are key extensions of anthropogenic environmental alteration, but they are also tools for mitigating the worst effects of projects like the development of sugarcane monocultures. Dams serve multiple uses. They can perpetuate the expansion of crops like sugarcane, but they can also support other forms of life. They are tools of capture but also of distribution. As Vaughn explains, in Guyana—a sugarcane colony— mid-twentieth-century dam projects, backed by capital and international development aid, "espoused" dominant, market-based "economic models for . . . regional development, thereby normalizing place-based climatic risks."[27]

One place-based climatic risk in the Nicaraguan sugarcane zone is intense tropical storms, like Nate, the one that swept through the area and "cleaned" the Río Jesús. Nate also flooded the Río Tecolapa, a few dozen kilometers south of Masachapa, in an isolated part of Montelimar's landholdings. The Tecolapa gorge is particularly steep around the village of El Sesteo. There is little doubt that the impact of the flood around El Sesteo was worsened by the presence of the irrigation dam and pump works just a half mile downstream. The system here, installed in April 1979, mere months before Somoza was deposed by the Sandinista popular revolution, is probably still the most impressive piece of industrial hardware at Montelimar, aside from the sugar-processing factory itself. The dam is some fifty feet high, and it pulls water from the Tecolapa into a series of hydraulic pumps that lift it more than a hundred additional feet up the gorge, where it spills into the concrete courses used by sugarcane irrigators and clothes washers.

The Montelimar Corporation did help with the cleanup of the riverside community after the flooding caused by Tropical Storm Nate, but the disaster amplified a long-standing grievance among the locals, one that AMBED had turned into yet another formal water-related complaint by Christmas 2017. Getting in and out of El Sesteo is always a challenge, and for those late-stage

CKDnt patients in the village who needed to reach the bus to the Managua dialysis clinic, more than an hour's walk away, it was particularly arduous, not least because they would have to cross the Tecolapa just above the irrigation dam. When the water was low, they could use a makeshift footbridge made of sandbags, but when the rains got heavy, the silt-choked dam could never open wide enough. When the high water swallowed the sandbags, patients in El Sesteo would have to strip off their trousers and shoes, hold them overhead, and ferry across.

Dialysis treatment happens three days a week, so behind AMBED's grievance about the Tecolapa dam was a point about the indignity of already-sick patients having to swim to access life-supporting treatment. AMBED counted it a victory when, more than a year after Tropical Storm Nate, the company agreed to create a notch, perhaps a dozen feet wide and as many deep, in the center of the dam. Under normal circumstances, the notch would allow a bit more water to flow out before being captured by the pump system, and in times of flooding, it might slow the water's rise. The precision of the cut makes an apt metaphor for the precise transactional trade-offs that tend to feature in corporate social responsibility efforts and climate mitigation measures. Whether an agreed-upon settlement like this restores bodily dignity is another matter. The silt beneath the surface remains.

On days when there was no dialysis, patients in El Sesteo and elsewhere would try to distract themselves as best they could. These were people who were used to working intensive shifts, and indolence was already something they tended to instinctively suspect. But as one man told me, dialysis made physical activity even more important. "I go walking because the doctors told us, 'Don't get lazy. If you get lazy, you'll be crippled,'" he explained. "So I go out in the morning, go down to the river and bathe . . . to exercise my body." In this account of the daily routine of caring for the body, in which the health benefit of exercise blended with the aesthetic benefit of cleaning, he routed us again through the unstable course of the dammed-up Tecolapa. It was important not only to get exercise but also, as the man explained, to sweat a bit.

As another hemodialysis patient told me, "We're drinking less water these days. For some people it's because of concerns about the quality, but for others it's because they can't. In [my] case, I can't drink too much. They told us in the hospital, 'You can only drink a half-liter of water [per day],' because the water accumulates in our bodies." He showed me his hand: "Look how it's swollen! Why? Because since Friday, last time I had the treatment, I drank water—Friday, Saturday, and today [Sunday]. So I'm full up!"

"I feel bloated," he continued, "because I don't urinate. It all disappears. . . . In three days, I urinate about one cc." In the recording, I can hear the shock I expressed at this, thinking back to how assiduously I worked to keep myself hydrated in the heat of the sugarcane zone, and how often I had to stop the car and ask Saúl and the others to wait for me while I looked for a suitable baño ecológico. Managing these internal flows was difficult, the man explained. "Sometimes you just want to have some *frito* [fried pork], and then you grab a glass of water." He made a chugging sound while he mimed drinking down his greasy, salty lunch. "Then after a while we have distended bellies because we can't get rid of the liquid until we get to the dialysis machine. The machine gets rid of that water."

Maybe it is not a surprise, then, that when I talked with people at Montelimar about CKDnt, our conversation seemed so often to get caught up in the subject of irrigation dams. Infrastructures like dams, as the environmental historian Richard White notes, have long been seen as tools for "[mixing] machine, nature, and society into a single metaphorical whole."[28] But perhaps it's not so metaphorical. Beaver dams—anthropology's prototypical example of more-than-human labor—are "natural" filters for the debris and waste tossed into waterways by humans.[29] The water below them is often cleaner than the water above. For this reason, beaver ponds have been rebranded by conservationists as "Earth's kidneys."[30] It is easy to imagine dialysis, too, as something that makes bodies metaphorically whole again, yet the challenge of keeping both outer body and inner blood free of impurities continued to be compounded by the realities of a plantation ecology in which rains and floods were ever more severe. Decades of deforestation and aggressive well drilling meant that the calculation that went into that notch in the Tecolapa dam must have included actuarial projections about the sugarcane crop's future water needs, set against the reality that—severe weather events aside—there was less water in Pacific Nicaragua with every passing year.

Dialysis, as any nephrology nurse will tell you, is a life-extending technology, not a cure. It does just enough to keep the organism functioning. It is not any more restorative than, say, the irrigation of a cash crop. It really isn't any wonder that at its clichéd extreme, a life support system (think of a ventilator or a heart-lung machine) turns a person into a "vegetable." But that is only an extreme. At a more ordinary level, on Nicaragua's plantations, to adopt a watery phrase from the anthropologist Kath Weston, the fragile architecture of dams and dialysis causes the kidney and the cane to "infiltrate each other's very substance."[31]

Consider once again the figure of the baño ecológico, and consider the fact that most of the people on dialysis in the sugarcane zone have trouble urinating at all. This means that all the inert wastes—the proteins and minerals and salts—that would normally flow out of their bodies have become trapped. Absorption of such wastes is not simply the work of a human body. A healthy renal and urinary system is always dependent on the absorptive capacity of the environment that surrounds it.[32] Long before CKDnt became a problem, for people living at Montelimar, that environment was built around cane. Questions about the contents of urine—the questions that sparked recognition of the epidemic in the first place—always must entail corollary inquiries about embankments: the silt building up in dammed rivers, the chemicals in communal wells, the creatinine building up in the blood, proteins building up in the urine, and the indignity of bathing and laundering in the same dried-up riverbeds used by pigs and horses.

One of the last AMBED events I attended took place in a ballroom of the Barceló resort, the beach hotel located on the grounds of Somoza's former palace, less than a mile as the crow flies from the Montelimar sugar mill. The general membership, including spouses and children, had been invited to hear an update from the Montelimar Corporation and a group of American scientists about the state of research on the epidemic. I spent most of the event standing on the side of the room. The place was full. Three or four buses had been rented to bring people to the event, which featured a catered lunch following the presentation. I placed myself on the outside of the crowd, taking a few pictures and wondering if my digital recorder would capture any usable audio from the echoes of the public-address system.

As I listened to the series of speeches, some scientifically substantive and others more in the key of public relations, my eye kept being drawn to the door of the lone bathroom in the ballroom. For the duration of the meeting, there was a line of AMBED members outside it. A weary-looking housekeeper stood at that door, and about every ten minutes, I would hear her quietly say "Perdón" to the next would-be user and let herself in to tidy it up, replace the paper, and wipe down the fixtures. Dozens of people used that toilet, and I do not think it is too much to interpret its popularity on that day as their attempt to extend the renal environment into the rarefied space of a luxury hotel, a subtle statement about their understanding of the inequities of water and waste management. There was as political a charge to the goings-on in the toilet as there was to those on the dais, where AMBED leaders like Don Alvaro Torres mingled uncomfortably with the engineers and managers who had once been their bosses.

The political ecology of sugarcane production and human health seems simple. Exploitation of natural resources like water compromises the bodies of those who work in the fields. It is both the cause of sickness and the cause of suffering after sickness sets in. Yet there is something about this that I find less than satisfying. This sort of explanation reproduces the very same artificial distinctions between life and nonlife, human and nonhuman, production and reproduction, nature and culture, inside and outside that give rise to problems like CKDnt in the first place. Questioning these divisions was precisely what I think AMBED's attention to the unstable embankments where the kidneys met the cane was all about. AMBED's work amounted to a dispersed effort to question what Povinelli calls the toxicity inherent to late liberalism. What was toxic was not just the haunting presence of agrochemicals in bodies and soils and waters but the premise that community concerns could be allayed by a more precise timing of irrigation activities, or a new water pump, or a twelve-foot notch in a forty-year-old dam.[33] Don Alvaro and his colleagues had kept taking me back to embankments like the edges of dams and canals, and sites like the mouth of the Río Jesús, to shed light on a problem that went beyond their bodies, to conjure a renal environment.

In a related way, the bathroom users at Barceló were using mass urination to push back against the efforts of the company and the dictatorships, past and present, that it represented, to disavow them.[34] It was not enough for the attendees to be counted, one by one, to receive their meal tickets, and feel the tide of abandonment turn. They also had to acknowledge their awareness of the fallacy behind the idea of the baño ecológico: that hydration, irrigation, urination, absorption, filtration had never been natural. The little bathroom in the five-star resort was just as "ecological" as any other.

4

———

Toxic Mediation

Many villages at Montelimar are separated from the cane by what residents refer to as a *cortina* (curtain) of trees. Were it not for the modest protection provided by a narrow stand of trees, residents say, the dust and smoke drifting from the sugarcane fields would be even worse than it is. For the Montelimar Corporation, what villagers call a curtain acts more like a fence. Legally speaking, any villager who breaches the curtain without company permission would be trespassing.

These tree curtains, as far as I have been able to establish, were created over time in a somewhat piecemeal fashion. Some of them are several decades old, and likely were planted when what is now the Montelimar plantation was a looser set of smaller fincas, owned by largely absentee oligarchs and operated by hired managers. The names of the villages correspond to the names of those fincas: names like Loma Alegre, El Zapote, San Diego, and El Apante. In each of these villages, you can still find not only evidence of deliberately cultivated tree curtains but also standing buildings that once served as worker housing, barns, offices, and storehouses. Today, depending on where you go, some of these buildings have been occupied by residents as houses. Others are conspicuously padlocked chambers where herbicides and other chemicals are stored alongside tools and machinery.

The tree curtains bear a resemblance to botanical borders elsewhere. Think of English hedgerows, or the legally mandated "living barriers" that separate soy fields from residences in Paraguay, or the "buffer zones" designed to keep soil fumigants contained within the industrial fruit operations of California. Depending on location and history, each of these borders carries a distinct set of meanings for the people who live in proximity to them.[1] In his work on Paraguayan soy, Kregg Hetherington documents the fragmentary nature of the living barriers, which were installed by law in the wake of antipesticide activism. Theoretically, they signify the government's will to protect its citizens from toxic industrial damage. But the law is patchy. The barriers are present in some landscapes and absent in others. In this way, they have become "the perfect symbol for the presence or absence of the state in the countryside."[2]

That is what curtains do, after all. They act as mediators between one sort of environment and another. They create separations in space not because they are impenetrable obstacles but because they are effective signs. In many Nicaraguan homes, curtains double as walls, marking the difference between sleeping areas and cooking areas, lending spatial order to everyday life. Curtains can even be media in a literal sense, for example, when they are impregnated with repellants to keep disease-carrying mosquitoes from menacing human inhabitants while they sleep. Whether in stage dramas or in everyday life, curtains obscure action from an audience, tantalizing it with glimpses and glares. A sliver of light pours through, air billows the fabric as a player (or is it just a stagehand?) hurries by. At Montelimar, the tree curtain had a similarly dramatic effect. When the leaves and branches of the curtain became discolored, residents knew that the sugarcane company's pesticide applicators must be active.

The Shriveled Plant Moment

A friend I'll call Mary labeled it "my shriveled plant moment." In 2003, Mary was part of a US-based development organization that operated in Goyena, the group of Indigenous villages outside León, which I described in chapter 1. Mary had witnessed plenty of dramatic scenes since she came to Goyena in the aftermath of Hurricane Mitch in 1998. But the shriveled plants, a cluster of brown, desiccated fruit trees, vegetables, and flowers in the garden of her friend Sonia, signified a different kind of disaster.

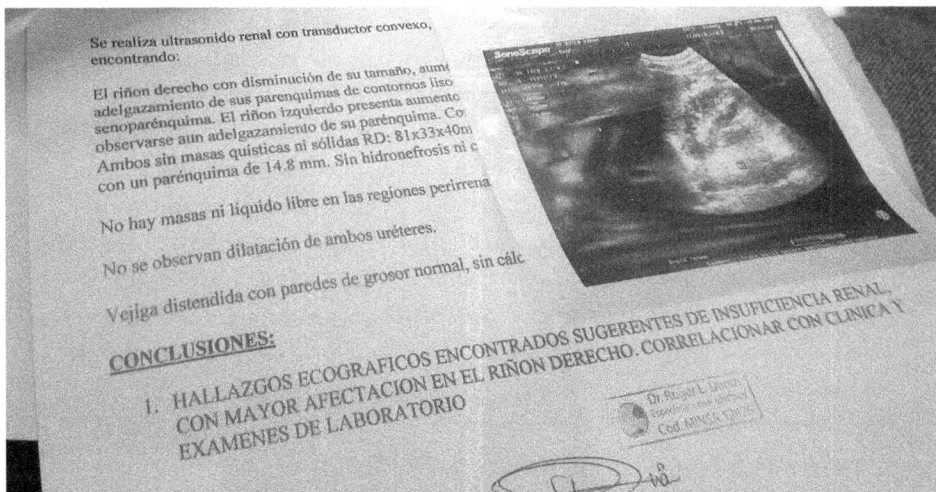

Se realiza ultrasonido renal con transductor convexo, encontrando:

El riñón derecho con disminución de su tamaño, aum[...]
adelgazamiento de sus parenquimas de contornos liso[...]
senoparénquima. El riñon izquierdo presenta aumento
observarse aun adelgazamiento de su parénquima. Co[...]
Ambos sin masas quisticas ni sólidas RD: 81x33x40m[...]
con un parénquima de 14.8 mm. Sin hidronefrosis ni c[...]

No hay masas ni líquido libre en las regiones perirrena[...]

No se observan dilatación de ambos uréteres.

Vejiga distendida con paredes de grosor normal, sin cálc[...]

CONCLUSIONES:
1. HALLAZGOS ECOGRAFICOS ENCONTRADOS SUGERENTES DE INSUFICIENCIA RENAL,
CON MAYOR AFECTACION EN EL RIÑON DERECHO. CORRELACIONAR CON CLINICA Y
EXAMENES DE LABORATORIO

FIGURE 4.1 A kidney ultrasound. Photo by the author.

Just before Sonia's plants started shriveling, the kidneys of many of the men who worked in the cane fields that surrounded Goyena had also started to shrivel. Grainy ultrasound images of damaged kidneys began circulating through the area (figure 4.1). These images were stapled to the discharge forms the men were handed as they started the journey home from hospitals and clinics. The front pages of these forms had one word printed in boldface: **EPICRISIS**.

Back then, doctors had no good explanation for the epidemic of renal failure, but for Mary and Sonia, the shriveled plants offered a clue. The villages in the area were increasingly being showered with agrochemicals, released from helicopters by the sugarcane company to promote the rapid maturation of the cane. During harvest time, houses were routinely enveloped in smoke that drifted from the fields, as company workers burned the brown stalks. Neither Mary nor Sonia had much medical training, but it made sense that what was happening to the plants and what was happening to the kidneys had something to do with what was happening to the sugarcane.

In Spanish, the word *epicrisis* means a clinical report, but more literally (in Spanish and English) it simply means "the crisis after the crisis." The shriveled plant moment, after all, seemed to come after the shriveled kidney moment. In the formal study of rhetoric, epicrisis refers to an annotation or speculation. The suggestion that toxic exposure was killing plants and people could not be proved. It was an "epicritical" association between events, based on a reading of signs in Goyena's landscape alongside signs in medical reports. When I went to Goyena to interview Sonia and others, they read those signs sent from shriveled plants and shriveled kidneys as harbingers of what they resolutely believed was a "crisis" in the sugarcane zone.[3] As we saw in chapter 1, it was this sense of urgency that led the people of Goyena to begin making their official complaints to NSEL, and which led sick and dying workers to organize themselves in the nearby town of Chichigalpa. A similar sense of urgency motivated AMBED. This chapter is about how people continue to make toxicity recognizable after the crisis, that is, after toxicity becomes a persistent and chronic element of everyday life. Since people first started piecing them together in 2003, the facsimiled ultrasound images of compromised kidneys and verbal and visual pictures of shriveled plants have kept recurring. What started as a moment has now become a genre.

Toxic exposure can be understood as a material condition, in which a body and a chemical meet through ingestion, skin contact, or inhalation. From this standpoint, exposure of a body to a toxin, like exposure of photographic film to light, can seem like a finite and measurable process. Scholars of environmental history, anthropology, and science and technology studies understand exposure in a less binary way.[4] Exposure occurs as much in the way it is mediated as in the way it is measured and quantified. Concepts of toxicity emerge through technical visualization as well as through artistic, poetic, and other forms of mediated communication.[5] Yet toxic mediation is never simply linguistic, and never only human.[6] It often happens through what anthropologists call *indexicality*.[7] Indexicality refers to the ways that some communicative signs possess "a material connection to the objects they represent. Instead of sharing qualities with their objects, they are impacted by them."[8] In the sugarcane zone, a kidney ultrasound and a shriveled plant make indexical reference to one another, as well as to invisible pesticides. Toxic mediation entails stringing together such signs. It entails following what Stacy Alaimo calls "a chain of material significations in which [illness] extends the body outward into a trans-corporeal space."[9] Just as an extended finger (the prototypical indexical sign) points to a tree or a flower and brings a viewer into closer proximity to it, the shriveled plant points to the presence of the otherwise unseen toxicant in the environment, bringing a viewer like Sonia or Mary closer to the toxic crisis in their midst. In one sense, the image of the plant *is* toxicity. In another sense, the shriveled plant, like the tree curtain, mediates the relationship between Sonia, Mary, and pesticides. The shriveled plant in this way *represents* toxicity.[10]

The beginnings and endings of toxic exposure are not as determinate as scientific models might propose.[11] For communities like those of the sugarcane zone, circulating stories, videos, and photos made toxicity thinkable and potentially actionable. The circulation of such stories and images helped expose the porosity of the botanical, legal, and economic barriers that separated them from plantations. For these communities, piecing together the signs emitted by garden plants and ultrasounds was a means of accounting for the impact of cane production on the world. As the architect and activist Eyal Weizman and his team found in an investigation of herbicide spraying by the Israeli military on the borders of Palestinian farms, videos and narratives speak to the ways in which such spraying enacts violence across political and economic barriers. This violence is as difficult to manage from above as it is to precisely predict or prepare for from below.[12] My invitation in this chapter is to think of the work of stringing together the signs of toxic exposure as a method of "toxic mediation."[13] Even when bodily injury seems to offer clear evidence of it, claims about toxicity are frequently mired in what Mel Chen calls "crises of objectivity." Toxicity is, paradoxically, both something people directly experience and a condition that requires mediation to become knowable and communicable.[14] Indexical associations like the one between the shriveled plants and the shriveled kidneys work along the edge of objectivity and conjecture. "Knowable toxicities" circulate along such edges, even if they cannot or will not be verified by laboratories.[15] This chapter examines toxic mediation at a variety of edges, including the ones between plantation and village, between human and plant or animal, between infrastructure and environment, and between the inside and the outside of the body.[16]

Exposing Exposure

With this in mind, let's return to the image of a low-flying helicopter carrying out aerial fumigation operations over the Montelimar cane fields (figure 4.2). I became aware that people took pictures of the pesticide helicopter before I first encountered one. This was not because these pictures, usually stored on cheap mobile phones, were closely guarded, or even because they were particularly controversial. It seemed mostly to do with the fact that they were so ordinary.

After several visits to the sugarcane zone, I was finally invited to peer over the shoulder of Yadier, a thirtysomething former cane cutter with stage 4 CKDnt. His tiny mobile phone screen rendered what looked at first like a picture of a fly that had landed on a cow's rump. The meaning of the pixelated pattern that shone back at me through the midday haze of a rainy season afternoon was anything but clear. We were seated in the patio of Yadier's house, which occupied a small plot of land about midway between San Rafael del Sur and Villa

FIGURE 4.2 The pesticide helicopter at Montelimar. Photo by the author.

el Carmen. His small farm was actually fairly distant from the cane fields. It was part of an older community whose residents kept a few cattle and chickens and raised corn, tomatoes, squash, and beans along a rugged, hilly stretch of a few dozen acres, hemmed in on one side by the Montelimar plantation's privately owned nature preserve. Yadier had captured the image of the helicopter during one of his thrice-weekly early morning trips to the main highway that ran through the plantation. Every Tuesday, Thursday, and Saturday, he would venture out at daybreak to meet the minibus that would take him and a dozen or so other former plantation workers with CKDnt to hemodialysis clinics in Managua. While hitchhiking along a dirt side road, he spotted the helicopter above a nearby cane field and took the picture. We got together a couple of days later, and he made a point of showing it to me, remembering that I had been asking to see one.

At the time, it seemed vital to my ethnographic research that I obtain my own copy of this image. It seemed like *proof* of something. That helicopter, after all, was known to carry tanks of a highly toxic substance (likely a formulation of glyphosate) in its belly. That substance, innocuously called a "ripener" by both Montelimar management and those who worked in the fields, was meant to help prepare the cane for harvesting. The practice of using helicopters to apply chemical ripeners to plants is somewhat new within Nicaragua's sugarcane industry, but pesticide drift and poisoning are far from new in the country. Well before the kidney disease epidemic began, and well before the advent of glyphosate as a tool in sugarcane production, thousands of Nicaraguans were sickened each year by pesticides applied both by aircraft and by hand. As we saw in chapter 2, aerial spraying during the height of Nicaragua's Green Revolution back in the 1960s left both physical scars and chemical residues in the landscape that were still felt in the 2010s.[17] If I'm honest, though, Yadier's photo did not actually show the pesticide falling out of the helicopter. Images like this turned out to be imperfect tools for exposing exposure, as it were, because they were indexical rather than conclusive.

It is useful to compare Yadier's fuzzy image of the helicopter with another kind of image. If you've read or seen a news story about CKDnt in a major media outlet, it is likely that the story found its way to a journalist thanks to the efforts of an organization called La Isla Network (LIN), whose work on heat stress mitigation we explored briefly in chapter 2. The founder of LIN, Jason Glaser, came to Nicaragua around 2007 as a filmmaker, hoping to expose the chemical harm done to workers in the banana industry, but he ended up staying because of the stories he heard about CKDnt.[18] Glaser built LIN's narrative and name around the story of a village he called the Island of Widows (La Isla de Viudas), a community surrounded by cane fields and beset by a wave of kidney disease deaths.

Although workers and others were mobilizing to confront the sugarcane industry well before Glaser's arrival, LIN explicitly takes credit for having "brought the world's attention to the CKDnt crisis, facilitating reports by major media outlets including *The New York Times*, *The Guardian* (UK), Al

Jazeera, and *National Geographic*."[19] Many of these stories of crisis feature LIN's collaboration with the photojournalist Ed Kashi. They include gripping portraits of former cane workers who are consigned to hemodialysis, along-side shots of funerals and mourning, and of the sweat-glistened backs of young men slashing their machetes against stands of charred cane.[20] Kashi's photographs have done quite a bit to give visibility to the CKDnt epidemic and to match viewers' understandings of it with the epidemiological consensus about its impact. The photos are effective because they juxtapose the risk-laden occupational space of the cane fields with the space of the village, a nonoccupational zone where care and hope struggle to offset suffering. The "About CKDnt" section of the LIN website states, "While Ebola has killed around 14,000 since its discovery in 1976, receiving billions in resources, CKDnt has killed many times more, but has received insufficient funding with which to confront a dire public and occupational health crisis affecting many times more people."[21]

The work by LIN is one example of a genre of global health storytelling that links imagery to established narratives about health crisis. Writing in the context of the Ebola outbreak that devastated three countries in West Africa in the early 2010s, Adia Benton suggests that visual representations of epidemics are effective tools for raising awareness in part because they smuggle dominant and unspoken notions of racial hierarchy into public consciousness.[22] Liberal responses to the violence of commodity capitalism also depend on this kind of normalized imagery. Through curated imagery of the Ebola crisis, Black suffering in West Africa becomes a matter of basic humanity, divorced from a history of chattel slavery and plantation agriculture on both sides of the Atlantic. Something similar happens with the suffering of brown Latin Americans implicated in the modern sugarcane market. Images of sugarcane production and the human suffering that results are oddly consistent across time and space, yet that consistency is rarely remarked on. The field is where injury happens; the home or village or clinic is where care and mourning happen. Stories about sugar production and its consequences reproduce stark divisions between farm and village, male and female, productive and reproductive, white savior and Black or brown victim.[23]

Kashi shoots on film. As the sociologist Ruha Benjamin notes, "Exposing film is a delicate process—artful, scientific, and entangled in forms of social and political vulnerability and risk. Who is seen and under what terms holds a mirror onto more far-reaching forms of power and inequality."[24] On the website of the Canon camera company, Kashi is quoted as saying, "I might have the spirit of an activist, but that's not what I do. I'm a storyteller."[25] In fact, he has taken part in ethnographic collaborations with academics, most prominently the geographer Michael Watts. There is tremendous value to this kind of photoethnography.[26] Such work is compelling not just because it vividly depicts suffering but because it promises a "thick" engagement with the quotidian aspects of life in places like the sugarcane zone.[27] Even for a skilled artist like Kashi, however, toxic exposure is difficult to photographically expose. Toxic exposure happens at multiple tempos. There is the immediate trauma of a skin burn or accidental ingestion, which would be ethically and practically difficult to catch on film, but there is also the longer-term damage of repeated, low-dose exposure, which lends itself more to narrative than to photography.[28]

Yadier's photo (a digital image, so only metaphorically "overexposed") wouldn't pass the rigorous tests of quality or craftsmanship that filter the contents of glossy newspapers, slick websites, or even academic books like this one. Like Sonia and Mary's shriveled plant story, Yadier's photo was not so much a proof of exposure as it was an indexical gesture to the possibility of exposure.[29] In place of the thick realism offered by artists like Kashi, blurry images and snippets of stories offer a form of what Rob Nixon calls "imaginative testimony." The purpose of imaginative testimony is not to provide explanation per se but to "invite apprehension": to catalyze an alternate sensibility about the material and social world.[30]

Image makers and storytellers, from globetrotting journalists like Kashi to engaged amateur observers like Yadier, work to close the temporal gap between an acute event (like, say, an instance of pesticide drift) and the harm it exacts (like, say, the death of a plant or animal or human person).[31] In this way, they offer an oblique challenge to the toxicological logic of regulators and corporations, who tend to treat chemical compounds as stable, knowable types. Chemicals are rarely thought of by these institutional actors as parts of the unstable and fluid ecologies in which people actually live.[32] Studies that have investigated the possible linkage between toxicity and CKDnt rely heavily, if not exclusively, on self-reporting of *workplace* pesticide exposure by officially contracted cane workers. They imagine toxicity as a discrete event, rather than an ongoing, slow disaster. Such conventional approaches to toxicity frame exposure as a problem—if it is a problem—that is limited to work, as defined by scientists, plantation owners, and management. In these narratives, CKDnt "hot spots" appear to cool at the edge of the cane fields. Stories and images like the ones about the helicopter or the shriveled plants, on the other hand, call into question the sharp distinction between industrial and nonindustrial space, working bodies and nonworking bodies. Mobile phones like Yadier's and software like WhatsApp and Facebook are as much a part of the ecology of the plantation as cane stalks, soils, water, pesticides, and tractors. To capture, store, and share images and stories is to participate in constructing that landscape.

Poisoned Dogs Take Three Months to Die

Using media like Facebook and WhatsApp, AMBED relentlessly documented its activities. Saúl often had his camera phone out to record conversations that were taking place in the field before I did, even though I as the anthropologist was ostensibly the professional collector of narratives and images.[33] We thus often ended up with parallel videos—something like an A-roll and a B-roll—of the same conversations or events.

In the video I'm re-viewing now, I notice that Doña Elba never misses a beat. Standing waist-deep in the stagnant section of the river that cuts through El Zapote, the same place where we found her in the previous chapter, she douses the pair of trousers in the coffee-colored water, snatches them out with a whipping motion, then slaps them onto the flat rock in front of her. Next, she pounds the brick of soap against the trouser legs, sweeping it across before crunching the fabric in her fists and sliding it across the hard surface. All the while, she's looking periodically up at the shore as her husband, Juan, tells us his theory about why dogs sometimes end up dead at the water's edge.

"They poison themselves," Juan explains. When no one was looking, they would run into the cane fields on the other side of the river looking for mice, rabbits, or rats. They might find one or two rodents to snack on, but Juan thinks they also find the little boxes of poison set out by the plantation managers to keep those same rodents from damaging the cane. But who can stop a dog from heading out for an adventure?

"They don't die for three months," Doña Elba interjects, tossing the soap-soaked pants into the water again for a rinse. She wrings them out and pounds them again on the rocks. "Those dogs go and eat up the poison, but it takes them three months to die." Doña Elba wants to clarify that dogs aren't poisoned in the way that you might expect: eating the wrong morsel of venomous bait and then dramatically keeling over. They get weak and lethargic, spending more and more time at her side by the river sipping water, rather than running through the yard—much less the nearby fields—chasing pesky rodents. "It affects the pigs, too," she adds.

"Not so much the pigs," Juan mansplains. "It's the dogs that like to run out there when you're not looking."

"That's because I keep the pigs tied up!" Doña Elba retorts, pounding the next pair of trousers with a heightened degree of intensity that seems to match her frustration. Then we all go silent for a while. I'm not sure what Saúl and Juan were thinking at the time, but when I watch the video again, I keep thinking about the paradoxical clash of rat poison (permitted in the plantation) and rat-hunting dogs (renegades from the village). They seem to tragically cancel one another out.

"The dogs die after three months," Doña Elba repeats, to no one in particular, or maybe for the benefit of our cameras, whose lenses are still resting on her.

She is sure about those three months, that lag between toxic exposure, illness, and death. Living in the sugarcane zone, it helps to think in terms of duration: the seasonal patterns of rainfall and drought, of planting and harvest, of washdays and market days. Doña Elba could tell you pretty accurately how many pairs of trousers she could clean with one brick of soap or one plastic pouch of bleach. She could tell you how many months it would take for the pig tied up behind her house to be fat enough to slaughter or sell. As for the prognosis of dogs that strayed too far into the field, Doña Elba must have spoken from a direct experience—or maybe, given how sure she was about those three months, more than one experience.[34]

That detail aside, what concerns me here is how that claim about the three-month duration—the temporal span of a particular, unremarkable sort of harm—circulates. One way to answer that question is to think about media. The media studies scholar John Durham Peters defines media as "vessels and environments, containers of possibility that anchor our existence and make what we are doing possible."[35] Media, which for Peters include physical elements like fire and water, are devices for "capturing" a variety of aspects of existence, the most important and fleeting of which is time itself.[36] Sugarcane plantations, in this formulation, are effective media because they capture so many temporalities. They effectively corral the seasonal growth and destruction of cane; the annual rains; and the daily labor of seeding, fumigating, and harvesting. The main value added to sugarcane firms by agrochemicals like glyphosate is the capacity of these toxic substances to rationalize and manage temporality. While glyphosate is most famously associated with the control of weeds—unwanted plants that disrupt the steady development of commodity crops (or lawns)— in the cane industry, it is used on the commodity crop itself. The helicopters that deploy it over the fields operate on a planting and cultivation schedule in which the development of stands of cane is carefully timed. When the ripener hits its mark, the cane stops growing. Thanks to glyphosate, sugarcane companies no longer need to project the pace of growth over time and wait for the opportune moment to begin the harvest. The chemical is a way of taming nature and, by extension, of lowering labor costs. Instead of hiring an army of workers to spread out across the plantation to bring in the cane, glyphosate allows the company to send teams of workers into targeted, chemically prepared zones. This chemical-temporal management scheme has echoes of the military strategies that have long relied on chemical arsenals.[37]

The rat poisons placed in the field perform similar temporal work. Immature cane is particularly vulnerable to pests, and cane is immature during the wettest parts of the year, precisely when the populations of small mammals are at their peak in the tropical dry zone. But there are some other temporalities that escape capture. These include, for example, the hunting and mating patterns of dogs. These temporalities get captured in other media, like my video; Doña Elba's and Juan's story; the dog's body; the soap and water; and the fluid borderland between village and field.

In his foundational work on the narrative aspects of epidemics, the historian Charles Rosenberg alludes to the opening of Albert Camus's *The Plague*, in which a doctor mindlessly brushes away the body of a dead rat with his foot. For Rosenberg, that rat's death indexes several things: how epidemics often begin with minor, almost forgettable incidents; how human health is inextricably bound up with animal health; and how "the implacable circumstantiality of an epidemic coexists with—in fact, necessarily invokes—larger frameworks of meaning."[38] I think Rosenberg's intention was to illustrate how human understandings of the supposedly natural event of plague was always and already mediated.[39]

To those conversant in the language of environmental justice, a story like the one about the slow death of a dog (or many dogs?) at El Zapote might easily fit into an already established narrative genre. Perhaps the most familiar genre of environmental justice storytelling is that of lives lived "downstream" of harmful industry.[40] Environmental justice movements, especially in the Global North, frequently use linear narratives about injury as evidence of a violent invasion of domestic space by wayward materials: the liquid, gaseous, or solid effluents of industrial production.[41] These materials become agents of environmental injustice when they do harm to the sort of reproductive life I discussed in the previous chapter: the working life of laundry, of course, but also of leisure and care. Together, the domestic spaces invaded by such toxicants, we are often told, constitute a definitive outside, a world that once lay beyond industrial production but that is now consumed by it. Many popular environmental justice stories fit Rosenberg's classic three-act dramaturgical structure for the "epidemic narrative," in which harm is revealed, the randomness of death is successfully managed, and a suitable public response is devised.[42]

Unlike the sharply rendered scenarios of epidemic narratives, stories like Doña Elba's—and many others in the toxic world—are nontotalizing.[43] These stories connect human bodies to other-than-human ones through what John Jackson calls "thin descriptions."[44] In its partiality, but also in its precision (*three months*), the story counters attempts to limit concern about toxicants to the increasingly circumscribed time-space of formalized field labor. It provides evidence not of the overwhelming power of corporate monoculture to shape environments but of the enduring, if unruly, presence of multiple forms of life in the plantation.

The dog dies in the story, after all, because the cane is so vulnerable to other furry creatures. Rodenticide remains a reliable part of the landscape because management still fears the damage that those other furry things might do. The fragility revealed in the story, then, is not just that of the damaged body but that of the landscape writ large—cane, community, dog, rat, laundry, helicopter, mobile phone, gossip, grievance. I've been calling this extended example "Doña Elba's story," but that's not accurate. Accounts like this one contain standard elements that can be slightly rearranged depending on the telling. A dog might become a cat, for example (or, heaven forbid, a poorly minded pig!); a box of rodent poison might be a carelessly discarded manual sprayer. But the central arc, in which a nonhuman creature violates the invisible line that separates the plantation from the villages and returns fatally poisoned to begin a slow march to death, remains fixed.

Voices from the Ground

Toxic research, too, depends increasingly on digital media. Over the course of doing the research for this book, I lurked on a listserv for CKDnt scientists. This was one of those newsgroups where researchers share and discuss recently published papers, find out about grants, and plan the occasional in-person workshop or conference. When the COVID-19 pandemic set in in mid-2020, field epidemiology on CKDnt came to a sudden halt. Like many scientific societies, the newsgroup started to organize online conferences and lectures to fill time during the involuntary hiatus. As the pandemic dragged on, one of the group's more active members offered to organize a webinar featuring Nicaraguan "voices from the ground," including those of former sugarcane workers. There was general enthusiasm among the group for this proposal. "Good idea to frame science with a context," wrote one colleague, echoing the consensus that the inclusion of such voices in the group's ongoing dialogue would provide a refreshing reminder for all of what was at stake in the research they did, and what would still be at stake when they returned to the field.

Within the science of CKDnt, the distinction between "occupational" and "nonoccupational" life tends to come alongside the more colloquial distinction between "cause" and "context."[45] In the proposed webinar, nonoccupational "context" becomes the ground, a world against which the occupational field of plantation work can be put into focus.[46] This rendering of figure and ground is common in global health projects. Calls by scientists for dispatches from the ground stem from a desire to do just what Rosenberg proposed: to situate epidemics within larger systems of meaning. This desire is common to many well-intentioned global health practitioners. Something important is probably going on in those villages beyond the stands of cane, but occupational epidemiology is not well positioned to take the measure of it. How convenient, then, that digital media—3G, Wi-Fi, camera phones, Zoom—can open this box and give texture and form to everyday life! It seemed entirely plausible to the scientists on the listserv that former cane cutters would be able to log into a video chat and share their stories.

It also makes sense that scientists see the role of digital media as giving "voice" to those whom they see their science as serving. This privileging of the individual voice reflects a broader dominant assumption about what counts as useful evidence. People on the ground may not have the capacity on their own to provide epidemiologically robust insights about the trajectory of CKDnt, but thanks to digital communication, their stories might help illuminate the human stakes of scientifically mapping that trajectory. For people like Doña Elba and Juan, however, the figure-ground relationship seemed bang-opposite. Goings-on in the cane fields—scientific, agricultural, medical—grounded nearly all aspects of existence, even for those like Doña Elba and her dogs who had no "occupational" link to it.

The advent of cellular phones, the internet, and other digital media in places like rural Nicaragua has been trumpeted as transformational for global health, in part because these media promise to shorten the social distance between experts, policymakers, and people who live "on the ground."[47] As far as I can tell, the "voices from the ground" webinar never got past the planning stages, but I still wonder what the folks on the listserv might make of a story like Doña Elba's. If they are like me, they would probably want to sympathize with her. They might be tempted to join her in mourning the unnamed canine victims of sugarcane's dependence on toxic chemicals. But here I must reiterate that Doña Elba's account of animal poisoning is striking in its lack of a sentimental edge. Her insistence that death by poisoning took three months was almost clinical. Such authority could only come from repeated observation—from seeing this story play out in the lives of several or many dogs, and from hearing the human companions of those dogs recount the ways that they died. The pattern of poisoning mattered more than the singular event of poisoning, or even of the individual sorrow at the loss of a companion. This patterning is the difference between genre and testimony. In genre, voice matters less than what Luise White calls "circulation, and the differences circulation reveals." It is circulation that "gives the genre its authority: a story that reports so many diverse experiences from so many different places must depict elements of social life . . . that hearers recognize and want to repeat."[48] Circulation, of course, requires a medium. The recording of conversations and events on digital devices is useful for establishing patterns and genres. Media like WhatsApp and Facebook systematically encourage short digital stories. Mobile phone networks, and the cheap phones that people commonly used in the sugarcane zone, also help steer would-be content creators and sharers toward an economy of presentation.

Return of the Shriveled Plant

In August 2019, the plantation's pesticide helicopter dumped part of its load of ripener onto a patch of tomato plants in a village on the northern end of Montelimar's land. A few days later, I met Doña Haydée, the woman who owned those plants. We were part of a large group that had gathered in the cool early morning in Villa El Carmen, waiting for a bus that would take us to a community meeting where Montelimar management would be present. Doña Haydée lived not far from Doña Patricia, the woman who had organized her neighbors in the land title dispute with the company I described in chapter 1. While Doña Patricia's land claims had been documented through official grievance forms, cadastral surveys, and numerous other governmental media, this version of the shriveled plant story found its home in a more direct documentary medium: Facebook.

Doña Patricia invited me to review Doña Haydée's account of what had happened. Facebook afforded a combination of the grainy, gestural imagery of amateur digital photography with the forensic, quantitative detail spelled out in Doña Elba's dying dog stories. In Doña Haydée's post describing the destruction of her plants, I would not have been able to identify the greenish-brown botanical remains in the pictures as dead tomatoes if the story of the helicopter had not also been included alongside it. The written story included the standard chain of signification of the "shriveled plant" genre: helicopter flies low; ripener rains down on the wrong side of the curtain of trees that separates garden plots from cane fields; ripener becomes herbicide.

Along the way, though, Doña Haydée did what other skilled wielders of the shriveled plant genre did. She supplemented the requisite elements of the structure with exact details. The incident had occurred on a Sunday, the one day of the week in which plantation operations supposedly should be suspended. There were precisely ninety-two tomato plants destroyed, and in the same area, a twenty-five-square-meter stand of yucca plants was also burned away. Anyone who saw the post could do the rest of the calculations, figuring out what ninety-two tomato plants and twenty-five square meters of yucca would yield on the market after harvest.

Even before this story went live online, the Montelimar Corporation had been forced by AMBED in the CAO-mediated dialogue meetings to recognize that sometimes the ripener might miss its target. The company had long since stopped claiming that pesticide drift would never occur. In fact, management seemed to take Doña Haydée's shriveled plant story quite seriously. No doubt, the story's presence on Facebook had something to do with that. Both Montelimar's field managers and its corporate social responsibility officers were well known to Doña Haydée and her neighbors. The day after Doña Haydée's post went up, a company representative was dispatched to her house, with another kind of mediation in mind. He asked her to remove the post and promised to compensate her with cash.

She refused.

To explain this refusal, it is worth thinking further about how stories—particularly online stories—constitute acts of toxic worlding. The digital pictures of the tomatoes symbolically represented Doña Haydée's home and community, of course, but they also indexed the (unpictured) chemical that had damaged the community. In a similar way, Yadier's helicopter photograph indexed both the chemical ripener and the plants—whether sugarcane or house plot crops—on which the chemical would eventually land. Doña Elba's slowly dying dog was an indexical gesture to the poison in the cane fields and the (possibly living, possibly dead) rodents that threatened the viability of the cane. Doña Haydée's brief written interpretation of the picture was indexical as well. By rehearsing the general familiar plot points of the "shriveled plant" story, she strengthened her particular claims about the ninety-two tomato plants and the twenty-five square meters of unharvested yucca. The post was indexical in one final way. In calling forth a relationship among pesticides, plant health, and human health, it pulled plantation and village—sites that sugarcane companies, the state, and international scientists insist should be thought of as distinct—into a "mediatized space," in this case, Doña Haydée's personal social network.[49] As social media begin to blur the line between mediatized and physical space, the act of "posting about" the activities of the plantation and its management (e.g., aerial pesticide application) became a new way of "participating in" the material life of the plantation.[50]

These indexical operations, which move from the aerial to the terrestrial to the chemical to the digital, gain purchase by manifesting what Deborah Thomas calls "co-relation," not linear causality.[51] The narrative told on Facebook obliquely rather than directly counters corporate and scientific claims about the lack of a connection between pesticides and CKDnt. Even on platforms like Facebook, the genre circulates in disjointed chunks, when the metaphoric "hot spots" of Internet and mobile telephone technology become available. Such hot spots tend to cool unpredictably in rural Nicaragua, when signals drop, when phones get lost, or when phone bills go unpaid. This means that the time between the initial authorship and the final reception of any particular post or message can be much slower than popular accounts of digital or social media activism might imply. Still, the Montelimar Corporation acted quickly to try to pull Doña Haydée's message off of the network.

The money the company offered was ostensibly a compensation for the cost of the ruined crop. When Doña Haydée rejected the offer, she rejected the premise that the harm she was describing on her Facebook wall was calculable in numbers. Her rejection of a personal payoff for erasing the story denied the company not only a short-term public relations victory but also a more long-term power play. By turning down the money, she made it impossible for the company to halt the story's circulation. The company seemed to recognize that the authority of the genre is reflected in the amplitude of its circulation.[52] Doña Haydée's refusal, then, was not a symbolic act that distinguished her as a selfless martyr but an indexical one that attested to the co-relation of the harm she suffered to the harm suffered by others, including the unnamed owner of the twenty-five square meters of desiccated yucca.[53]

Signs of Obligation

In the summer of 2019, residents of several villages around Montelimar who were affiliated with AMBED were invited to hear a scientist from a US university give a briefing on the efforts being made by his research team and others to understand the CKDnt epidemic. The upshot of his presentation, not surprisingly to those of us who had heard the dominant scientific story before, was that no one knew for sure why so many people were getting sick. During the question-and-answer period that followed, the subject of aerial herbicide spraying came up repeatedly. The American scientist expressed his sympathy over the destruction of people's garden crops, and he even conjectured that the chemical in question might be glyphosate (something I never heard management admit). But he quickly reminded the audience that there was no conclusive evidence of a connection between the spraying and CKDnt. As far as I could tell, the scientist was telling the story as most any responsible person in his field might. Epidemiologists are careful not to get ahead of their data. Still, I could see the managers of Montelimar squirming in their chairs. Even if the science was "on their side" when it came to pesticides and CKDnt, management was clearly not happy that their invited guest was having to hear about the shriveled plants.

Then a woman from one of the villages took her turn to ask a question. She said, "I realize that you don't know if the chemicals make our husbands sick, but it does seem dangerous for the children to be showered when the helicopter comes overhead." While some others had spoken at high volume and in impassioned tones, she addressed the scientist in a voice so calm that the once-raucous room grew quiet as everyone strained to hear her. "Children are curious," she explained. "They want to go out and *see* the helicopter."

People started to smile and nod. What she said was true. The low-flying, sleek helicopter was an understandably fascinating sight for young children. It was one thing to witness it on the tiny screen of a cheap camera phone and to hear adults retell snippets of the shriveled plant story, but quite another to see it for yourself, unmediated. She went on, "But then you look at the plants and you think, this must not be good for them. So I accept that we don't know about the kidneys, but it seems like we should keep [the pesticides] from falling on our children's heads. We don't know when the helicopter is going to come, and we can't ask them to stay inside under the roof all the time." The unspoken corollary to this, of course, was that you couldn't grow tomatoes or squash or mangoes or avocados indoors either.

The woman's point was that while the house lots adjacent to Nicaraguan cane fields are not, strictly speaking, the property of workers and their families, multiple generations have occupied them, seeing their homes and the plantation as virtually interchangeable. In legal terms, this land is not entirely under corporate control, but in practical terms, it is not entirely independent of corporate control either. This liminality is the messy outcome of a transition in Latin American cane production from the vertically integrated finca system, in which companies provided workers with land and housing in company-owned dwellings, to a "new style" plantation in which labor was partially external-ized.[54] The woman's public invocation of the shriveled plant genre invited the epidemiologist to think of the houses and gardens where workers live and raise children as part of the overall architecture of the plantation, along with more familiar components like irrigation systems, processing mills, and aerial "ripening." Houses are situated just a few meters from cane fields, and plantation roadways double as village thoroughfares.

This pattern of settlement reflects a long-standing arrangement between plantations and those who work them. For example, what the feminist philosopher and critic Sylvia Wynter calls the "plots" cultivated by enslaved Africans on Caribbean sugarcane plantations were sites of remarkable crop diversity. Such plots provided a means of subsistence and thus a means of reproducing the plantation labor force, but they also formed ecological counterpoints to the surrounding monoculture. The cultural and emotional significance of these spaces for workers tends to be ignored in histories of the Euro-Atlantic economy generally and in histories of the enslavement of Black Africans specifically. The ambiguous ecological and economic relationship be-tween plot and plantation, Wynter argues, can sometimes be a source of alien-ation. At other times, that ambiguity can be useful in projects for solidarity and resistance.[55]

Wynter uses the term *plot* in two ways: in its agricultural valence as the physical ground on which plantation laborers cultivate crops and in its literary valence as a structure for narrative. When Wynter was writing in the 1970s, most histories of capitalism told a linear, progressive narrative in which white figures like plantation owners and scientists were the protagonists, if not the heroes. In these histories, plantation laborers and their descendants were ren-dered minor, passive, sometimes invisible characters.[56] This sort of plot, like Rosenberg's epidemic narrative, is hatched from above, from the point of view of the architects of a gridded, ordered modernity. The counternarratives that emerge from the lived-in worlds of laborers, by contrast, are views from some-where. These stories do not teach history in a neat, orderly, linear fashion. Much like garden plots, they can look unruly and undisciplined to the eye of an industrial engineer. These stories evoke what Thomas calls "co-relations," by which she means both connections between people and the nonhuman world, and correspondences between events—the kinds of correspondences that can-not be apprehended by modern science (perhaps especially epidemiology).[57]

If plots are of the plantation and not beyond it, it becomes harder to dismiss the spraying of plants and children as mere accidents. By ceding the point that there was no evidence of a linear connection between the helicopter, the chemicals it carried, and CKDnt, the woman's public retelling of the shriveled plant story highlighted a more troubling link between plantation workers' long-standing dependence on subsistence plots and the sugar industry's more recent dependence on aerial pesticides. Pesticide use didn't seem to reinforce an ethical alienation of plot from plantation, but a possible ethical connection.[58]

In their work on inviting apprehension with US environmental justice groups, Nicholas Shapiro, Nasser Zakariya, and Jody Roberts discuss strategies for eliciting ways of sensing the environment that go beyond (or lurk below) the strict enumerative parameters of fields like environmental toxicology.[59] These include dramatization and storytelling, activities whose aim "is not to provide counter or alternative facts, but to reimagine what the appropriate questions (and therefore facts) might be in the first place."[60] In the sugarcane zone, visual, dramatic, narrative, and digital media are not just ways of sensing the environment. They are ways of participating *in* the environment.

Coda: Data and Stories, Photographs and Movies

To address their concerns about water quality, AMBED's leaders and I approached the occupational health unit of the medical school at the National Autonomous University of Nicaragua in León. The unit had long been a participant in a variety of CKDnt-related research projects, and I had become interested in the work of an environmental scientist I'll call Licenciada Palacios. She worked in a laboratory that occupied a long, narrow series of rooms in an outbuilding of the medical college. There, she ran a variety of tests and experiments, but her passion was water and humans' right to a "consistent and clean" supply, no matter where they lived.

On our first visit, Saúl and I were captivated by a small contraption that Lic. Palacios had arranged on one of the lab benches. It turned out to be a portable water quality monitoring kit, constructed of simple and easy-to-find materials. It was created by an industrial design team from the Polytechnic University of Madrid, and Lic. Palacios's lab was invited to pilot it in late 2017. The little device, which included low-cost materials like PVC pipes, plastic food containers, and simple electrical nodes, would permit communities to take samples of their local water and keep them at a suitable temperature for testing in a local clinic or laboratory. At the time, universities like the National Autonomous University of Nicaragua (UNAN) campuses in León and Managua were the only places where such tests were possible, and sampling still relied on expensive sampling and incubation equipment.

Animated by the prospect of helping people in places around the sugarcane zone take action to learn about their own water, we invited Lic. Palacios to collaborate with us. Like many would-be promoters of "citizen science," we were attracted by the cheapness and simplicity of the device we had seen in her laboratory.[61] Lic. Palacios soon helped us moderate our expectations. The kit we had seen was still very much a prototype, and besides, she insisted, a community water-monitoring project could not be overly invested in the collection of data. It had to be holistic. The Spanish word she used was *integral*. Water quality could be affected by pesticides, to be sure, but as soon as one started investigating that problem, others would surely interfere. "Where are their latrines? What about their livestock? Do they also use chemicals for gardening? Do they understand the limitations of water testing?" Over the spring of 2018, she helped us design a participatory water-monitoring pilot project for the village of El Apante, complete with a plan, budget, and draft memorandum of understanding between her laboratory at UNAN and my home university. Then in April of that year, normal life in Nicaragua ground to a halt, as the country entered a protracted period of political unrest, sparked by protests against the environmental and social policies of the government of President Daniel Ortega. For more than a year, I was unable to safely travel to the country. I kept the memorandum, the work plan, and the budget, but the project remained undone.

As the political crisis began to abate, the Montelimar Corporation resumed its own periodic water tests. Every now and then, I would receive a picture or photocopy via WhatsApp of an impressive-looking laboratory report, broken down into testing categories: fecal coliforms, heavy metals, certain chemicals (though not the glyphosate that was being used as a cane ripener). Almost without fail, the reports show no evidence of dangerous levels of toxic chemicals, and almost without fail, they show some evidence that more mundane local events such as leaking toilets or wayward pigs or horses were causing bacterial infiltration of the supply.

"A report like this is like a photograph," Lic. Palacios once explained to Saúl and me. "Water behaves like a movie." Her point was that no single picture of water quality could suffice. Her comment causes me to think about the expectations, practical and imaginative, that are generated by the technologies used to document exposure. Documentation of exposure depends on the generation of data by pulling toxicants out of their surroundings, while conveying the experience of exposure depends on putting toxicants back in: of re-mediating them.

5

——————

Working Conditions

When I met him, Yadier—whom I introduced in the last chapter as a photographer of pesticide helicopters—was in his late thirties. After he came down with CKDnt, one of the first things he did was visit his local branch of the National Institute of Social Security (INSS). An INSS doctor took a detailed case history, asking him about his work and what it entailed. Yadier told him a typical story. He had started working as a teenager and had been given various tasks at Montelimar, many of them involving long, arduous hours, and nearly all of them putting him in proximity to agrochemicals. Based on this history, the INSS officially classified Yadier's condition as "work-related" (*laboral*). This classification entitled him to a small subsidy for hemodialysis treatment and medications. Yadier was fortunate. With the money he was saving on health care, he could plausibly imagine what the CAO, the Montelimar Corporation, and residents of the sugarcane zone blandly termed *alternatives*, economic projects beyond the plantation. After his CKDnt diagnosis, Yadier was no longer able to earn money working in the cane fields, so he started raising chickens in a loose cooperative association with his neighbors.

Actually, even before he got CKDnt, Yadier already had a few chickens on his small farm, which was located a few miles from the Montelimar mill. For years, Yadier and his wife had kept a fluctuating flock of *gallinas indias*, free-range yard chickens whose colors ranged from brown to black to red. Anyone in the area could tell you that the meat from a gallina india was superior in flavor to the meat that came from the commercial chickens—uniformly white-feathered—that Yadier was now raising in a coop he had built with the assistance of Nicaragua's Ministry of Agriculture and Forestry. While the gallinas indias were feisty, multicolored fixtures of the domestic landscape, destined for Yadier's wife's stewpot, the commercial chickens Yadier and his neighbors were growing were uniform and fungible, not unlike the stands of sugarcane visible on the horizon. They were destined to join thousands of others on the wholesale market.

Yadier kept meticulous records about his commercial chickens. He could tell you how much he invested week by week in specialized feed, in the construction and expansion of the coop, in special warming lights for newly hatched chicks, and even in vaccines to prevent viruses like influenza. The life of the flock was mapped out in budgets, projected growth charts, and market trends, the software and hardware for an agrarian future. Here was a scaled-down version of the kinds of accounting and measurement technologies being used at the Montelimar Corporation to track both the steady growth of the sugarcane monoculture and the health of the workforce.

This little chicken business was aimed at economic growth and a modicum of profit, but its viability depended on cooperation between Yadier and his neighbors. Each associate in the enterprise had to dedicate land to the project, and each had to do the kind of close accounting that Yadier showed me when I visited him to see the operation for myself. Like so many cooperative associations across Latin America, the enterprise relied on a dynamic process of "commoning," a diverse set of exchanges of labor time, money, land, paper, accounting skill, and much more. The market value of the chickens depended on a host of nonmarket exchanges.[1]

There were limits to this project. Yadier figured that if he and his neighbors were successful, they might be able to raise a few hundred chickens at a time, maybe as many as a thousand, but space was not infinite. He still grew corn and squash, and he kept a few pigs and a horse or two in addition to the gallinas indias, which did not demand the careful financial investment required of the commercial flock. The gallinas indias would subsist on foraged bugs and cast-off corn kernels, and if they were going to die prematurely, the culprit would most likely be a predator, not a virus. If the white commercial chickens seemed like the animal avatars of an entrepreneurial future, the multicolored gallinas indias seemed like those of a passing campesino lifestyle, preserved for the sake of nostalgia, or at least better-tasting soup.[2] Another way of seeing the relationship between these two kinds of chickens is as a coexistence between two forms of social security. They seem to fractally encompass the divides between capitalist and noncapitalist safety nets; between the working conditions of the campesino landscape and those of the manufactured, standardized, and closely audited plantation.

More than twenty-five years after sugarcane companies first started collecting data on workers' kidney function, CKDnt is still not definitively considered an occupational disease by the INSS. Throughout the period of my research, the INSS continued to designate some CKDnt cases as occupational (*laboral*) and others as nonoccupational (*común*). Those like Yadier, whose disease was classified as laboral, could claim free medical benefits, while those whose disease was classified as común could not. This chapter is about how people at Montelimar reckoned with this bureaucratic division, and how the onset of CKDnt rearranged not only workers' understandings of the ethical obligations of corporations and the state to provide them with care but also their understandings of their obligations to one another.

In a general sense, people facing CKDnt were concerned about what caused the disease, but in a more specific sense, they were concerned about working conditions, the terms under which bodies are recognized as working bodies, and environments are recognized as occupational environments. Knowledge about working conditions is produced in several places at once: by corporate management, by the state institutions that regulate them, and by workers themselves. One way of defining social security is as the setting and maintaining of working conditions. Social security becomes all the more complex when, as in the sugarcane zone, individual work histories (and by extension individual medical case histories) blur standard sociological and medicolegal binaries: corporate and collective; wage work and piecework; subsistence and market; occupational and nonoccupational.

This blurring is evident in individual stories like Yadier's, and in intergenerational stories like that of Don Tomás, a forty-seven-year-old man who had stopped working at Montelimar around 2010. When Saúl and I met them one late September day in 2017, Don Tomás told us about the pressures that had led him to abandon his job at a relatively young age, before the onset of CKDnt. Like others in the Nicaraguan cane industry, Montelimar workers only get paid a full day's wage if they harvest a daily allotment, what they call a *tarea*. If a worker fails to complete their tarea, a field manager can cut their daily pay in half. As in other agricultural contexts, this piecework system incentivizes dangerous levels of exertion in extreme heat.[3] Much like Yadier, Don Tomás recalled being denied personal protective equipment when he worked as a fumigator and herbicide applicator, and he told stories about field managers encouraging people to return to work even when they felt sick from the effects of the chemicals. Some of those same field managers would hand out ibuprofen or acetaminophen for aches and pains on the job, making it possible for workers to meet their daily tareas.

A little while into our meeting, Don Tomás introduced us to his son, Pedro, an active worker who had fallen sick with symptoms of kidney disease several times over the previous two years. In 2015, a company doctor had sent Pedro to a private clinic for a kidney ultrasound, after his creatinine level rose above 5.8. As I explained in chapter 3, since the late 1990s, when kidney disease rates appeared to spike in the sugarcane zone, company medical clinics have closely monitored workers' kidney function biomarkers, including the levels of the waste protein creatinine, in their blood. Just before we met that day in 2017, Pedro's symptoms returned, and he was given two days off from work to recover. Now those two days had passed. As Don Tomás recounted his son's work history for my digital recorder, Pedro was getting bathed and dressed to go to the mill and report back to the human resources office. He had to attest that he was still feeling sick and request new kidney tests, he told us, lest he be fired for abandoning his job. Pedro had to work to be sick, and be sick to keep working. He stood a better chance of having his condition classified by the INSS as work-related, or laboral, if he could stay employed. Workers were more likely to be able to access biomedical knowledge and state disability benefits if they presented themselves as loyal employees, and if they presented their bodies as available for exposure to heat, chemicals, and dust.

Over time, workers developed a remarkable understanding of the relationship between exertion, chemicals, the consumption of water and analgesics, and kidney function. As Don Camilo, another longtime cane cutter and a member of AMBED's board of directors, explained, "When I worked in the [field], I carried two big bottles of water, and when I went to urinate, it came out clear, clear. So I said, 'I'm OK.' Then it started to come out almost black, so I went to the [company] laboratory, and asked, 'What's this?'" When Don Camilo's urine started sending him disturbing signals, his first act, as Pedro's had been, was to visit the company's medical laboratory. His next was to visit the INSS. When Don Camilo was initially diagnosed with CKDnt, however, the INSS classified his disease as nonoccupational, or común. He refused to accept this decision, and his family gathered enough money to hire a lawyer to help dig into company records to prove that he was working during the time that his disease likely first took hold. As the lawyer made his petitions, Don Camilo's wife, who also worked for the Montelimar Corporation, made regular visits to the company human resources office to plead for help in dealing with the INSS. The family spent more than three years working its way between company and INSS offices before Don Camilo's CKDnt classification was finally changed to laboral.

As the stories of Yadier, Pedro, Don Tomás, and Don Camilo attest, disease classification in the sugarcane zone entailed a multiway exchange between workers, neighbors, families, corporations, and state. Classifications were far from given. Rather, they emerged out of a blending of plantation labor with aspects of the "commoning" work that characterized Yadier's chicken cooperative.

Disposability and Care

At first glance, the relationship between CKDnt and work seems easy to explain. In western Nicaragua, where sugarcane plantations are among the only reliable employers, there is a labor surplus, which means that companies can use early detection of kidney dysfunction to cut ties with workers as soon as their bodies succumb to dangerous conditions. As Julie Guthman explains, this kind of corporate monitoring reflects a broader global condition of industrial agriculture, in which laborers remain "valuable . . . because they have been constructed as disposable and thus readily left behind when they become sick or less productive."[4] Worker disposability is often understood as an essential, if hidden, element of monocrop production, one that is enabled by public policy. In the United States, for example, undocumented Latin American migrant workers are legally excluded from many basic social protections, including social security.[5]

It is noteworthy, then, that for decades, the Nicaraguan state has sought ways to *ensure* the future of the rural poor and of the national economy: to use the bureaucratic mechanism of public welfare to turn working bodies and working environments into subjects of regulation and care. Indeed, social security is arguably a Latin American product. Manuel Israel Ruiz Arias, a former director of the INSS, credits the South American revolutionary Simón Bolívar with introducing the concept of "social security" to the lexicon of government in 1819, some sixty years before Otto von Bismarck implemented a social safety net in Germany.[6] The premise of such safety nets is that the state must protect its most vulnerable citizens across the life course. The INSS, like most modern social security systems, ties entitlements to labor. The French anthropologist Marcel Mauss portrayed social insurance of this type as an elaborate form of reciprocity, one that acknowledges that "the wage does not cover society's obligation to the worker."[7] The bureaucratic design of social safety nets, however, tends to favor frugality in the allocation of benefits. Deservingness is determined by officials who are incentivized by rigid regulations to limit the distribution of entitlements. The result is that state care can maintain rather than assuage structural violence.[8]

The establishment of modern social security schemes has not erased older ways of making labor-based claims to food, land, and health care in Latin America, those "moral economic" entitlements based on reciprocal relations between landowning patrons and the peasant and smallholder "clients" who work for them. An insistence on such obligations, as seen in the work that Don Camilo and his family undertook to change his común classification to a laboral classification, continues to be a way for the poor to hold employers and landowners to account.[9] Moral economic obligations were also central to the operations of nonplantation enterprises like Yadier's chicken business. To social security and moral economic considerations, a global economy in which the behavior of large companies has come under increased public scrutiny has given rise to practices of "corporate security." In an age in which human rights and environmental concerns are unavoidable, companies must express limited degrees of care for the communities in which they operate, but they do so frugally. After all, they have a responsibility to their shareholders to limit their liability.[10]

The corporate impulse toward frugality had immediate and devastating effects in the early days of the CKDnt epidemic. Until the CAO intervened on behalf of workers' groups at NSEL and later at Montelimar, detection of the disease in company clinics nearly always led to swift and unceremonious dismissal. In the years after sugar companies first started monitoring kidney function, scores of workers were fired, or, in their words, "tossed into the wind," "left out on the street," "abandoned," with little recourse to occupational health or injury insurance.

Worker disposability is not an inevitable feature of the rise of monoculture or the emergence of a post-Fordist global economy. It is "a historically constituted social fact, which can manifest itself in a variety of ways."[11] As CKDnt became more widely acknowledged, and as it became more clearly connected to sugarcane production, disposability ceased to seem like an inevitable part of working life in the sugarcane zone. Thanks to broad recognition of a possible connection between work and CKDnt, disposability had shifted from an inevitability to a possibility. Workers still feared the prospect of abandonment, but they also creatively leveraged systems of corporate and state care, along with kin and community ties, to hedge against that abandonment.

Cabra. Campesino. Combatiente. Número.

Don Alvaro Torres was diagnosed with CKDnt in 2010. Back in the 1970s, when he was just a teenager, he started working in the sugarcane fields near his home outside Villa El Carmen as a *cabra*, or informal helper, accompanying his older brothers as they cut cane during the annual harvest. When Don Alvaro was young, the plantation now known as Montelimar was a loose federation of farms owned and operated by landowners loyal to Nicaragua's dictator, Anastasio Somoza Debayle. Somoza Debayle himself owned a sizable portion of the land under cane in the region, and his palatial beachside estate, which also went by the name Montelimar, was as much a local landmark as the ingenio. Families like Don Alvaro's considered themselves campesinos, working their own land while supplementing their incomes with cash wages from sugarcane labor.

Somoza Debayle inherited the plantation-mill complex at Montelimar from his father, Anastasio Somoza Garcia. As we saw earlier in this book, Somoza Garcia was a self-described economic liberal and modernizer who reimagined the agricultural belt of Nicaragua's Pacific coast as the crucible for the nation's economic future.[12] In this future, a nation of campesinos would progressively become a nation of workers (*obreros*).[13] During his rise to power in the 1930s and 1940s, Somoza Garcia separated himself from political strongmen of previous eras by styling himself not as an oligarchic patrón—a leader who cultivated loyalty by doling out the favors and benefits associated with agrarian moral economies—but as the country's "laborer in chief," or *jefe obrero*. Somoza Garcia cultivated loyalty by tapping into an emerging class consciousness, particularly among the rural poor.[14] Over two decades, he consolidated power by deftly dividing and subdividing the interests of the country's nascent rural workers' movement and its conservative landed elites, staving off left-wing socialist unionization with one hand while building social protections for workers into the law with the other. Most prominently, Somoza Garcia promised to include agricultural laborers in a new national pension and disability scheme. The scheme was written into the Nicaraguan constitution in 1955, and a few years later, the INSS was born.

During the Somoza era, Nicaragua's sugarcane workers did begin to access INSS benefits, but coverage was wildly uneven. Even when they reached massive scales, the major agro-export industries in Nicaragua (cotton, sugarcane, tobacco, sesame, peanuts, and coffee) continued to rely mostly on seasonal laborers, and on long-standing systems of kin-based patronage, to recruit and retain them.[15] Even today, workers who show up each year for the sugarcane harvest support themselves, as Yadier did, through small farming: growing a variety of food crops, tending cattle, and maintaining flocks of chickens, ducks, and geese.

Many workers at Montelimar started out as cabras. One explanation I received for the use of this term is that goats (*cabras*) consume the weeds and grasses that grow beneath crops like cane and suck valuable nutrients from them. A human cabra, then, might do some weeding, fetch water, and in other ways absorb the tremendous physical stress of the job of harvesting sugar, allowing the adult, formally employed worker to whom he was attached to meet his daily cutting quota. Cutting cane has been compared by occupational health experts to running a half-marathon in ninety-plus-degree weather, six days per week, for weeks on end. It saps energy, and it demands a discipline that a field manager, or *capataz*, cannot instill on his own. But to call the cabra a "child laborer" would be misleading. The cabra is as subject to the orders of the capataz as he is to those of his adult relatives.[16]

The figure of the cabra bridges the reciprocal, noncapitalist obligations that attend family and kinship with the extractive imperatives of modern industrial production. The cabra embodies other, murkier dimensions, including both extralegal exploitation (as an "informal" laborer, a cabra could make no claim against a sugarcane company for injury or wage theft; as a child, he was subject to potential abuse, or special treatment, at home) and the kinds of patron-client-inflected moral economics often associated with Latin American plantations (if he worked hard, the same cabra could reasonably expect an overseer or field manager to formally hire him when he came of age). When they were hired and became officially listed on the books of the company and the INSS, cabras turned into *números* (numbers). A formally hired person would henceforth refer to him- or herself as a número. Overnight, their futures became factored into company and state actuarial figurations about investment and risk.

Within the life histories of individual cane workers like Don Alvaro, then, two facts about sugarcane labor coexist. Seen as originating in the figure of the cabra, one's status as a worker derives from a kind of entangled existence, in which social security came from a combination of plantation production and subsistence from small family plots. Seen as originating in the figure of the número, one's status as a worker derives from an "autonomous" existence, in which labor power is compensated through state-regulated wages and benefits.[17]

Don Alvaro himself expected to become a número, but in 1979, the Sandinista revolution deposed the Somoza dynasty. Anastasio Somoza Garcia, who seeded the idea for the INSS, had been assassinated in 1956. In the years between his death and the 1979 revolution, his sons Luis and Anastasio Somoza Debayle oversaw the transformation of the country's Pacific landscape from a loose patchwork of small and medium-sized farms to an increasingly consolidated series of monocultures—cotton, sugarcane, wheat, sesame, and peanuts.[18] This transformation, as we saw in chapter 2, was part of an initiative by entities like the US government, the Rockefeller Foundation, and the World Bank to grow Latin American economies through monocrop agriculture— one that continues to this day. Over the course of the 1950s, 1960s, and 1970s, Nicaraguan smallholders found themselves with less and less land, making field labor increasingly necessary, if never sufficient, for survival.[19] The social security system that Somoza and his sons created did not keep up with this growth. In fact, in its first twenty-five years, the INSS "was characterized by zero growth."[20] Expanding plantation companies used the seasonality of labor, a diminishingly small rural literacy rate, and nonmonetary benefits such as food and medicine to keep many of their operations off the books.

Partly in response to this socioecological crisis, peasants, students, and urban and agrarian workers' movements united under the banner of the FSLN to overthrow the Somoza dynasty in 1979. The FSLN's political platform in the 1980s was beset by its own internal divisions. Leadership was split between a group of pro-peasant *campesinistas*, who advocated for the establishment of agricultural cooperatives and the protection of small and medium-sized farms from industrialization, and a group of modernizing *decampesinistas*, who (somewhat in line with the Somozas' vision) saw the conversion of rural peasants into wage earners as an inevitable and economically desirable outcome.[21] The decampesinistas pushed for the nationalization of roughly half of the country's sugarcane sector, including the Somozas' Montelimar plantation, which was renamed the Ingenio Julio Buitrago, after a founding FSLN member who is remembered, interestingly enough, as the "father of the *urban* resistance."

Formal, paying jobs on the Julio Buitrago plantation were given to combat veterans of the revolution and the subsequent US-orchestrated contra war, including Don Alvaro Torres. The INSS, renamed the Institute for Social Security and Welfare, was expanded massively during this same period. Some seventy-five thousand rural people, including all those at the state farms, were enrolled.[22] But as Santiago Ripoll explains, decampesinista assumptions about the appetite of rural workers for embracing the state farm model were overly optimistic, and many workers, particularly former revolutionary fighters, demanded access not just to work but to land.[23] Eventually, workers like Don Alvaro were given assurances that they would be more than just números. They were given an ownership stake in the Julio Buitrago plantation itself, in addition to plots where they could grow their own crops. Social security now included not only the family ties that helped bring new generations of cabras into the workforce but also the moral economic obligations between *combatientes* and the state that were born out of the revolutionary moment. Just like the cabra system, this sense of manifold obligations never fully went away. Throughout the negotiations mediated by the CAO, in fact, Don Alvaro continued to think of the sugarcane complex at Montelimar as something that he could claim, thanks to his work both as a cabra and as a combatiente in the revolution, as a kind of patrimony.

For Don Alvaro and other Montelimar residents of his generation, the land concession to combatientes and the conversion of campesinos into partners in the state farm joined the cabra and the número in a stew of facts about working conditions. Nicaragua's revolutionary government invested in sugarcane, in part, because the idea of modernization through industrial monoculture had become cemented into the national development telos, and in part because plantations had long been viewed by campesinos as sources of stopgap security, places where a benevolent patrón might be sought when medical, economic, or other needs arose. By making workers vested coproprietors of state plantations, the revolution deepened a long-standing sense that a sugarcane firm's duty of care to its workers extended into the family plot itself.

This recognition was short-lived, and when the revolution ended in 1990, the government hired consultants from Price Waterhouse to orchestrate the sale of nationalized plantations like Julio Buitrago to private buyers. The postrevolutionary government did try to avoid the reentrenchment of the Somocista oligarchy in the countryside by formalizing the land rights of both the ex-combatants and the thousands of farmers and villagers who lived in the environs of cane, cotton, sesame, and peanut plantations along the Pacific coast.[24] Even a few of the Sandinista-era cooperatives managed to survive into the twenty-first century. At the time of its sale, workers at Julio Buitrago were granted a 25 percent stake in the plantation, but that concession was quickly forgotten.[25] It was not until 2012, some twenty years after the sale, that some of the men and women who worked the Ingenio Julio Buitrago were paid a small sum in recognition of the sale, but Don Alvaro and his neighbors still talk of the sale and the disappearance of what they call *el 25 por ciento* as a theft of a revolutionary gain by rich bankers and unscrupulous political leaders.[26]

The plantation now known as Montelimar changed hands twice between 1990 and 2000, when it was purchased by its current owner, a murky conglomerate called the Nicaraguan Shipping Consortium (Consortio Naviero Nicaragüense, or NAVINIC). These changes of ownership made establishing chains of responsibility for worker welfare much more difficult. NAVINIC continued to hire field laborers from the surrounding communities, but it frequently relied on subcontractors, who failed to report weeks of work to the INSS and failed to act as caring bosses. And just to confuse matters further, when the CKDnt epidemic emerged, NAVINIC changed its legal name to the Montelimar Corporation. During the 1990s, enrollment in the INSS among rural people plummeted from its revolutionary period high of seventy-five thousand to around three thousand.[27] This meant that by the time the CKDnt epidemic began, many of the workers seasonally employed by sugarcane firms were not paying into the national social security system at all, even if the pay stubs they collected from a revolving cast of subcontractors said otherwise. They would not become aware of this until they became too sick to work.

This situation is not unusual. Indeed, evidence suggests that the entrenchment of state protections for agricultural laborers in Latin America has actually deepened social and economic precarity, precisely because subcontracting permits companies to game the system.[28] Seasonal work is by definition not constant work, which means that if a worker's relationship is increasingly with a series of contractors and not a single sugarcane company, any inconsistency in treatment or in accounting becomes harder to correct. A retired worker I interviewed explained it like this. Back in Somoza's time, he said, if you had a problem (an illness, a missing paycheck, a missing INSS record), you went straight to the administration and you dealt with the administration. But by the 1990s, subcontractors were making access to administration more difficult. "No hay patrón," he said. "No hay patrón. Because the contractor doesn't know you are . . ." You were just a número. The condensation of an array of bifurcated identities (campesino-cabra, cabra-número, número-combatiente, combatiente-owner) into a single number elided a fundamental sense among workers that persons and things that seem unitary and individual exist in the world as relational and immanently divisible.[29] Social security systems depend on such condensation. Workers like Don Alvaro maintained a capacious sense of what social security meant. Social security emanated from bureaucratic registries, the obligations of the state to armed combatientes, the debts owed to clients from patrons, and the kin relationships that structured the cabra system.

Campesino, cabra, combatiente, número. The story of the CKDnt epidemic in Nicaragua illustrates that economic and ecological simplification are not the only sources of plantation violence.[30] These are joined by the bureaucratic simplifications of social welfare schemes like the INSS.[31] Simplifications are built into the architecture not just of the companies that produce and process monocrops but into the architecture of the nation-states that regulate those companies. Such simplifications are supposed to be helpful, for if it were impossible to tell whether an illness was work-related, or if there were not a legal way to categorize an injury as the result of industrial negligence, workers would be further disempowered. The problem is that while workplace injuries are frequently thought of as discrete events, acute disruptions to the everyday cycles of industrial labor, injury is perhaps better seen as a process rather than an event.[32] This is not to say that categorical bifurcations or bureaucratic regulations are inherently bad. Indeed, as Andrea Ballestero's examination of water regulation in Costa Rica shows, they are indispensable to the ethical work of human rights and environmental protection.[33] In the case of CKDnt, however, the process of determining what counted as a work-related condition turned out to be an arbitrary and violent one.[34]

Routine Tests and Arbitrary Conclusions

Doña Cynthia and Don William lived in a settlement tucked on a hillside above the small town of San Cayetano, halfway between the Pan-American Highway and the Pacific coast. I met them on a rainy day in mid-July. Don William was in his late forties, which meant that he first showed signs of CKDnt rather late in life by comparison to others with the condition. He had worked at the company long enough to be able to retire with full benefits. While legal retirement age varies in Nicaragua, sugarcane workers who had put in enough time could begin collecting benefits through the INSS at age fifty. If he lived to age sixty-two, Don William would be able to draw an additional old-age pension through the INSS, and if, as was more probable, he did not reach that age, Doña Cynthia would be entitled to a small widow's pension.[35]

Nicaragua has a two-tiered health care system. The national Ministry of Health runs public clinics and referral hospitals to which every citizen, regardless of employment status, has full access. Those who are formally employed pay portions of their salaries, called *cotizaciones*, into INSS accounts, and employers also contribute to the INSS on workers' behalf. Cotizaciones are akin to the payroll taxes that workers pay in other countries. For those who have experienced occupational injuries, who are retired, or who have reached old age, payment into the INSS confers entitlement to care at a network of semiprivate hospitals and clinics, all of which are considered superior to the public ones run by the health ministry.

The INSS is a fragile institution for several reasons, the most obvious of which is demographic. The size of Nicaragua's intermittent, cash-based, "informal" workforce continues to dwarf that of the documented INSS-contributing "formal" workforce. In 2017, a report by the International Monetary Fund (IMF) estimated that some 80 percent of Nicaragua's workers did not pay into the INSS, and though efforts have been made by successive governments to grow the client base by encouraging people outside the formal workforce to contribute, the massive disparity remains.[36] This means that the "social" part of "social security" has always been severely limited. The solvency of the INSS has not been helped by the fact that successive governments have raided its reserves for short-term giveaways to loyalists.[37] In April 2018, partly because of this chronic instability, the government of Daniel Ortega, encouraged by the IMF, proposed a hike in INSS employee contributions and a reduction in retirement benefits. In the wake of these proposals, a simmering opposition to Ortega's government boiled over, and Nicaragua fell into a national political crisis marked by weeks of public protests and severe reprisals by the National Police. Hundreds of people were killed in the unrest, and hundreds more were jailed. The country has not been the same since.[38]

Don William and Doña Cynthia were not on the front lines of the 2018 protests, but they were well aware of the vicissitudes of Nicaraguan social security. Workers like Don William kept close tabs on the number of weeks they had been employed, and stacks of pay stubs documenting cotizaciones were as ubiquitous in their homes as sachets of instant coffee. In the legal language of the Nicaraguan labor code, a workplace injury is a *riesgo laboral*, a clear, calculable risk, an event that might (probably) happen to a certain percentage of workers in the future.[39] Yadier, the poultry entrepreneur whose story opened this chapter, gave the example of his uncle Arlen, who lost a finger in a harvesting accident. Arlen's was a working finger, and the machinery that took it was part of a working environment. There was little ambiguity there.

But CKDnt was not, or at least not always, an occupational injury. As Ruiz Arias, the former INSS director, explained in the Nicaraguan public affairs journal *Envío* in 2010,

> Work-related risk insurance . . . seeks to protect workers from the moment they set off to work until they come home at night. . . . If the

worker ends up disabled he/she also receives a pension and on reaching old age has the right to two pensions: for disability and for old age. The work accident . . . must be reported in order for the worker to claim benefits. If it is a "white" accident, an unreported one with no apparent symptoms, INSS won't consider it a work-related illness or accident even though health problems appear later on. The same is true if it is a non-serious and unreported "red" accident (because there is blood).[40]

CKDnt subverts this neat bifurcation. It is neither "white" nor "red." There are symptoms, but no discrete accident, and unlike the loss of a digit or a limb, there is no blood spilled.

While tests at the company clinic were starting to show worrying signs of kidney injury, Don William held out hope that if he could stay employed for just a few more months, he could count on the retirement benefit from the INSS. Continued employment would also make it more likely that the INSS would choose to classify his condition as laboral. If a worker's kidney disease was to be considered laboral, they had to meet a few criteria. They would have to have worked in sugarcane for at least two years. They would have to have done these two years of work under the current ownership of the plantation, and to receive any kind of INSS benefit, they would have had to have worked for at least 26 consecutive weeks during that time. To receive a full pension, they would have to show a total of 150 weeks of documented work. And, of course, the INSS would have to feel confident stating in an official medical record that plantation working conditions had something to do with the condition of the patient's kidneys. All this meant that if Don William was laid off and then reported his CKDnt case to the INSS, it would be much more likely that it would be classified as común.

The terms *laboral* and *común* are both statements about the spatial and temporal limits of modern plantation labor. They are ways of setting working conditions on what João Biehl calls the "frugal" terms that link the work of public medical care, oriented to preserving life, and corporate behavior, oriented toward accumulating wealth.[41] Companies like Montelimar needed to get workers with suspected CKDnt off their books, in order to make it less likely that INSS doctors would classify their condition as laboral. It was one thing for nearly everyone in the sugarcane zone to assume that CKDnt was caused by industrial sugarcane production; it was quite another to underwrite that opinion in the official records of the social security system. As long as mortality and morbidity records on CKDnt remained ambiguous on the causal question, sugar companies could limit their liability. The causal ambiguity also benefited the fragile social security system. The financially strapped INSS could not possibly cover every case of CKDnt if it classified them all as laboral. The bureaucratic bifurcation between laboral and común was built atop the political bifurcation between campesino and obrero, the workplace bifurcation between cabra and número, the conceptual bifurcation between formal and informal labor, and the structural bifurcation between semiprivate INSS and public Ministry of Health services.

At the Montelimar company clinic, Don William's kidney function was assessed through a variety of laboratory procedures, as it had been many seasons before. His blood was tested for the presence of creatinine, which helped doctors determine his estimated glomerular filtration rate (eGFR), and his urine was examined for evidence of unusually high levels of electrolyte sediments such as magnesium and phosphorus. His eGFR turned out to be consistently low, while his sediments were high. These could be signs of an acute kidney injury, something more chronic, or both. Don William continued to take the tests for several weeks, sometimes receiving a few days of sick leave, and sometimes feeling (and testing) well enough to work.

When we met, Doña Cynthia did most of the talking. "The last exams that [the company doctor] sent [Don William] to get," she remembered, "had to be done in Managua, at a particular laboratory. So the company took them in a microbus. . . . They must have had some kind of arrangement, because they sent a group of them, not just [William]." At that laboratory, Don William and a group of his coworkers underwent more blood and urine testing, and then they piled back into the microbus to go to another laboratory for ultrasounds. "And with these exams, they were able to certify that [William] really had the disease," Doña Cynthia continued. "They had diagnosed it here [at the plantation], but there they confirmed it."

Ten days after that trip to Managua, Don William and several others who were on that bus were laid off. What Doña Cynthia still couldn't get over was the excruciating slowness of the experience. For two months, Don William had been reporting back to the company clinic, hoping that his kidney values would stabilize. The tests in the private laboratories in Managua, however, showed no improvement. Don William received the news of his firing just two months shy of retirement. Even if the INSS did not choose to classify his CKDnt as laboral, full retirement benefits would have included a decent pension. Doña Cynthia reasoned that the company wanted to give the INSS good reason to classify his disease as común.

In the interview recording, I am clearly confused. Surely, the company would have wanted Don William to be able to retire comfortably, I suggested.

"Of course they know," Doña Cynthia replied, a bit impatient. "They know how old the workers are, and they know how many cotizaciones they have. The company knows perfectly well who is close to retirement and who isn't."

What felt violent about this situation was not just the firing but the arbitrariness of the company's decision. "In fact, I *went and I told them*, 'Look, why don't you just let him work these two months, just until his retirement?'" Doña Cynthia continued. She and Don William had heard that a handful of CKDnt patients who worked under field managers or sector engineers that were known to be particularly good bosses had been able to petition for low-stress work over those final few weeks or months, allowing them to qualify for retirement. Even though that sort of arrangement was anything but guaranteed, the figure of the beneficent upper manager (for all intents and purposes, a patrón) allying with workers against the austerity of the state remained a powerful one.

The Gift of Disease Classification

When I spoke with CKDnt-affected workers around Montelimar, several of them concluded their accounts of their journeys through the INSS by saying something to the effect of "and they gave me an enfermedad laboral" or "they gave me an enfermedad común." It was as if the disease classifications, which one might expect to be forensic or technical descriptors, were instead the end results of some kind of long-term exchange.

And why shouldn't they? After all, social security systems like the INSS rely on mutual contributions by workers and employers, who expect the state to provide care in return. Questions about what counts as a workplace injury, and what counts as a working environment, turn out to be questions of exchange, and by extension questions about the recognition of persons.[42] What was confusing about the bifurcation of CKDnt cases into the categories of laboral and común was that it seemed to rely on a conceptualization of work that diverged from the way that men and women who had actually spent their lives in the cane experienced life in the sugarcane zone in the decades leading up to the onset of the CKDnt epidemic.

The rise of attention to occupational disease over the twentieth century, which came thanks in large part to organized labor, has come at a cost, namely, that medical scrutiny of workers' bodies often furthers the dehumanization of those bodies, all while masking the broader set of economic and political forces that cause harm.[43] Bodily conditions can be bifurcated into occupational and nonoccupational categories, but the process of embodiment cannot. The kidneys are physically affected by sugarcane production long before they become visible to corporations or state social security institutions.[44] Unlike limbs or even brains, kidneys are only indirectly enrolled in work. There is "intellectual labor," and there is "manual labor," but to my knowledge no category called "renal labor" exists. The kidney's services as an interface between a body and its environment are something of a biophysical donation by the worker to capital. No one is hired for the quality of their kidney function, but they can be fired for it. It is thus no wonder that workers talk of the fate of their bodies not through the technical idiom of exposure but through the social idiom of exchange.

Those like Don William, whose CKDnt was classified as común and stayed that way, could still receive a disability payment through the INSS, since INSS doctors agreed that they *were* physically unable to work, but they would have to seek medical treatment through the public health care system, run by the Ministry of Health. The IMF's 2017 report on the INSS notes that ministry's service is inferior to that of the INSS, not least because the public health system has no capacity to provide dialysis care, something that all CKDnt patients eventually need.[45] This meant that those whose CKDnt was deemed común would have to spend their own disability pension money to pay for treatment.

Blended with the bureaucratic arbitrariness of the INSS, the arbitrary patriarchal benevolence of the plantation created a nasty brew. David Graeber has argued that "bureaucratic procedures . . . are invariably ways of managing social situations that are . . . founded on structural violence."[46] This insight is useful for understanding the bureaucratic itineraries of sugarcane workers and of the life-altering difference between the words *laboral* and *común.* Those itineraries alert us to "[structural] violence's capacity to allow arbitrary decisions, and thus to avoid the kind of debate, clarification, and renegotiation typical of more egalitarian social relations."[47] As the stories told by Don Camilo and Doña Cynthia suggest, such renegotiation still happened in CKDnt cases. Some people *could* convince an INSS doctor to change a classification from común to laboral, and some people *could* convince a field manager to let them eke out the last few weeks of work before retirement. The problem was that the chance of entering into such "egalitarian" relationships with either the state or management was random.

The arbitrariness of care on the plantation is not just a feature of a hierarchical structure that puts management and INSS officials above workers. It is a feature of the very "red" and bloody germ of plantation capitalism itself: the control of labor through the threat of direct physical violence.[48] I am not saying that workers at Montelimar were physically abused on the job. What I am saying is that to understand what makes CKDnt into a social crisis, it is essential to understand structural violence as the historical outcome of enslavement and indenture, labor processes that have always included both the threat of arbitrary violence and arbitrary gestures toward caring "egalitarian social relations."

Occupational Disease and the Problem of Simplification

Occupational disease is typically framed, both in the Nicaraguan laws I summarized here and in most modern tort systems, as a discrete event. In US law, "a claim of injury relies on a prior, uninjured body." This legal bifurcation between the injured and the uninjured, as Lochlann Jain notes, makes regulating harm done at work by toxic substances, or accretive exposure to heat and dust, exceedingly difficult.[49] These exposures present a temporal problem: How to pinpoint the "prior" in a body like Don William's?

If the starting point of CKDnt is debatable, the disease itself is not. Doctors know it when they see it, and even in places like Nicaragua, where biopsies and other complex procedures are hard to perform, they rarely dispute the diagnosis. But there is a void where a definitive causal mechanism should be.[50] The emergence of this void can be traced to the very design of the occupational environment, one saturated with toxic chemicals, where temperature control and hydration are erratic, and—most important of all—where the experiences and knowledge of the people getting sick are systematically devalued.[51]

Are such conditions occupational or not? This seems to be the question. A clear answer seems like it would have meant a great deal to a couple like Doña Cynthia and Don William. Ever since company doctors at NSEL first attempted to study the disease in sugarcane laborers in the 1990s, the science of CKDnt has been consumed by the task of determining the extent to which the disease is related to work. Even though a causal mechanism for CKDnt remains elusive, the ostensible correlation between the disease and sugarcane production is undeniable. CKDnt is a sign of an eco-bio-social dysbiosis, one with dire consequences for the future of the sugar industry, in Nicaragua and elsewhere. If more and more workers are coming down with a devastating disease, companies and governments might want to stay ahead of the problem. Since plantation companies have been systematically disavowing their responsibility for the violence done in the name of commodity crop production for centuries, it is not surprising that they, and the states that support them, are looking for ways to cut their losses.

Even with full knowledge of the risk of CKDnt, throughout the course of my research, people in the sugarcane zone continued to take jobs in the harvests. They continued to take those jobs even when they knew there was a strong likelihood that the work would shorten their lives. Like Don William and Pedro, many continued to return to work because the plantation was their primary source of medical attention. To presume that they were simply exploiting themselves because they had no choice would be a mistake. Anthropological research in plantation contexts illustrates that complex, more-than-capitalist relations—including the kinds of "egalitarian" ones that Graeber alludes to in his work on bureaucratic violence—are essential to the persistence of monocrops.[52]

My analysis of the stories of CKDnt patients' journeys through the INSS leads me to conclude that the question of whether CKDnt is "occupational" or not, while epidemiologically interesting, is overly narrow. After all, we already know based on decades of research that industrial farm work is dangerous. Answering the occupational disease question for CKDnt tells us nothing about how, even as they continue to strain against the ecological limits of soils and water tables and against the biophysical limits of human bodies, monocrop systems persist. Indeed, efforts to determine whether diseases like CKDnt are occupational or not actually help perpetuate the violence of monoculture—and not just because these questions are hard to answer. To treat work in sugarcane as an "occupation," as a job and nothing more, is to reinforce one of the very things that makes plantation life violent: its tendency to perpetuate itself through social and ecological simplification.[53]

We must ask what the bifurcation between occupational and nonoccupational disease does, and for whom. What sort of politics of work does it imply? What if the continued recurrence of questions about whether and when agricultural labor is dangerous is itself a political technology, a way of extending the unnatural life of the plantation by treating it as if it were interchangeable with any other form of production?[54] What if that recurrence is part of a long-standing modernist push to bifurcate work from life? And what if such a push occludes the more-than-capitalist activities and moral economic obligations on which both plantation agriculture and rural life still depend? In Nicaragua, as we will see in chapter 6, CKDnt seemed to matter as a problem not so much of work but of the *end* of work: its temporal ending, prompted by the onset of disease or retirement, as well as its moral implications, including how a worker's loyal service to a company, or a company's faithful provision of care, should be valued.

As much as monocrop agriculture can be caricatured as an animated force that aspires to occupy more and more land and to consume more and more bodies, monocrop agriculture depends on the idea that it, too, has limits: that there is a space that lies beyond it—a space where illnesses just happen. Think of the ways that the agro-industrial complex in the United States has historically leveraged the politics of legality and citizenship to limit its obligations to migrant workers from Latin America. Call it accumulation by disentanglement.[55]

Uncertainty about the status of bodies as working, and environments as occupational, has been a major obstacle to the development of modern welfare states in Latin America, where agriculture still takes up a dominant slice of GDP. The past century of Nicaraguan history is marked by efforts to tame that uncertainty: to do the work of convincing all concerned that commodities like sugar, spaces like sugarcane fields, units of human labor power, and the conditions of kidneys are all discrete and more or less interchangeable things. To be discrete and interchangeable, they must have physical limits. A field can only carry so many stalks of cane; a worker can only harvest so many kilos in a day; and a corporation can only manage fields and workers at a certain scale.

At the onset of the CKDnt epidemic, international lenders from the World Bank and national agricultural regulators had come to think of sugarcane plantations as discrete, regulated spaces, the kinds of spaces where workers' time was neatly kept, where they paid into the social security scheme, and from which the INSS would help them cleanly eject after injury or retirement. The case of CKDnt illuminates some of the limitations of both the modern corporate-state welfare complexes that aim to deal with the problem of workplace injury, and of the conventional critiques of those complexes. The twinned fragility of social security systems and industrial production systems is a hallmark of the epoch Kim Fortun calls "late industrialism," a time when the autonomous, atomistic existence of things, facts, and bodies is coming into question—at least in those pockets of the Euro-Atlantic world where people may have once found stories about that autonomy convincing.[56] When the fiction of autonomy breaks down, strange new pathologies arise—long COVID, cancer clusters, endemic asthma, multiple chemical sensitivities. Economic, industrial, and state fragility is refracted back onto bodies in the form of more precarious conditions, more injuries, and fewer options for preventing them, or so the thesis goes.

But for most working-class people in Latin America, factual, objective, or personal autonomy was never a given.[57] For many, existence was and remains irrevocably bound up with messy colonial formations—like plantations—and with noncapitalist forms of debt and obligation like those of Yadier's chicken cooperative. What is violent here is not the breakdown of a stable, autonomous existence but the effort to will the imaginary of autonomous existence into a matter of fact. As Nicaragua's social security system struggles for solvency due to chronic underfunding and decades of political corruption, workers make appeals for justice and for health care based less on liberal notions of bodily autonomy than on an insistence on the entanglement of flesh and environment—on the persistent blurriness of the divide between the occupational and the nonoccupational environment. The simplification of CKDnt as an occupational problem is thus part of the broader set of simplifications on which late industrial agriculture relies. Violence stems not from the division of work from nonwork, but from the fragility of that division, and the lengths to which the state and capital interests will go to preserve it.

6

Plantation Patienthood

During the harvest season, the microbus that takes hemodialysis patients from the sugarcane zone to Managua would sometimes get trapped between slow-moving semitrucks packed with freshly harvested brown cane. The routes of the harvest and the routes of treatment paralleled one another, at least until they reached the Pan-American Highway, where there was a not-yet-built evangelical church that hosted its more enthusiastic congregants for all-day outdoor Sunday services. At that junction, there was a decent family restaurant that advertised a miniature zoo, consisting of an anemic menagerie of caged birds and monkeys, where Montelimar's managers and engineers lunched on *quesillos* or fried fish. At the junction, the cane truck would bear left along the Montelimar fields, which stretched north at least as far as the village of Ojo de Agua. The microbus would go right, beginning the climb into the capital. If a former Montelimar worker were lucky enough to have their CKDnt diagnosed as "occupational" (laboral), and if that worker could prove they had worked for the company for at least two years, then they could qualify for subsidized transportation to a hemodialysis clinic. Three times a week, qualifying ex-workers would board the bus and take the two-hour journey.

By many measures, those who made it onto the bus were the lucky ones. Nicaragua's capacity to treat the growing number of individuals with end-stage renal disease (ESRD) was inadequate when the CKDnt epidemic was first recognized at the turn of the twenty-first century. CKDnt emerged in parallel to an explosion in the rate of type 2 diabetes. The Ministry of Health's nephrologists could not keep up. In 2020, Nicaragua had roughly four nephrologists per million residents, while countries in Latin America average eighteen per million. Both numbers are too low, but this means that most Nicaraguan ESRD patients will likely never meet a kidney specialist. Because access to kidney transplant is nearly unheard of (a handful—like fewer than twenty—are performed in Nicaragua every year), this also means that, as in other parts of Latin America, Nicaragua's hemodialysis facilities operate at full capacity, constantly. For those who need hemodialysis, it helps to live in or near Managua because that is where a majority of the machines are.

Technically, there are two kinds of dialysis treatment available in Nicaragua. When the CKDnt epidemic was first recognized, peritoneal dialysis (PD) was promoted as a promising option by many medical experts. In PD, a patient has a catheter surgically inserted into their abdomen and self-administers a dialysate fluid to remove the wastes previously filtered by the kidneys. As long as the equipment and fluid are available, a person can theoretically survive for years on PD, even if, as was the case with most CKDnt patients in Nicaragua, their primary clinics and doctors are located far from their homes. The thing that makes PD attractive, however, is also its biggest drawback. The catheters used for PD can invite infection, especially when housing and water quality are substandard, and in the early years of the epidemic, more than a few CKDnt patients in Nicaragua died after their PD inserts became infected. As a result, new CKDnt patients started to refuse PD. Some insisted they would rather die of kidney disease than be poisoned by the treatment.

By the time my fieldwork began, hemodialysis had become the overwhelmingly more common way to manage late-stage CKDnt at Montelimar. In five years of researching the disease and meeting patients, I interviewed exactly one person who used PD. Hemodialysis involves the filtration of blood by an external machine over several hours, three days per week. It has been the subject of numerous anthropological studies. Ethnographers often speak of hemodialysis wards as platforms for understanding the social worlds that ESRD engenders.[1] Standard treatments for chronic conditions, especially ones like ESRD that require patients to adopt rigid routines, can bring people who may otherwise have little in common into novel "biosocial" communities.[2] For those who are similarly marginalized by dint of race, age, or citizenship, the quest to access treatment forms the bedrock of a politics of patienthood.[3] The work of AMBED can be interpreted through this lens, but the dialysis ward turns out to be a poor setting from which to study the social world of CKDnt. CKDnt patienthood is best understood from the plantation itself, because CKDnt patienthood, as it is structured in Nicaragua, is really about the survival of the plantation.[4] The plantation, threatened by its own excesses, is the other, unnamed patient being healed by the limited provision of dialysis care.

Dialysis is often portrayed by medical doctors as a tool for the "management" of disease, but anthropological accounts reveal how, from the perspective of ESRD patients, dialysis is better understood as the management of death.[5] The term *management* is neither incidental nor insignificant.[6] As we have seen, by the 2010s, sugarcane companies in Nicaragua and financiers from the World Bank and the IFC had come to recognize the CKDnt epidemic as a threat to the expansion of the sugarcane business. Like monocrop growers in other contexts, sugarcane producers in Nicaragua operate on very thin margins. Improper management of the slow deaths of workers with CKDnt (there was no chance of saving them) would do harm to the viability of their business model.[7] Another reason why management might be an appropriate way to understand CKDnt is that in the sugarcane zone, theories that circulated in the community about the etiology of CKDnt were also theories about industrial management. The two key elements in those theories—that the company made excessive and irresponsible use of toxic chemicals in the cane fields and that field-level supervisors put pressure on cutters, seeders, and fumigators to work lengthy shifts in stifling heat with insufficient access to water and shade—located the root causes of the disease in managerial decisions about production.[8]

More broadly, the parallel journeys of a microbus packed with very sick workers and of semitrucks packed with charred or chemical-soaked cane stalks can be read as emblems of the way that climate crisis induces new industrial forms of managing death. By agreeing to provide former employees with transportation to the hemodialysis clinic, firms like the Montelimar Corporation were acknowledging the extent of the CKDnt epidemic in the labor force, but these firms were also turning human life support into a new terrain of managerial control. Plantations have always been technologies for modulating and managing death, both human and otherwise. What is important is not merely that the production of soy, or cotton, or sugar involves organized death; rather, what is important is *how* such production organizes death.[9]

If life support is really technological oversight over death, then the company's willingness to provide transportation to dialysis services might be understood as a form of what Achille Mbembe calls "necropolitics," the "subjugation of life to the power of death."[10] My aim in this chapter is to examine what meanings people rescue from these dark conditions. Understanding how people's entanglement with the sugarcane complex persisted up to and past death provides insight into the ways that planetary health, for those on its front lines, entails learning new ways to grieve irrevocable loss.

Fungibility, Moral Economies, and Liberal Settlements

Fundamental to the making of sugarcane as a fungible commodity was the rendering of laboring bodies, too, as fungible: interchangeable, malleable, and individually meaningless.[11] This conflation of plant and human fungibility has its origins in the transatlantic slave trade, and as Tiffany Lethabo King suggests, assumptions about the fungibility of the Black body in particular were essential to the making of the sugar plantation complex.[12] Theorists of plantation life and its aftermath as experienced by Black, Asian, and Indigenous people in the Americas consistently point to what Stephen Marshall calls "the subjective and intersubjective experience of fungibility."[13] This experience was characterized by a recognition that enslaved persons had no sovereignty over their own deaths. Elaborating on this point, Mbembe explains that because they were valued only for their labor power, the enslaved on plantations experienced "a form of death-in-life."[14]

Today's Nicaraguan sugar plantations share some features with the slave plantations of the Caribbean or North American colonial era, but as I explained in the last chapter, they began as something more like haciendas, in which workers still were not exactly free but could make claims on landowners as clients to patrones. Invocations of a mutual obligation of patrones to clients, always a common feature of health crises, became essential modes of survival after the onset of CKDnt.[15] At Montelimar in the early twenty-first century, the company health clinic was the place where workers went when injured on the job and when they had routine health needs. Their appeals to corporate care were infused with nostalgia for the hacienda, where workers' lives and labor power were not fungible. At least in their ideal form, systems of patrón-client exchange are premised on the possibility that a worker's life is specific and valuable and individual, and that a worker's death could, with the help of a patrón, be properly memorialized.[16]

The eventual agreement of the Montelimar Corporation to offer free rides to the dialysis clinic for a small subset of former workers could be seen as a revival of a hacienda-style moral economic reciprocity, but it is more appropriate to see the agreement as an attempt at a liberal, corporate management of death. The agreement emerged from the CAO and the World Bank's view of companies like Montelimar as corporate persons with a responsibility to their shareholders to limit their liability, and of workers as "free labor," persons whose value to the company was, primarily, as willing providers of labor power. Free laborers are neither slaves to masters nor clients to patrones. The responsibility of management to free labor is set by the terms of the wage relationship, and nothing more.[17] This legalistic arrangement shapes how disputes get resolved, and it modulates the level of involvement companies might have in the ends of workers' lives. The provision of subsidized transportation to the dialysis clinic—only for those who could prove two years of consistent employment, with pay stubs—was a version of the restitution paid by a defendant to a plaintiff. It was a liberal settling of accounts. It made the production of sugarcane commensurable with the production of any other fungible good, precisely by treating laborers and corporation as two parties who had freely entered into a contract.

Even those Montelimar workers who did receive the benefit of bus travel to the dialysis clinics did not fully buy into this liberal logic. Instead, as they rumbled back and forth to Managua, closer and closer to death, they continued to make claims on the company that exceeded the individualized relationship of free laborer to free employer. On the bus routes in and out of Montelimar, a specific form of necropolitics emerged. Amid the dynamic tension between liberal settlement, patrón-client care, and fungibility, Montelimar residents refused to accept the bus service as an unambiguous good. They availed themselves of it, but as this chapter shows, their way of embracing the bus and all it represented was less a form of acquiescence to the life support logic of the plantation than part of a broader process of grieving the human and nonhuman deaths that had come to consume the landscape.

Patient/Passenger/Payload

AMBED's first meeting was held at the home of a former Montelimar employee, whom I'll call Mauricio. When I met him a few years later, Mauricio was about my age, in his late thirties, and my photographs and videos from that encounter remind me that he wore a bandana over his head, and that he participated in the interview from a hammock hung under a metal and wood shelter in the center of his mother's patio. Mauricio was the first ex-worker to join AMBED's general membership, and he was the first to get on the dialysis bus. His wiry frame, topped by a cat-shaped face, gave way to arms that were a maze of distended veins. A large bandage covered his right pectoral muscle where one of the tubes entered his body. But he seemed energetic as he spoke with me, Saúl, and Don Camilo.

The theme of that conversation, as it was in so many conversations with Montelimar hemodialysis patients, was a *queja*, a grievance. Mauricio's queja was not about the arduous dialysis sessions but about the bus journey.

"There are twelve of us on our bus," Mauricio began. They picked him up at 8:00 a.m. (his village, which abutted the main road to Managua, was the first stop) before continuing through the area to find the others. His dialysis session began at 11:00. "Only I go to that clinic," Mauricio explained. "Juan and Hector go to Monte España . . . and what's his name . . . ?" He looked at his wife Teresa, who sat behind him.

"Felipe."

"Right, Felipe . . . he goes to another one." He named the locations where the others in his cohort were dropped, to the best of his recollection.

Due to the patchiness of Nicaragua's dialysis resources, with machines and qualified nurses spread out in private hospitals and clinics across Managua, the groups who boarded the bus in Montelimar would be divided during treatment. They might be hooked up to a machine alongside a neighbor or two from Montelimar, but they might be joined by CKDnt patients from NSEL, the massive cane plantation to the north. More likely, though, they would be sitting with diabetes patients or others whose case histories did not include plantation labor.

"And they come back to pick you up, right?" Saúl asked, continuing our discussion of Mauricio's treatment routine. We were getting to the grievance.

"Yes, but sometimes at three or four [in the afternoon]. They go on errands; they give them papers, orders to go collect people, collect money, other things. So they come for us at three or four, when I finish [my session] at 12:45!"

We were hearing a version of this grievance a lot, about how the bus did double duty as an errand vehicle. A trip to the bank; a pickup or drop-off for an office staff member; even, as more than one patient reported, collection of a load of agrochemicals, which were hoisted onto the roof rack for the ride back to the plantation.

Former plantation workers were now plantation payload.

Grievances about the bus journey back and forth from treatment help underscore how the onset of CKDnt constitutes less a break or rupture than an extension of plantation life. In ethnographic work in the trauma wards of Indian hospitals, Harris Solomon shows how technologies of life support such as dialyzers and ventilators "remake social relations" through "economies of movement." The efficacy of life support depends on what he calls "moving commitments," the coordination of actions from several dispersed figures, including family, doctors, nurses, technicians, and even ambulance drivers.[18] Mauricio's brief account of his bus routine, like his longer case history, is a story of moving commitments. By this point, the sequence of events that led him to hemodialysis should be a familiar one, but here is a recap. He began work on the plantation at age fifteen, working alongside his father as a cabra before joining the labor force as a paid worker. His commitments to his family, as with many of his comrades, were played out within the economy of the plantation, where movement was essential. A worker who wanted to stay employed had to be flexible. Mauricio was assigned many kinds of duties during the years in which he was employed, from seeding to cutting to cleaning to mill work, but he spent a lot of time as a fumigator, working with harsh agrochemicals and little personal protective equipment. His account of finding work, being diagnosed with elevated creatinine, traveling back and forth to the company clinic and to the INSS hospital in Managua, being laid off, and later scrounging his pension and care benefits all entailed working to situate himself and his body within the rhythms of the plantation.

When work ceased prematurely for people like Mauricio, it was the bus, as much as the dialysis machine itself, that became what Solomon calls the "hinge" between the plantation and its outsides, between public and corporate care, between life and death.[19] To begin the journey, patients knew, was to enter the final phase of a fatal disease. It was to commit oneself not so much to a way of living but to a way of dying. Expressions of doubt about the quality of the bus, uncertainty about its ethical goodness, and resistance to its managerial demands were a means by which patients, their kin, and their former work comrades strove not to survive CKDnt—because no one would—but to respond to it. In this sense, these expressions of doubt constituted a version of what Lochlann Jain calls "elegiac politics," a kind of necropolitics from below, an attempt to "account for loss, grief, betrayal, and the connections between economic profits, disease, and death in a culture that is affronted by mortality."[20] The general preoccupation among CKDnt patients and their families with the quality of the bus service situates end-stage disease management within the plantation environment that I have described in the previous chapters. This was an environment that was consistent in its violence but inconsistent in the means by which that violence was acknowledged and redressed.[21]

There is something audacious about patients who leverage grievances, especially patients who are among a minority of those with a given condition who count *as patients*. Many Nicaraguan people with ESRD, including most people with CKDnt at Montelimar, would never see the inside of a hemodialysis clinic, or the inside of that bus. Mauricio's protest could be interpreted as not just audacious but excessive.[22] He had to wait a few hours, but he got a life-extending treatment!

But Mauricio knew something about the limits of the corporation's commitment to life support. He bemoaned the boredom and indignity of having to spend extra hours waiting for the bus, but more than that, he questioned the corporate frugality that the bus represented.[23] The Montelimar Corporation, like other plantation enterprises, was oriented at once to the continued, efficient extraction of capital (keeping those cane-carrying semitrucks on schedule) and to the regulation of life at a population level. These priorities rarely align harmoniously.[24]

"Together We're Gonna Wait Around and Die"

Silvio was Don Alvaro Guerrero's nephew. His house sat on a farm road that led from the hill town of Diriamba down to the village of El Sesteo. At least, that is what I was told. I have never been able to find that road on a map. For those who know their way around the sugarcane zone, El Sesteo marks the southern edge of Montelimar, where the cane fields spill into the gorge of the Río Tecolapa. Most of the village is on the northern side of the river, and on those maps I have been able to find, the road ends at the river's edge, a few yards upstream from one of the plantation's major irrigation dams. A good truck, like one of the Toyota Hilux models favored by wealthy Nicaraguan city dwellers, politicians, and plantation engineers, could ford the Tecolapa at low water and get over to the south side of El Sesteo. A motorcycle could get across, too. So could a horse, but not a Hyundai Accent, so when we visited in August 2019, we went on foot. On the south side, twenty or thirty houses formed a chain of small farms and extended the riverside canopy of trees a kilometer or so upland, before giving way to a tract of mostly bald cattle range.

Soon after I arrived back in Nicaragua in August 2019, Don Alvaro Guerrero had gotten word from his brother Jorge, Silvio's father. Silvio was unwell. He had been a cane cutter for several years at Montelimar, and all signs pointed to CKDnt. Silvio's brother Luis had succumbed to the disease the previous year.

The younger pair of brothers, Silvio and Luis, were close. They had been neighbors and coworkers, joining each other on the daily trip to the remains of an old finca at Vista Hermosa to meet their field manager and receive their fieldwork assignments. Their father and uncle, Don Jorge and Don Alvaro Guerrero, had once done the same, but in retirement—Don Alvaro's brought on by CKDnt and Don Jorge's by a desire to remain on his tiny farm—they had a more strained relationship. Nevertheless, when Luis fell sick, Don Alvaro and AMBED had helped him get access to food aid, pension benefits, and free dialysis services. Jorge was grateful to his brother, if not effusively so, for this assistance during Luis's final few months of life, but he kept his distance. Jorge never did show up at AMBED's biweekly meetings.

By August, though, Jorge got in touch with Don Alvaro, inviting him to bring Saúl to visit. When we got to Silvio's house, the last one on the road before the cattle range took over, we found him lying in bed, barely conscious. As I waited in the doorway, I heard Silvio whisper to Don Alvaro and Saúl that he thought this was it. His limbs were bloated with retained liquid. He was exhausted, he said, *rendido*.

When CKDnt came for him, Silvio decided he would let it come. Better to expire here at home with his wife, Ydalia, and their two small children, working the little garden and helping his father and mother tend to theirs. Initially, Jorge did not object when Silvio told him he wanted nothing to do with hospitals, nothing to do with AMBED, and nothing more to do with the Montelimar Corporation—certainly nothing to do with that bus.

Together, the family would wait around for Silvio to die.[25]

Don Alvaro and Saúl remained inside with Silvio for a few more minutes, trying to talk him out of his despair. Meanwhile, I found myself pacing outside the house, treading between neat rows of immature garden plants. Ydalia stepped outside as well, not really to keep me company but to try and calm an upset child whose crying seemed to have had more to do with a stubbed toe than a sense that his father was contemplating death. She saw me over by the garden and let the little boy, now over his injury, toddle out into the neatly swept yard. We did not speak for the first few moments. By now, I was accustomed to the emotional reserve of CKDnt spouses, and I knew I had no way of knowing from her countenance how upset she might be about what was happening to Silvio, who lay a few feet from where we stood. But silence seemed rude, so I tried asking her what sorts of plants I was looking at. She quietly identified them: tomatoes and sweet peppers mostly.

"Do you sell them?" I asked, trying to play the disinterested anthropologist to stave off the gravity of the goings-on inside.

"We eat them," she answered bluntly, betraying frustration with my question by looking down at the short green rows beneath our feet. This was a kitchen garden, a supplement, a life support, not an income stream.

Before the conversation could get more awkward, Don Alvaro and Saúl emerged, ready to offer a summation of their bedside assessment. "Silvio is gravely ill," Saúl stated, repeating the headline that had brought us there. "He says he doesn't want any treatment, but he can live if he wants to. We can get him to a nephrologist."

Ydalia was quiet for a moment before she responded, "Maybe he should go, but he's weak. We don't have any transport, any money." As our collective consideration of the limitations of cost and distance mingled with the limitations of a patient's will, I began scanning my phone for the number of one of the few nephrologists in the Ministry of Health, a young doctor I had met at a conference the previous spring.

"Don't worry," Saúl implored. "We can get him to a hospital, but he has to believe it will help him. He thinks that if they try to remove the liquid, it will kill him, but it's not like that." Ydalia shrugged. Maybe if we could convince Papa Jorge, and maybe if we could arrange a truck. Maybe there was time. Throughout this brief exchange, she never outwardly embraced the sense of urgency that Saúl was suggesting best fit the situation, but she didn't reject the offer of assistance.

We half-jogged toward the river to reach Jorge's house. Like Ydalia, Jorge was hesitant. He feared that an emergency visit to the nephrologist would kill Silvio, his last living son. And if it didn't, then the next step was hemodialysis, and he knew that was a temporary fix. He wondered whether this was the time to draw the Montelimar Corporation back into their lives, or to remain on the family's side of the river.

Saúl and Don Alvaro were undeterred. "We're going to call Gregoria in human resources," Saúl insisted. Gregoria was Montelimar's HR director, its point person on the CKDnt situation, and its principal interlocutor with AMBED. She was responsive on the phone, if limited in her power within the company.

Our half-jog back to the river continued, as Saúl and I checked our phones. Saúl's pinged first, and before we made it to the Hyundai, he had put Gregoria on notice about the situation. Over the next hour, as we lumbered toward San Rafael del Sur from El Sesteo, calls flew back and forth. Unable to connect with the one nephrologist I sort of knew in Nicaragua, I tried to take notes on the half of the clipped phone conversations I overheard from the Hyundai's passenger seat:

> SAÚL TO GREGORIA: Is there a pickup truck available? . . . No, we need it today. . . . Yes, he's affiliated with AMBED. . . . Yes, he'll be ready, the family will be ready.

> DON ALVARO TO JORGE: Look, the truck is ready to come for you. . . . I don't know, maybe two hours. . . .

> SAÚL TO JORGE (*a few moments later on the same call*): Yes, they can save his life, señor. You can go with him and speak to the nephrologist yourself.

By the time I got home that night, Silvio was on his way to the hospital, and after a short stay for recovery, he was enrolled as a hemodialysis patient.

Although the progression of is variable, with some patients able to maintain decent kidney function for years after diagnosis and others, like Silvio, reaching ESRD within months, the tension between resignation and urgency in Silvio's case merits closer attention. Silvio and his family had a front-row seat for CKDnt's emergence as an epidemic in the sugarcane zone, yet the family's reaction to his condition seemed so passive. As Silvio lay on what he construed as his deathbed, they described his situation not as one of a life in crisis, or emergency, but as one of a life exhausted, rendido.

Grief and Grievance

I wonder about how to piece together complaints like Mauricio's, about the indignity of waiting around for the bus, and the willingness of Silvio and his family, in or near extremis, to wait around to die. Silvio's wife and father were as prepared to grieve on their own terms and in their own homes as Saúl and Don Alvaro and Mauricio and dozens of others were prepared to fight to get Silvio on the road to the dialysis clinic.

For Silvio to become visible as a patient, the family's grief had to be reframed in the liberal language of "grievance," the pursuit of a specific, recognizable redress for a specific, recognizable condition. In chapter 1, we saw how AMBED creatively managed a tension among the demands of grievance-making, place-based knowledge of the ground, and a Christian faith in divine grace. Plantation patienthood entails another tension, between grievance and grief. While it is important to understand why people opt to seek biomedical attention for progressive, fatal conditions like CKDnt—to refuse to die without putting up a fight—it is equally important to consider the reasons why they might not—why they might choose, together, to wait around and die.

Getting to the bus from El Sesteo required that Silvio wake up at 3:00 a.m. The nearest pickup point was an hour's walk away—an hour, that is, after he crossed the Río Tecolapa. As I explained in chapter 3, the Tecolapa frequently flooded, thanks to the presence of an irrigation dam downstream, which meant that Silvio often had to wade across the river rather than use the makeshift sandbag footbridge the neighbors had constructed. Once he reached the road, he would have to get dressed again and walk (or, with luck, hitch a ride on a horse cart or motorcycle) to the larger village of Vista Hermosa. At 5:00 a.m., the bus would arrive to pick up CKDnt patients. This would be Silvio's morning routine, three days a week. He knew from watching Luis how exhausting the journey would be, and he knew dialysis was no cure. Given all this, a hesitancy like Silvio's—to even try to access dialysis—makes sense.

Treatment cessation is often cited as a leading cause of death for hemodialysis patients, and more than a few of the many recipients profiled in the ethnographic record have questioned the capacity of the procedure, life-preserving as it is, to sustain a quality life. Once enrolled, patients can feel the onset of a kind of social death even before physical death arrives. In this way, hemodialysis "threatens to overcome and . . . to *become* the life that it extends."[26] Commitment to hemodialysis disembeds bodies from place, abstracting them from social and ecological ties. One of the things that makes dialysis challenging is its time-limited efficacy. Every person who comes to the clinic is facing a certain physical decline and death. Dialysis can extend life. It cannot save or restore life. Though its limitations are obvious in places like Nicaragua, where kidney transplant is out of the question for all but the wealthiest patients, the pressure to opt in to dialysis remains high. It may be even higher in such resource-limited contexts. While refusal or treatment cessation among dialysis patients is common in the Global North, in the Global South, the leaders of organized patient movements for access to dialysis, like AMBED, are understandably confounded by the prospect of patient burnout.[27] Treatment activism depends on the cultivation of a will to live. A common anthropological analysis of technologies of survival is that they are grounds for a particular kind of vital life politics.[28]

Close attention to instances of refusal, hesitancy, or "noncompliance" points to a different analysis. Survival can be evidence of a will to live, but it is also the name we give to the form of life that remains after the demise of a prior set of material conditions for existence: to the form of life that accepts the nearness of death. There is value in examining the sociality that emerges in the space between grief and grievance. From the perspective of people with CKDnt, plantation patienthood can be read as a matter of anticipating and managing death, of grieving for oneself and for others. What made this an ethical and existential challenge was the knowledge that the more activism and advocacy succeeded in drawing sugarcane companies and the state into the project of providing life support, the more sociality started to take a corporate form.[29] To become a patient was to be pulled back into the plantation, that "sprawling (and overlapping)" set of "biological, economic, and social systems" that keeps even healthy bodies from ever being or feeling whole.[30] Silvio and his family pondered the collective costs and benefits of waiting around to die, of never getting on the bus. They tempered a grievance with grief, perhaps, because they knew that grief was something the corporation could not (or would not) interfere with.

In the Black Atlantic studies tradition, plantation grief centers as much on the acute destruction wrought by runaway production (injury, death, abuse in the field) as on the slow, accretive violence that undermines processes of reproduction (birth, family separation, lost ancestors).[31] While Nicaragua's plantation history is one of debt bondage and patron-clientage rather than outright enslavement, that sense of life's fungibility resonates, captured in the commonplace description of CKDnt patients as exhausted (rendido).

Exhaustion, or *rendimiento*, was an apt way of categorizing what was happening to Silvio. His kidneys were physically exhausted, by any medical standard. Exhaustion, as Elizabeth Povinelli notes, can be thought of as both something "produced by and then reabsorbed into the system," such as the toxic chemical waste that may or may not have triggered the CKDnt epidemic, and that which is "produced when trying to create alternative ethical substances."[32] Seen in this way, rendimiento is more than a depletion of physical energy or capacity in an individual. It is a relational category, a condition that Silvio inhabited along with his wife, along with his father, along with his departed brother, and along with the landscape in which he lived. To petition plantation management for benefits was to suggest that the plantation had unmet obligations to its workforce, obligations that had to be settled. The Spanish verb *rendir* can connote physical exhaustion, but it also relates to management and exchange. The settling of accounts in business, for example, is referred to as a *rendición de cuentas*. Rendimiento implies what Mareike Winchell calls "obligation not only as a practice bound to human life span and economic calendars but also as [a] model for addressing past injustice."[33] Those who would be counted as CKDnt patients had to appear on the Montelimar Corporation's employment rolls, and by taking the opportunity to become passengers on the dialysis bus, they reentered the corporate accounts as different kinds of expenditures, offset, one presumes, by the public relations and economic benefits that accrue to companies that can demonstrate a commitment to "social responsibility."[34] In other usages, *rendir* can connote personal sacrifice, the kinds of reciprocal obligations demanded of survivors by a death in the community, and of the dying to be present for those who remain, all while (at Montelimar anyway) contemplating the unrepayable blessings bestowed by God. Grief entails all of these: a loss of physical strength, a settling of accounts, a giving up of life or property for something or someone else, and a submission to the demands of reciprocity. If we think of grief in this way, as simultaneously exhausting and generative of obligations, we might come to a better understanding of the ambiguity of plantation patienthood. Seen as a doubling of grief and grievance, plantation patienthood is difficult to characterize either as resistance to the structural violence of plantation conditions or as resignation to it.

The Occasional Patient

"How often are you drinking these days?" Don Alvaro Torres asked Jairo. The question was less clinical or judgmental than gently ribbing. We hadn't come to Vista Hermosa, the settlement directly upland from El Sesteo, looking for Jairo in particular. It just turned out that Jairo, who was drunk, had been hard to miss.

"Solo en ocasiones," Jairo replied, feigning offense that Don Alvaro would think him a habitual drunkard. Jairo's joke hit its mark. Translated to English, the phrase *solo en ocasiones* can mean either "only occasionally," as in a vague "now and then," or a more precise "only on certain occasions."

"Ocasiones!" Saúl bellowed. "Birthdays, holidays . . ."

"Tuesdays!" Don Alvaro chimed in, completing the joke. Beneath the laughter, though, was a concern about the relationship between Jairo's reliability as a drinker and his dedication to treatment.

"Look, Jairo," Saúl began, "you were supposed to be on the bus this morning." The bus had come and gone hours ago, which meant that Jairo risked more than a hangover when he opted to spend Thursday evening and part of Friday morning imbibing. "If you don't show up for treatment, how can we help you?"

Jairo was neither apologetic nor combative, and I don't think this was because he was numb to the problem Saúl laid before him. The truth was that he had been a faithful client of the dialysis bus, most of the time. His explanation for his "occasional" bender and subsequent choice to miss the bus sounded pretty well reasoned. Sometime in the previous couple of weeks, he had managed to find part-time, informal work back on the plantation, helping apply herbicides in a patch of cane across from the *pulpería* where we now sat. A field manager had offered him a bit of cash and provided him with a backpack-mounted hand sprayer to do the work, off the books.

If this petty violation of labor standards merited shock and outrage, Don Alvaro and Saúl didn't let on. They listened calmly as Jairo explained that the work he was asked (and paid!) to do was much the same as the work he had done before he was diagnosed with CKDnt. To be sure, what the capataz offered by way of compensation was less that what he had earned before, but Jairo confessed that he enjoyed the work.

"But you have to be careful, Jairo," Don Alvaro admonished. The strain of being out, even for a few early morning hours, in the heat and the sun would accelerate the decline of his kidney function. Don Alvaro was echoing the advice doctors gave to patients diagnosed with CKDnt: avoid exertion, remain sedate, and watch your diet by avoiding sugar, alcohol, and greasy foods. Forget about what toxicants might be in that herbicide sprayer. Too much physical activity would lead to a faster progression of the disease. Nausea would lead to fatigue, fatigue to swelling and pain, and all this would stress compromised kidneys. The assumption built into these recommendations was that at home, there would be family members or neighbors to provide care and to make up for the loss in earnings occasioned by the diagnosis.

Jairo clarified that it was not as if he was out there every day, like before. He wasn't signing on for a seasonal contract, or any contract. This work was, to use the term with which he (jokingly?) described his drinking pattern, "occasional." And it was welcome. Jairo could not just turn over breadwinning to his mother or his wife, the latter of whom worked on the plantation already. Here at Montelimar, he was a known "human resource." If he wanted to contribute to the care of his family, picking up the sprayer again was easier than looking for work in the seaside tourist town of Pochomil, more than a forty-five-minute mototaxi ride away, on a good day.

One might object here that Jairo was not thinking of his wife, his mother, or his children. In spending his underground wage on alcohol, surely he was thinking of himself. Despite the advanced stage of his disease, Jairo was one of the lucky ones. He was one of a minority of plantation patients to whom dialysis was available. As Saúl and Don Alvaro kept reminding him, by skipping treatments, he was hastening his own death. If these were the choices he made, he would not live long.

But how long he would live was unclear. CKDnt patients tend to reach ESRD at a young age, and while the progression can be quick, patients have lived for years with the aid of hemodialysis. While Jairo's choice to seek informal plantation work meant that he missed more than a few hemodialysis sessions, he had probably observed what most people in Nicaragua had: that the disease, to an extent, could be self-managed. The medical literature on patients who opt out of dialysis, or opt never to seek it at all, tends to focus on the pros and cons of providing treatment to elderly patients or patients for whom ESRD is a sequela of diabetes. Again, the focus is on whether continuing (or even starting) hemodialysis promotes or detracts from quality of life.[35] CKDnt patients on sugarcane plantations are a distinct patient population. None are "elderly" by the terms of nephrology journals, and many enjoyed good health relative to the general population before being diagnosed (i.e., they had steady incomes, had no diabetes or heart conditions, and were not obese). People with CKDnt, at least by the second decade of the epidemic, when my research began, had had time to bear witness to the temporal unpredictability of the disease. Places where dialysis is not universally available, and where transplant is virtually unthinkable, make interesting "natural experiments" on survival possibilities. For every story about a person who didn't last six weeks after starting hemodialysis, or who succumbed to a secondary infection after beginning peritoneal dialysis, there were people like Jairo, whose choice to take the bus "occasionally" would have made him a statistical anomaly in any study of survival rates that bifurcated patients into groups of "on dialysis" and "off dialysis."

To be an occasional patient was another way of enduring while refusing to subject disease to the frugal logics of corporate management. It was another way of making moral economic demands on the company. To be legible to the Montelimar Corporation's corporate social responsibility mechanism, people like Jairo were asked to treat their condition as a fundamental break with the past. By this logic, if they wanted to retain any hope for a good life, patients had to submit to the demands of treatment. When patients become subject to strict therapeutic itineraries, deviation from those itineraries can signal noncompliance, even immorality. Anthropological explanations of compliance and noncompliance often turn to the social, economic, and political structures that make patient adherence to therapies difficult or impossible.[36] In sketching the cases of Mauricio, Jairo, and Silvio, I have already named a few: the distance between the village and the town where any hope of low-stress, low-exertion labor lay; the economic trade-offs between sticking to long-term treatment (even subsidized treatment) and earning short-term cash; the cruel system of resource provision that made cheap beer and liquor easier to find than healthy, nutritious food.

But if we look again at Jairo's embrace of ocasiones, a different explanation might transpire. To me, it is not too much to think of his return to plantation work on this occasional, informally timed basis as a form of participating in that doubling of grievance and grief, a way of reckoning with the fungibility that the plantation simultaneously imposes on working bodies, crops, and land.[37] By working in the margins of the labor force, Jairo was questioning the isolation and extraction from home and environment that ethnographers of dialysis have identified as a motivator for treatment refusal elsewhere.[38] Why limit the benefits he and his family could extract from the Montelimar Corporation to a bus ride? Why not milk the company for a few more córdobas by fumigating weeds in the cane? Occasional patients countered the frugality of corporate care with a more capacious approach to extending quality of life.[39]

Companions

Over the course of 2017 and 2018, AMBED formalized Mauricio's queja about the bus doing double duty as a patient carrier and as an errand vehicle into a written grievance, which it submitted to the corporation and the CAO. Eventually, via the mediation process, AMBED succeeded in making the bus schedule more reliable. By 2019, my notes indicate that fewer patients were being forced to wait as the bus picked up supplies, office workers, or other nonmedical items from Managua. By that time, the Montelimar Corporation had identified a point person for the bus service, a handsome young HR specialist I'll call Emilio. Emilio turned out to be popular among the hemodialysis patients, and it started to seem like the bus problem was being "managed" (there is no other word for it) rather smoothly. Harmonizing patient demands with the company's priorities, though, remained a challenge.

Hemodialysis is grueling. A session can leave a person tired, disoriented, and nauseated, and Nicaragua's dialysis clinics lack the support staff to provide food or physical comfort. In response, Montelimar patients had started bringing companions with them to Managua. They did not ask permission to do this, but it appeared not to bother Emilio, who was said to be something of a natural when it came to corporate social responsibility. He answered phone calls promptly, even after hours, remembered people's names, and appeared to know when to bend the rules to assuage conflict.

Then, in the summer of 2019, Emilio took a new job, off the plantation. A few weeks later, on a Saturday morning, a new HR official boarded the bus when it stopped in front of the mill and informed the riders that starting on

Monday, only patients would be permitted to board. From then on, companions would banned.

When I heard about this development, I was in Villa El Carmen with Don Alvaro Torres and Doña Iris, recording a conversation with a woman named Anna and her sister, Julia. Their father was one of the CKDnt bus riders. Within a few minutes of our gathering on Anna's porch, the topic of conversation turned to companionship. While the epidemic disproportionately affected men, women overwhelmingly served as bus-riding caregivers and as advocates. They told me that when their father began dialysis, there was not yet a bus service. Patients were on their own. Before the bus became an option, their family spent more than 7,000 córdobas per month (more than US$200) in transport back and forth to the clinic. They felt they had no choice. As Anna explained:

> I had to be there to ask, "Papa, do you need some water? Here, have this juice, have a little bread," you know? There are times when they finish [the treatment] and they don't want to eat. So in my bag I bring a little bread. Sometimes he says, "No, I don't want to eat," and a little while later, I say, "Now, are you going to eat?" And I have to watch to make sure they don't leave nauseated, or with pain. If he does, I go back, I look for the doctor.... One has to be there for one's relatives, so they don't feel alone.... Emotionally, we're not all the same. Some of us get depressed more easily than others, so one has to travel with their patient.

"And in the hospital, they encourage it!" Julia interjected. "They don't want the patients sent to the clinics alone!"

But when every patient brought a companion with them, conditions on the bus became crowded. Earlier that week, Gregoria, the head of HR, had boarded the bus and taken camera phone pictures of the crowd. Some patients were left standing in the aisles, gripping the overhead storage rail for balance—a physical feat familiar to any Nicaraguan public transport rider but much more difficult for one weakened by ESRD. It was hard enough to balance on the journey up to Managua, but on the way back, it was torture. Gregoria's version of the justification for banning companions was that the patients had to be protected from injury. An overcrowded bus was a liability for corporation and patient alike.

Don Alvaro had heard Gregoria's side of things, but he thought that something else was going on. "The new manager—the one who replaced Emilio— boarded the bus yesterday and in what I'm told was a very hard manner said that the owners, the administration of the mill, the managers, weren't aware of what was going on in the bus. And he wouldn't have that because it's the upper management that authorize the use of the bus for dialysis." Unlike his predecessor, the new manager was unwilling to look the other way about the presence of companions on the bus. According to a strict reading of the agreement that AMBED had signed with the Montelimar Corporation, companions were not in fact authorized, but riders had brought them along anyway. Management had come to see this as excessive. Too many people on the bus posed a safety issue, but additional payload also presented an issue of economy: more people meant more fuel, more time on the road. If the bus was no longer allowed to pick up supplies and ferry office staff from the city to the mill, why should relatively healthy companions get a free ride? By the time of our conversation, the outright ban on companions had been delayed, pending AMBED's formal grievance asking to amend the original agreement and establish companions as legitimate riders, even if that meant finding a larger bus— maybe, Doña Iris suggested, one of the yellow Bluebird buses the company used to move work teams from field to field.

AMBED's appeal would hinge not just on the letter of the original settlement the group had signed but on a dual commitment of plantation management to former workers, and of family members to one another. Much of our conversation with Anna and Julia revolved around the etiquette of bus riding. In their view, able-bodied companions *should* give up seats to weaker patients. But the new bus manager should also learn to treat riders with respect, as Emilio had done. At one point in the conversation, Doña Iris began instructing the two other women about how to use their mobile phones to make clandestine recordings of the new HR manager when he rudely chastised the companions, as he tended to do, for taking up space and for wasting company time and resources. These recordings, she was sure, would embarrass management into making the companions a permanent part of the payload. At the same time, the patients would do more to regulate themselves. She proposed appointing a leader for each dialysis group, someone who would ensure that patients were prioritized for seating.

The bottom line was that companionship was not excessive. As Don Alvaro put it, "I think that as a family member, one should feel glad to know that they fought to support a relative up to the end, the last moment, because after that, what? You're bringing flowers to a grave, no? But there are people who want to do this but can't because of their resources, their limitations."

Don Alvaro was speaking of a duty of care that arises out of a proximity between corporation and community, a proximity defined by death rather than life. One thing that was certain was that the company was not going to purchase flowers, or even a coffin. Maybe this was why people in the sugarcane zone were already so adept at recording funerals and burials on their camera phones, much as they documented the flyovers of the pesticide helicopter (see chapter 4). Don Alvaro drew a line connecting companionship during dialysis and graveside visitation not only because these were typologically similar obligations but also because, even though it was never spoken out loud, everyone knew that inviting a patient to take a drink of juice, slipping a little salt under their tongue when their blood pressure dropped, or giving up a seat on the bus as it wound down the mountain into the sugarcane zone was life support or, more accurately, a form of extended palliative care, the part of grief that begins before death itself.

Dying as Plantation Labor

Attention to stories about plantation patienthood affords a better understanding of the compromises, the partial measures, and ultimately the unrestorative ways in which people in the sugarcane zone enact life support amid irreversible ecological damage. As they worked to keep the question of CKDnt's causality open—maybe a toxic exposure, maybe a heat exposure, maybe a chronic lack of water—people in the sugarcane zone struggled to create space for multiple ways of being affected by CKDnt. Life support, then, was neither something that was simply granted to patients by the corporation or the state nor something that patients had to learn to cherish without question. Like any item of exchange, life support implied manifold relationships. These included strained kin networks, an uneven and unsatisfying form of corporate care, the ordinary work of growing food for subsistence, and, of course, a life-sustaining technology, the hemodialysis machine that operated, for a while anyway, as an artificial kidney.

Plantation patienthood, like plantation labor, is hard work. Many years ago, the anthropologist Roger Lancaster drew the title for an ethnographic monograph from a commonplace Nicaraguan saying: Life is hard.[40] In that book, set in the waning days of the Sandinista revolution, Lancaster uses narratives about intimate life, family formation and dissolution, sexual relations, work, and leisure to chart how people living in the aftermath of extraordinary events navigate the slippery space between the uncertainty of ordinary survival and the seeming surety of impinging structural conditions. In the cases Lancaster examined, the hardness of life came from the brutality visited on the poor by dictatorship, civil war, and the US economic embargo against the Soviet-supported Sandinista regime. The slow violence of plantation production at

Montelimar has culminated in a particular version of that hardness.[41] The genius of Nicaraguan endurance after the revolution, and after the rise of the corporate plantation, is a refusal to let hardness become suffocating. In his work on necropolitics, Mbembe points out that even as enslaved plantation workers were treated as fungible tools, they found ways "to demonstrate the protean capabilities of the human bond," to live lives that exceeded the presumptions of fungibility on which the plantation was founded.[42]

Attention to patient stories helps push back against a tendency, both in medical treatment and in ethnographic analysis of patienthood, to extract bodily conditions from ecological ones. What I think this material may help us appreciate is the slipperiness of the categories and terminologies we have come to use to think about people and their bodies—laborer, patient, caregiver, manager. In many ways, the logics of corporate sugarcane production become clearest not when we forensically investigate how it does immediate harm, in the forms of toxic poisoning or environmental damage or workplace injury, but when we look at efforts to limit that harm. Plantation violence emerges as much in the careful management of slow death as it does in the wanton perpetration of acute abuse. The management of death entails a toggling between fungibility, patron-client reciprocity, and liberal legal liability limitation.

The idea of the "socially responsible" corporation arguably has its roots in two myths. One is the myth of the plantation as a moral economic system, where mutual obligations mattered and where bodies were specific and historical and individual rather than interchangeable and fungible. The other is the myth of free labor, in which work is imagined as an abstract outcome of a contractual relationship between equal parties. Those two myths each perpetuate a third myth: that labor can be a pathway to full humanity for people (e.g., Indigenous, Black, women, queer) whose humanity is constantly questioned by dominant systems of knowledge and power.[43] When stirred together, as they were at Montelimar, these myths make it seem natural that access to dialysis should be connected to a documented history of plantation work—that dying slowly in that managed, medicalized way was a kind of plantation labor.

Attention to people's ambivalence about the dialysis bus may help us understand how these myths work in tension with a myth that haunts corporations of all kinds: the myth of the fungible body, the illimitably interchangeable and expendable laborer. Contemporary corporate social responsibility schemes, including those promoted by the World Bank and the IFC, constantly confront the problem that capital accumulation in agribusiness depends upon the disappearance of dead laborers into the accounts, along with pesticides, seeds, water, and energy. As sugarcane production becomes more mechanized and more dependent on chemicals, opportunities for work are, ironically, drying up. Thanks to these technologies, there are fewer jobs than ever on Nicaraguan sugarcane plantations, which means that the very possibility of a labor-based form of advocacy or solidarity may be decaying along with the bodies of people with CKDnt. Eventually, unless a new commitment emerges, there will no longer be any people with CKDnt who meet the Montelimar Corporation's accepted criteria for dialysis services. Continued on-site kidney function tests will weed out those whose bodies are too compromised to put to work and ensure that reaching the threshold of two years of employment will be all but impossible. At that point, the question of CKDnt's status as an occupational illness will have been successfully pushed outside the imaginary boundary that separates the plantation from its outside.

Conclusion

When I was a graduate student, my adviser recommended that I avoid writing in the "ethnographic present," which means speaking of a subject as if it existed in a perpetual now and claiming that cultural forms are somehow static. This remains good advice for a variety of reasons. This book, like many contemporary works of anthropological ethnography, is a kind of history, even if it is about how the members of AMBED and the residents of the Montelimar sugarcane zone worked to imagine futures amid a devastating epidemic. By way of a conclusion, I want to take a moment to think further about the temporal dimensions of CKDnt, of Nicaragua's sugarcane boom, of chemically driven monoculture, and of planetary health.

On one of my first visits to Montelimar, Saúl insisted that we take a break from our visits to CKDnt-affected communities and drive into the interior of the plantation for some real anthropology. Somewhere off the road that connects the village of El Apante to El Borbollón, the municipal reservoir serving the town of Villa El Carmen, there is a small, mostly dried-up riverbed, with a tiny hut sitting just above. The signs welcome visitors to the "Archaeological Site of the Pozo de Danto Forest Reserve." Down in the riverbed are petroglyphs that, archaeologists reckon, were carved into the rock by Chorotega people between 800 and 1350 CE. There are faces, full human figures, a few images that look more like they could be monkeys, and a rendering of what the informational sign on the riverbank calls the Cruz Americana, the "American Cross," "a symbol of orientation to the four cardinal directions."

Here, amid the vast stands of cane, was evidence of the land's past occupation by Indigenous groups who relied on this and many other rivers for clay, stone, fish, and, of course, water. Here was a kind of ruin, evidence of a past settlement and a bygone way of living on this landscape. When scholars think of the state of the planet today, they frequently speak in terms of ruins. CKDnt seems like a paradigmatic example of late capitalist "ruination," a sign that the heyday of industrial monocrop capitalism is approaching its end. If workers are dying in such numbers, surely this is what some CKDnt scientists have argued is a tipping point for this form of production.[1] But such a view may be overly optimistic; after all, places like western Nicaragua have been sites of plantation-based ruination for centuries.[2] The sugarcane boom of the early twenty-first century is just the latest chapter. The violence runs deep. Problems like CKDnt may be signs of a profound pathology in monocrop production, but monocrop production has always been pathological. Workers, already low-paid and racially marginalized, have always carried a disproportionate risk of bodily harm due to faulty machinery, pesticide exposure, and chronic repetitive stress.

In most years, there is no water running beneath the petroglyphs. In reviewing the pictures I took all those years ago, glimpses of the faded remains of Chorotega presence in what is now the sugarcane zone, I am reminded of an article written by the journalist Francisco A. Guevara Jerez. The subject was Nicaragua's rural water crisis.[3] As an epigraph to a lengthy scholarly explanation of how a country that, despite its numerous aquifers, freshwater lakes, rainforests, and rivers, has become associated with a generalized thirst, Guevara Jerez quotes "Canto de la Guerra de Las Cosas" (Anthem of the War of Things), by the Nicaraguan poet Joaquín Pasos:

> Water is blood's only eternity.
> Its strength, made into blood. Its restlessness, made into blood.
> Its violent longing for wind and sky,
> made into blood.
> Tomorrow they will say that blood became dust;

tomorrow the blood will be dried.
Neither sweat, nor tears, nor urine
Will be able to fill the void of an empty heart.
Tomorrow they will envy the hydraulic pump of a throbbing toilet,
The living constancy of a faucet,
The thick liquid.
The river will take charge of the destroyed kidneys
and in the middle of the desert the cross of bones will ask in vain for
water to return to the bodies of men.

These words read like a contemporary meditation on climate change and its ravages on bodies and landscapes. Life transfers to the toilet and the faucet. Deserts are all that remain. Pasos wrote these apocalyptic verses, complete with explicit reference to "destroyed kidneys," some three-quarters of a century before the CKDnt epidemic emerged. I quote them here because they mention destroyed kidneys, and because they offer an oblique commentary on the charge in the field of planetary health to restore Earth's "life support systems." The poem looks forward to a future in which people and the Earth they once knew no longer exist. "When you reach old age, you will respect stone," the poem begins, "if you reach old age, if any stone is left."

Like many of the people whose lives are pseudonymously portrayed in this book, Pasos died young (he was thirty-two and was never published in his lifetime). I can find no clear record of this, but perhaps he linked his own mortality to that of the planet because the "destroyed kidneys" mentioned in the poem were his own.[4] Songs of the apocalypse like "Anthem of the War of Things" could be warnings to their audiences, but they also could be wishes for an ending. In a way, it would be nice to think that war, environmental destruction, and the human exploitation that drives them are coming to a self-induced conclusion.

In some ways, that is what the call for a new planetary health, sounded by the Rockefeller-*Lancet* commission in 2015, attempts to do—manifest an ending to a way of understanding the relationship between human life and nonhuman life that has proved ultimately "self-devouring."[5] As the historians James Dunk and Warwick Anderson write, "Planetary health represents our current response to what might be called the dark side of development, progress, and the 'civilizing process,' a means of contending with the consequences of our species' incessant assault on the planet's life support systems."[6] Dunk and Anderson add that while the movement for planetary health has been spearheaded overwhelmingly by "well meaning white male experts from the Global

North," it must begin to incorporate the insights of people from the Global South, women, and Indigenous people.[7] I agree—white, male, and northern as I am—and hope that this book and the story of CKDnt in Nicaragua prompt consideration about what such insights could offer.

Here are some possibilities.

AMBED and those who are affiliated with it recognized the apocalypse not only as the comeuppance for the overreach of plantation capitalism but also as the inevitable end that was always destined to come. Their search for nonsecular accountability in the face of certain death signals a belief that action in the face of irreversible destruction must start from a position of noninnocence. For medical anthropologists, persistent health disparities between farmworkers and nonfarmworkers substantiate the critical claim that economic inequalities can become embodied conditions, but attention to nonsecular accountability projects points to a slightly different story.

For people in the sugarcane zone, a diagnosis of CKDnt presented a puzzle. To make a claim to be an injured worker was at the same time to make a claim to participation in the deterioration of the broader environment. The question was how to do both: to talk about a body injured at work, and to talk about the damage to a landscape that transcends the occupational. Anthropologist Alex Blanchette, in his study of the toxic plumes of dust that swirl well beyond the industrial meat operations of the US Midwest, argues that this form of pollution is the product not just of corporate activity but of the labor of the very people who may later be affected by antibiotic-resistant microbes lodged in that putrid air. Blanchette uses this example to call attention to "how the actions of some people are made to more directly and disproportionately bear the weight of remaking and maintaining volatile worlds."[8] Building on observations like this one, I have tried to show that a movement for health in an age of irreversible environmental change requires a rejection of models for living that presume the possibility not just of ecological equilibrium but of social and environmental settlement.

In this way, AMBED's approach to confronting the epidemic reflects an observation by the French social theorist Georges Canguilhem. This book has described AMBED's efforts to achieve a kind of environmental justice, and how those efforts met awkwardly with both the efforts of an industry to limit its liability and the efforts of scientists and lawyers to explain a mysterious illness. In an essay titled "The Problem of Regulation in the Organism and Society," Canguilhem notes that while the organism has been seen as a metaphor for society, and vice versa, there is one big difference between the two. When it comes to (human) organisms, people may debate the nature of what ails them—in other words, the cause of a disease may be uncertain—but "no one [debates] the ideal of the good," healthy body. By contrast, Canguilhem explains, "the existence of societies, of their disorders and unrests, brings forth a wholly different relation between ills and reforms, because for society, what we debate is how to know its ideal state or norm."[9] Canguilhem explains that a human body is made up of organs, which have been usefully compared to social institutions and even the organizational structure of factories, but what distinguishes the organism from society is that the organism has the capacity for self-regulation built into it. Its ability—within limits, of course—to overcome disturbance is built in, integral. Societies do not possess this self-regulating function. Justice is not a natural function of society but something that must be imposed on it from the outside.

Ecological theory once turned on a notion similar to the one that Canguilhem identifies about the organism, namely, that ecosystems were self-righting machines. But amid climate crisis, this notion of dynamic equilibrium has to be questioned.[10] We live on a planet where no stable state of equilibrium exists: one where, as the poet Pasos might have it, the flows of water through a toilet are as "natural" and contingent as the flows through a stream. We live on a planet where even the immortality of stones is dubious.[11] What AMBED seemed to recognize is that the body is surrounded by other organisms, and that the arrangements among them are always in the making. AMBED was a group of engaged participants in that making, but one lesson their story might offer to planetary health is that, as I have argued, "environmental activism" is not a large enough category to encompass what grassroots collective action for planetary health could be. AMBED's activities may have been less dependent on the sharp distinction between the organism and society than Canguilhem might have supposed, but AMBED was nevertheless less committed to a kind of environmental justice.

This leads me to a second potential takeaway from the preceding chapters. In short, the movement for planetary health must develop more sophisticated and complex ways of conceptualizing work. The making of occupational environments is at the same time the making of occupational subjectivities. In addition to establishing a clear border between the human and the natural, modernization in Latin America was also a project of establishing a clear border between work and nonwork, working environment and nonworking environment, body at work and body outside of work. Diseases of unknown causes underscore the fragility of these borders. They leave open the possibility that illness is not just a technical matter but a moral one. As Sarah Besky and Alex Blanchette put it, "Like the 'nature' shifting beneath our feet, work . . . is a fragile category of practice tied to and changing within the worlds where it unfolds."[12]

And yet one of the shortcomings of efforts to address the novel pathologies that result from industrial modernization is that work continues to be treated as a stable, undifferentiated category, defined and delimited, by and large, by employers and financiers. The twenty-first-century plantation persists through its frugality, its constant struggle to limit its own spatial and human exposure. The same kinds of economic calculations that make it highly remunerative to use glyphosate to mature cane—calculations that also permit plantations to employ fewer and fewer people—perpetuate a process of what Jasbir Puar calls "debilitation," "a practice of rendering populations available for statistically likely injury."[13] The toxicity of plantation agriculture emanates not just from the pesticides but from the account books and financial projections of companies and states. But the Nicaraguan sugar industry is dogged by its own history—by things like the existence of cabras, the grainy records of lost garden crops stored on cheap mobile phones, and the fleeting collective recovery of environment and society precipitated by the Nicaraguan revolution. All these kept Montelimar entangled in obligations of care that exceeded its increasingly streamlined industrial design.

At Montelimar, the borders between plantation and nonplantation space are anything but clear. Personal histories of work at Montelimar exemplify an idea put forward by the environmental historian Linda Nash: it is in "those landscapes"—like plantations—"that are typically taken as symbolic of the human alienation from nature" that an entanglement between humans and nonhumans is most apparent.[14] There is no biosecure perimeter on a sugarcane plantation, and even if there were, no one could stop pesticides from drifting. And, of course, the social relations that plantation agriculture relies on are more than just those of labor to management. They include family connections, political ties, and more than capitalist relations of gift exchange and mutual aid. Nicaraguan sugarcane workers live in and around the plantation, and they can rightly claim the very occupational environment that they believe has harmed them not as an external environment but as something they built, their patrimony. The CKDnt epidemic thus poses a threat not just to the ability to do plantation work but to the ability to imagine nonplantation alternatives. The work of planetary health, as I suggested in the introduction, entails much more than conventional occupational health paradigms would assume.

Finally, I hope that this book might expand how we think about life support. *Life support* is a key term in planetary health, but it is frequently treated as a function, as in the phrase "life support system." Both AMBED and the residents of the sugarcane zone had good reason to question the integrity of life support systems, and in each chapter, I have illustrated how they did so. Taken together, these chapters give us a picture of life support not as one closed system but as a set of interconnected, open ones. In this sense, life support encompasses the collaborative, noninnocent practices that sustain collective existence. I say that the ethic of life support is "noninnocent" for specific reasons. AMBED took action without believing that the damage done by sugarcane production could ever be fully rectified. Noninnocence is not nihilism or cynicism. Rather, it is a commitment to repair that acknowledges the impossibility of a cure.[15] For AMBED, life support included things as simple as getting from place to place in the plantation zone and processes as byzantine as seeking benefits from the Nicaraguan social security system. Life support included the work of securing biomedical treatments, but it also included the more-than-medical effort to confront a disease for which the exact cause remained unknown, and for which there was no possibility of a cure.

The barbed wire fence that protects the evidence of the ancestral presence of Chorotega people in the riverbeds of the Montelimar sugarcane zone is flimsy. Pasos, who may have encountered those same pictographs in his short life, warned his readers that they, too, would eventually disappear. This book has concerned itself with a set of projects aimed not so much at preserving evidence of a threatened way of life but at figuring out how to live life under threat. Much of that work takes the form of archaeology and archive: the contemplation of mineral and protein deposits contained in urine and blood, the layered accretion of chemical deposits in soils and bodies, the decaying stacks of unanswered grievance forms. It is tempting, then, to think that evidence for the ultimate source of the harm done to sugarcane plantation workers' bodies lies underfoot, in the ground or in the diminishing water table.

But I would be remiss if I did not close by turning our attention in a different direction. Maybe you can't hear it, and sometimes you can't even see it, but the helicopter is there, dropping the chemical ripener down on the cane. I feel compelled to end where I began, with the haunting of the helicopter, because one of the most consistent refrains among sugar plantation residents, from the beginning of the epidemic, has been to ask why aerial fumigation, which is so clearly dangerous and damaging, remains necessary to production. That helicopter is a kind of temporal black hole, where memories of past regimes of agricultural accumulation and land seizure—memories of methyl parathion and DDT—mesh with visions of a future where fewer and fewer people will need to give their bodies to the cane—at least not directly. The efficiency of chemical ripening promises more, cheaper, and, if Monsanto's corporate parents at Bayer are to be believed, safer agricultural futures.

While the term *climate crisis* is often deployed as a means of sparking a sense of duty and responsibility among the wealthy and powerful, its material correlates in our lives are often hazy: a warmer winter, an unexpectedly timed hurricane, a summer picnic disrupted by clouds of opportunistic mosquitoes. For some, COVID-19 was a wake-up call, but a casual glance at an airport or city jail indicates that life in the Global North is quickly and alarmingly returning to "normal." It seems like a simple observation, but when people at Montelimar point to the helicopter and back at themselves, they are questioning the wisdom of such a return. Looking up and out, they can see not only into a history of agricultural violence but into a future where the crops of empire—sugarcane, cotton, oil palm, soy—will be stretched to their limits.

If we want lessons about how to make climate change feel real, how to endure destruction while still questioning its logics, we may not need to look to laboratories, think tanks, or celebrity soothsayers urging us to pay attention. To see the world as it is, one needs only walk to the edge—of a shortened life, of a chemically prepared cane field, of a dried-up tropical riverbed—and look up. The answer may be silently floating overhead.

Acknowledgments

This book was made possible thanks to the cooperation of the people of Montelimar. Víctor Hernández taught me as much as anyone about the sugarcane zone and its history, and I am grateful to Edwin Cáceres, who provided hours of companionship, numerous introductions, and friendship. In the summer of 2015, very much by accident, I met Jean Silk in Managua. Jean helped open multiple doors, and she introduced me to Olivia Kaplan. I thank Jean and Olivia for showing trust and confidence in me, and for aiding me in getting my fledgling fieldwork off the ground. Kris Genovese provided key guidance, and she remained available even as the situation in Nicaragua became challenging. Additional thanks for practical support to Aurora Aragón, Marvin González-Quiroz, Juan José Amador, Daniel Brooks, Madeleine Scammell, Jason Glaser, Elyssa Noce, Emily Wright, Edipcia Roque, and Eréndira Vanegas.

During many of my field trips to Nicaragua for this project, I was involved in parallel research alongside Jae Fisher. Jae's intellectual dexterity and encyclopedic head for theory continue to inspire me. Through Jae, I became close to the members of the Jubilee House Community, where we spent many happy hours discussing Nicaraguan politics, telling good and bad jokes, and benefiting from Jae's mixology skills. Thanks as always to my oldest Nicaraguan collaborators and advisers, Haydée Abarca and María de Jesús Zepeda. Like all Nicaraguans, they have weathered a tumultuous political and social crisis since 2018, but they always made time to help me.

Research and writing require financial support, and the bulk of the funding for this book came from a Wenner Gren Foundation research grant. Additional research was carried out thanks to the support of the National Science Foundation project "A Political Ecology of Value" (award no. 1648667). Further funding was provided by the University of Edinburgh Munro Lectureship

Committee and Research Development Fund, as well as an Overseas Development Assistance grant from the UK Department for International Development. Faculty travel and research funds provided by Brown University and Cornell University were also essential to the project. A TOME grant provided by the Cornell University Library supported open access publication.

While researching and writing this book, I held three separate academic positions. At the outset, I was a faculty member at the University of Edinburgh. I conceptualized the project with the help of multiple colleagues and workshopped early written material with the "candlelit seminar" group. A special thanks is due to Lucy Lowe, with whom I coauthored an article in *Medical Anthropology* ("Social Justice as Epidemic Control") featuring some preliminary research for this project. At the nearby University of Durham, Tom Widger was an enthusiastic co-thinker, and though the conversations we had back in 2015–16 did not materialize in the grant we had hoped for, they were transformational for me. Most especially, I wish to thank Jamie Cross and Alice Street, who both continue to be treasured colleagues and dear friends. In 2018, I moved to the Watson Institute for International and Public Affairs at Brown University. Watson provided me with space and support to complete the final stages of research. Ed Steinfeld, Patsy Lewis, Andrew Schrank, Nick Ziegler, Margaret Weir, Prerna Singh, Aarti Sethi, and Bhrigu Singh all provided advice and warm companionship during my two years in Providence. Cornell University, where I have now worked for five years (longer than in any of my previous institutions), has been a wonderful professional home. Faculty and staff in the Department of Anthropology and the Mario Einaudi Center for International Studies have been a huge source of support.

The writing for this book began during a School for Advanced Research seminar in 2016, organized by Alex Blanchette, Naisargi Dave, and Sarah Besky. Subsequently, I presented research related to this book at the University of Oxford, Brown University, the University of Stockholm, the University of Wisconsin-Madison (thanks to the Center for Culture, History, and Environment !), the University of Toronto (thanks to Kevin O'Neill), the University of Hong Kong (thanks to Robert Peckham), the University of North Carolina at Chapel Hill (thanks to Bryan Dougan), Rhode Island College, Bryant University, the University of Pennsylvania EnviroLab, University College London, the University of Pennsylvania Department of Anthropology, the University of Texas at Austin, the University of Birmingham/Warwick Biocultural Diversity and Obesity Unit, the CERMES3 lab at the Centre national de la recherche scientifique in Paris, and, last but not least, the Agrarian Studio at Cornell University.

The 2022 "Alterlife" and 2024 "Multi-Elementalisms" workshops provided some of the most helpful feedback I received on the manuscript. Participants included Lochlann Jain, M. Murphy, Kristen Bos, Miriam Ticktin, Mel Chen, Hannah Landecker, Joe Masco, Cal Biruk, Nick Shapiro, Bishnupriya Ghosh, Cori Hayden, Nadia Gaber, Sheyda Aboii, Paras Arora, Rachael Healy, Nicole Mabry, Galen Joseph, Kelly Knight, Gabeba Baderoon, Joe Klein, and Victoria Nguyen. The "Future of Facts in Latin America" project, organized by Andrea Ballestero, Eden Medina, and Kregg Hetherington, also merits special mention. Thanks to Emily Maguire, Pablo Gomez, Vivette García Deister, Gabriela Soto Laveaga, Diana Bocarejo, Ignacio Siles, Rosana Castro, Eduardo Dianderas, Melanie Ford, Javiera Araya, and Katie Ulrich.

The following individuals directly and indirectly made this book possible: Claire Wendland, Paul Nadasdy, Sharon Hutchinson, Poulomi Saha, Fábio Zuker, Emilia Sanabria, Marina Welker, Jean Segata, Towns Middleton, Kathleen Millar, Noah Tamarkin, Jamie Lorimer, Jenny Goldstein, Jason Cons, Jonathan Padwe, Juno Parreñas, Stacey Langwick, Amiel Bize, Zoë Wool, Paul Kohlbry, Sahana Ghosh, Wenfei Xu, Jonathan Boyarin, Ashley Carse, Noah Theriault, Nikhil Anand, Ramah McKay, Hannah Brown, Alex Blanchette, Peter Little, Abby Neely, Jason de León, Amelia Moore, Austin Zeiderman, Ann Kelly, and Javier Lezaun. Finally, an ultraspecial thanks to Vincanne Adams. Vincanne, I hope you see the imprint of your scholarly spirit in this book.

I am grateful to the editors and anonymous reviewers of the journals *Medicine Anthropology Theory* and *Tapuya: Latin American Science, Technology, and Society*, as well as to the *Fieldsights* blog, the blog of *Environment and Planning D: Society and Space*, and the *Edge Effects* blog.

The series editors Vincanne Adams and João Biehl helped usher this project into Duke University Press, where Ken Wissoker, Kate Mullen, Courtney Leigh Richardson, and Michael Trudeau made the development process feel supportive and seamless during 2023 and 2024. Thanks to Susan Ecklund for copyediting so carefully. The manuscript was transformed by insightful readings from Kregg Hetherington and one anonymous reviewer. I am truly thankful for the years of support and conversation that Kregg has offered. He is a model of collegiality and generosity.

There were moments in the darkness of Ithaca winters and the depths of pandemic inertia when I did not think I would complete this book. The continued love and support of my extended family in Alabama, Georgia, and South Carolina, as well as the companionship of Sidney, Momo, and

Chuck-D, helped me see it through. But no one is more deserving of appreciation than Sarah Besky. Wonky academic textbooks can't really double as love letters, but I hope this book is a reflection of both Sarah's inspiring intellect and her love and care through turbulent and tranquil times. This one's for you.

Notes

PROLOGUE. LIVES WORTH SUPPORTING

Portions of this prologue were published in Nading, "The Plantation as Hotspot."
    1. Whitmee et al., "Safeguarding Human Health," 1997. "Anthropocene" is the name
that scientists have given to the geological epoch brought on by irreversible, human-
induced change to the Earth's geological and atmospheric systems. See Crutzen, "Effects
of Industrial and Agricultural Practices"; Steffen et al., "Anthropocene." The Rockefeller-
Lancet report is implicitly critical of the twentieth-century development ethos that saw
the improvement of human health as naturally compatible with the steady growth of
economies, measured through gross domestic product (GDP) indicators. See Murphy,
Economization of Life; Farman and Rottenburg, "Measures of Future Health"; and Livingston, *Self-Devouring Growth*.
    2. Whitmee et al., "Safeguarding Human Health," 2008. The rise of planetary health
follows on from the roughly twenty-year period in which states, universities, and supranational organizations organized around the notion of "global health." In some ways,
planetary health represents a pivot to a more explicitly environmental posture, and in
its emphasis on measuring and mitigating the effects of climate change, it is also distinct
from the One Health and Eco Health movements, which have tended to focus on the
pathways of zoonotic disease transmission and, to a lesser extent, overlaps between the
health of key ecosystems like forests and farms and the health of humans. See Dunk
and Anderson, "Assembling Planetary Health"; Brown and Nading, "Human Animal
Health"; Brown, Cueto, and Fee, "World Health Organization"; Packard, *History of
Global Health*; Craddock and Hinchliffe, "One World, One Health?"; Chabrol and
Gaudillère, *Introduction à la santé globale*.
    3. CAO, "Complaint of CFI Project 32253." The International Finance Corporation
goes by the English abbreviation IFC. In Spanish, its name, Corporación Financiera
Internacional, shortens to CFI.
    4. CAO, "Complaint of CFI Project 32253," 1.
    5. Nading, "Ethnography in a Grievance"; Johnson, "Nicaragua's Latest Revolution."
    6. International Finance Corporation, "Disclosure—Ingenio Montelimar."

7. Patel, "Long Green Revolution." Hetherington, in *Government of Beans*, builds on this idea to suggest that the Long Green Revolution ushered in an age of "agribiopolitics," in which the regulation of human life, through the idiom of health, became entangled with the regulation of the lives of commodity crops.

8. Laveaga, "Beyond Borlaug's Shadow."

9. Zubrin, "In Defense of Biofuels."

10. Faber, "Sea of Poison"; Faber, "Imperialism, Revolution, and the Ecological Crisis."

11. Butler, "Nicaragua Forest Information"; Mayer, "Conceptualizing Settler Colonialism in Nicaragua."

12. Thompson et al., "Most At-Risk Regions."

13. As the medical anthropologists Hannah Brown and Ann Kelly have argued, "Disease risk is not . . . 'located,' in the sense of being a feature of a particular kind of place. . . . Rather, it is locational . . . arising from particular configurations of social, biotic, and material conditions" (Brown and Kelly, "Material Proximities and Hotspots," 287).

14. Sorensen and Garcia-Trabanino, "New Era of Climate Medicine," 694.

15. Solomon, "Life Support"; Kaufman, *Ordinary Medicine*; Biehl and Adams, *Arc of Interference*.

16. Whitmee et al., "Safeguarding Human Health," 1973. For an alternative reading of this point, see Hinchliffe, Manderson, and Moore, "Planetary Health Publics."

17. As critical global health scholars (and maybe my students!) will recognize, panel 14 vastly oversimplifies the AIDS story. Despite widespread availability of HIV drugs, it is not clear that the movement for treatment access has fundamentally addressed political or racial inequality, partly because the provision of therapy is so narrowly implemented, and partly because other basic aspects of public health still receive too little attention (see Kalofonos, *All I Eat Is Medicine*; Yi Dionne, *Doomed Interventions*; Biehl, *Will to Live*).

18. Adams, *Metrics*.

19. Carse, "Ecobiopolitics of Environmental Mitigation."

INTRODUCTION

1. The disease that forms the backdrop to this book has been known by several names over the past twenty years, including Mesoamerican nephropathy (MeN) and, more commonly, chronic kidney disease of unknown causes (CKDu). Using the term *chronic kidney disease of nontraditional causes*, I join other researchers and advocates who hold that emphasizing the "unknown" in discussions of the epidemic risks deferring investigation and critique of the likely sources of harm to workers and communities, namely, the drastic ecological transformations that have come along with the making of monocrop landscapes in Nicaragua and elsewhere.

2. Anderson and Dunk, "Planetary Health Histories," 769.

3. Whitmee et al., "Safeguarding Human Health."

4. Horton, *They Leave Their Kidneys in the Fields*; Holmes, *Fresh Fruit, Broken Bodies*; Besky, "Exhaustion and Endurance."

5. DeLoughrey, *Allegories of the Anthropocene*, 7.

6. Hecht, *Residual Governance*.

7. Agard-Jones, "Bodies in the System"; Trouillot, "Making Sense"; Scheper-Hughes, *Death without Weeping*.

8. Besky and Blanchette, *How Nature Works*; Farmer, *AIDS and Accusation*; Farman and Rottenburg, "Measures of Future Health"; Livingston, *Self-Devouring Growth*. White reminds us that "labor rather than 'conquering' nature involves human beings with the world so thoroughly that they can never be disentangled" (*Organic Machine*, 7).

9. Fortun, "Poststructuralism, Technoscience," 314.

10. Moore, *Anthropocene or Capitalocene?*; Mintz, *Sweetness and Power*; Mintz, *Worker in the Cane*; Moran-Thomas, *Traveling with Sugar*.

11. Guthman, *Wilted*, 10.

12. Besky, *Darjeeling Distinction*; Hetherington, "Beans before the Law."

13. Blanchette, *Porkopolis*.

14. Guthman, *Wilted*; Hetherington, *Government of Beans*.

15. Grover, "Too Hot to Handle."

16. Whitington, "Fingerprint, Bellwether, Model Event."

17. Mitman, *Breathing Space*; Lorimer, *Probiotic Planet*; Lamoreaux, *Infertile Environments*; Murphy, *Sick Building Syndrome*; Kenner, *Breathtaking*.

18. Lock, "Recovering the Body."

19. Here, I am paraphrasing an observation made by the anthropologist and writer Amitav Ghosh, who has argued that mass migration out of vulnerable areas such as the Sundarbans of the Bengal Delta should not be viewed as consequences of climate change but as a manifestation of climate change itself (Ghosh, "Embattled Earth").

20. Smith, *From Fish to Philosopher*, 3.

21. Smith, *From Fish to Philosopher*, 10.

22. Smith, *From Fish to Philosopher*, 3.

23. Baker, "Chronic Kidney Disease."

24. Like other medical anthropologists who have studied chronic kidney disease (e.g., Hamdy, *Our Bodies Belong to God*; Crowley-Matoka, *Domesticating Organ Transplant*; Kierans, *Chronic Failures*), I aim to use ethnographic storytelling to highlight a "conviction on the part of people who face some of the worst health conditions on the planet," namely, as Charles Briggs and Clara Mantini-Briggs write, "that their ideas could play a crucial role in making a healthier and more just world" (Briggs and Mantini-Briggs, *Tell Me Why My Children Died*, 1). Briggs and Mantini-Briggs wrote these words in the context of another medical mystery—a rabies epidemic that devastated an Indigenous Warao community in Venezuela. As in the stories I will tell in this book about the Nicaraguan sugarcane workers and others affected by CKDnt, the search by the Warao for answers was at the same time a quest to be seen and heard not merely as "victims" but as active producers of knowledge. Elizabeth Povinelli, following William James, puts it another way: "The poor 'who live and feel' the regions of existence sucked dry of value 'know truth' as an actuality. They are always, even if immanently, opposing the dominant (if ultimately sterile) ideas of bourgeois philosophers and statesmen" (Povinelli, *Between Gaia and Ground*, 5).

25. Horton, *They Leave Their Kidneys in the Fields*; de Silva, "Drinking Water"; Senanayake, "Towards a Feminist Political Ecology"; Kierans, *Chronic Failures*.

26. Yusoff, "Indeterminate Subjects," 92.

27. Hetherington, "Concentration of Killing."

28. Gunatilake, Seneff, and Orlando, "Glyphosate's Synergistic Toxicity"; Seneff and Orlando, "Is Glyphosate a Key Factor?"

29. Haunting in this (metaphoric) sense is the feeling of being repeatedly visited by a troubling presence, of both a troubling past and an uncertain future. Such a presence may provide openings for imagining and enacting justice. See Good, Chiovenda, and Rahimi, "Anthropology of Being Haunted"; Derrida, *Specters of Marx*.

30. Guthman, *Wilted*.

31. McKittrick, "Plantation Futures," 10; Li and Semedi, *Plantation Life*.

32. Walker and Wade, *Nicaragua*; Quesada, "Brief History of Violence"; Gobat, *Confronting the American Dream*. This formulation emerges from Black feminist frameworks, as well as from the work of anthropologists of the plantation who attend to the specific ways in which racial and gendered violence manifests itself across different monocultured spaces (Besky, *Darjeeling Distinction*; Jegathesan, "Black Feminist Plots"; Wynter, "Novel and History"; Davis et al., "Anthropocene, Capitalocene").

33. Trouillot, "North Atlantic Universals."

34. Tsing, "On Nonscalability"; Mintz, *Sweetness and Power*.

35. Tsing, "On Nonscalability," 512; Spillers, "Mama's Baby, Papa's Maybe"; Marshall, "Political Life of Fungibility."

36. Medical anthropology and critical food studies have gained a notable amount of traction in global health—at least at the level of college curricula—in part because of the allure of the "suffering stranger" (Butt, "Suffering Stranger"; Biruk, "Ebola and Emergency Anthropology"). Elsewhere, Anna Tsing writes of the need in global capitalist supply chains for suitable, transposable "figures." Figures like the injured male farmworker are as essential for food justice and labor advocacy as they are for fair trade certifiers and corporate social responsibility consultants (see, e.g., Holmes, *Fresh Fruit, Broken Bodies*). These human figures form a fractal dyad with recognizable commodity crops like cane, packaging a story about runaway capitalist growth, its consequences, and its solutions. As Tsing puts it, "Businessmen, policy makers, voters, trade unions, and activists . . . use concrete figurations to imagine which projects might succeed" (Tsing, "Supply Chains," 152).

37. Wolf, "Specific Aspects of Plantation Systems"; Mintz, *Worker in the Cane*.

38. Gould, *To Lead as Equals*.

39. As Elizabeth Ferry defines it, a "'moral economy' entails a parallel, often unwritten set of moral prescriptions over economic activities and their proceeds that contrast with official often elite or managerial prescriptions" (Ferry, "Geologies of Power," 424; see also Scott, *Moral Economy of the Peasant*; Thompson, "Moral Economy of the English Crowd"; Rueda Estrada, "Campesinado Migrante").

40. Gould, *To Lead as Equals*, 29.

41. Gould, *To Lead as Equals*, 30.

42. Nash, "Devil in Bolivia's Nationalized Tin Mines"; Taussig, *Devil and Commodity Fetishism*.

43. This narrative arc tracks with the ones in perhaps the two most famous anthropological accounts of sugarcane in Latin America, Sidney Mintz's *Worker in the Cane*

and Nancy Scheper-Hughes's *Death without Weeping*. In those books, the authors recount how by the 1960s, mechanization and industrialization in Puerto Rico and Brazil led to a loss of jobs and an onset of a sense of abandonment, not to mention a renewed contemplation among workers about the role of God in their lives. Nicaraguan workers' descriptions of exertion followed by abandonment reflected what Maya Mayblin, writing about Northeast Brazil's sugarcane zone, calls "the drama of work . . . as a form of sacrifice, a veritable spillage of bodily service to others" (Mayblin, "The Way Blood Flows," 547).

44. Cooper Owens, *Medical Bondage*.

45. I was able to piece together this genealogical relationship with a few clicks of a mouse, while thirteen of the sixteen women who suffered under Sims remain unnamed. No one needs to fight to build public statues of my ancestors, as many are doing now to celebrate those women's memory, because my ancestors' names and faces are preserved on the internet. I can think of few better examples of the banality of white supremacy.

46. I wish to express my gratitude to the historian Rachel Dudley for (albeit unwittingly) provoking me to do some genealogical digging. I imagine that many of us in academia who descend from white plantation slaveholders know intuitively that we are still reaping the benefits of that institution, but at the risk of distraction, I feel compelled to state what I know in concrete terms.

47. Fortun, in *Advocacy after Bhopal*, calls this kind of meeting-in-process an "enunciatory community."

48. Li, *Will to Improve*, 12.

49. Tironi, "Hypo-interventions," 443.

50. Graeter, "Infrastructural Incorporations"; Auyero and Swistun, *Flammable*; Lora-Wainwright, *Resigned Activism*. Other plantation scholars have pointed to the ethical, economic, and political compromises that are emblematic of plantation life. "Weapons of the weak" tend to be wielded alongside a host of creative strategies for ensuring social reproduction, accessing resources, and otherwise sustaining everyday existence. For contemporary workers, tactics can entail sabotage not just of industrial farm machinery or plants, as in classic renderings of weapons of the weak, but of fellow plantation workers and satellite residents (Scott, *Weapons of the Weak*; Li and Semedi, *Plantation Life*; Scheper-Hughes, *Death without Weeping*). The work of enduring and reproducing life, then, becomes integrated into the work of reproducing the plantation itself (Besky, "Exhaustion and Endurance"; Jegathesan, *Tea and Solidarity*).

51. Fortun, *Advocacy after Bhopal*, 16.

52. Actors' roles in open systems are "continually being reconstituted through the interaction of many scales, variables, and forces" (Fortun, "Poststructuralism, Technoscience," 296). Ethnography in the mode of "open system analysis conjures and temporalizes its 'object,' both synchronically and diachronically, recognizing diverse forces of change and diverse ways change happens" (Fortun, "Figuring Out Ethnography," 169–70).

53. Hecht, *Residual Governance*, 8; Livingston, *Self-Devouring Growth*; Marya and Patel, *Inflamed*.

54. Clare, *Brilliant Imperfection*, 15 (emphasis in original). See also Shotwell, *Against Purity*; Wool, "in-Durable Sociality."

55. In their critique of the concept of planetary health, Farman and Rottenburg make clear that unlike global health, planetary health cannot be one single thing—though the name implies a deep interconnection and a singular planet (Farman and Rottenburg, "Measures of Future Health," 3).

56. Jackson, *Thin Description*, 94.

57. "Identity," as Wendy Brown notes, is created on edges, where borders and oppositions are established (Brown, *Edgework*, 60).

CHAPTER 1. GRIEVANCE, GROUND, AND GRACE

Portions of this chapter were published in Nading, "Ethnography in a Grievance."

1. CAO, "Agreement," 2.

2. Neely and Ponshunmugam, "Qualitative Approach to Examining Health Care."

3. Guevara, *Guerrilla Warfare*, 56.

4. Gobat, *Confronting the American Dream*; Quesada, "Brief History of Violence"; Walker and Wade, *Nicaragua*; Grossman, "The Nation Is Our Mother."

5. As Allewaert writes, "The entanglements that proliferated in the plantation zone disabled taxonomies distinguishing the human from the animal from the vegetable from the atmospheric, revealing an assemblage of interpenetrating forces . . . an ecology. This ecological orientation departs from an eighteenth-century political and aesthetic tradition distinguishing persons, in particular, white colonial subjects from the objects and terrains they surveyed" (Allewaert, "Swamp Sublime," 341). Her observation is resonant with Sylvia Wynter's much earlier argument that the life lived by Afro-Caribbeans, enslaved and free, on the "plot" was a political and conceptual foil to the stories told about them from the linear perspective of the plantation (Wynter, "Novel and History"; see also chapter 4).

6. Allewaert, "Swamp Sublime," 343.

7. Spillers, "Mama's Baby, Papa's Maybe"; King, "Labor of (Re)reading Plantation Landscapes"; Povinelli, *Economies of Abandonment*, 108.

8. I did not explicitly set out to do an engaged anthropological project, but collaboration, which included the sharing not only of data but also of the costs of food and fuel, became the defining feature of my research with AMBED. While the Montelimar Corporation was always aware of my presence, and I never felt threatened, there is certainly a degree of risk in this methodological choice. As Scott Knowles has pointed out, whether they are acute or slow, disasters tend to summon calls for documentary investigation, usually by various kinds of elite scientific experts. Precisely what such investigations will yield is always uncertain. They might be politically co-opted by corporations or states, they might "pave the way for legal proceedings," or they might simply "channel the anger of interest groups" (Knowles, "Learning from Disaster?," 78). The ethnographic challenge is in part to resist the urge to turn complex associations like AMBED into ciphers for fixed categories of political or social action. AMBED's willingness to independently navigate the zona was part of a set of pragmatic and ethical commitments to place. This work was also a form of what Wendy Brown, drawing on Michel Foucault, calls "local criticism," which "articulates potency and humility vis-à-vis both the complex powers producing the present and the difficult task of apprehending this present" (Brown, *Edgework*, viii).

9. Lancaster, *Thanks to God.*

10. This outcome is similar to the emergence of a "biological citizenship" in Ukraine, as described by Adriana Petryna, but in this case, what was being reasserted was an assertion of rights and visibility tuned to a corporation, rather than to a nation-state (Petryna, *Life Exposed*).

11. See McKay, *Medicine in the Meantime*; Biruk, *Cooking Data.* As Annelise Riles notes, "documents provide a ready-made ground for experimentation with how to apprehend modernity ethnographically" (Riles, *Documents*, 2). Documentation can also, as M. Murphy argues, "arrange and gather data about interventions in the world toward the possibility of making something different happen" (Murphy, *Economization of Life*, 80).

12. I draw on Elizabeth Povinelli's argument about ground, that "ancestral catastrophes are past and present; they keep arriving out of the ground of colonialism and racism rather than emerging over the horizon of liberal progress. Ancestral catastrophes ground environmental damage in the colonial sphere rather than in the biosphere; in the not-conquered earth rather than in the whole earth; in errancies rather than in ends; in waywardness rather than in war; in maneuvers, endurance, and stubbornness rather than in domination or resistance, despair, or hope" (Povinelli, *Between Gaia and Ground*, 3). I also draw on two excellent works of political anthropology, Kregg Hetherington's *Guerrilla Auditors*, which examines campesino claims on land and citizenship in a Paraguayan state that never fully considered them to be eligible for it; and Nikhil Anand's *Hydraulic City*, which shows how urban claims to a "right to the city" are always temporary, and frequently dependent on the illiberal economy of patronage and mutual aid.

13. Hetherington, *Guerrilla Auditors*; Little, *Toxic Town*; Anand, *Hydraulic City*.

14. The Sutiaba (or Sutiava) community has received too little attention in English-medium scholarship on Nicaragua (but see Gould, *To Lead as Equals*; Gould, "¡Vana Ilusión!"). The Goyena group managed to retain traditional land tenure rights in an area of western Nicaragua that is heavily dominated by mestizo landowners (Torres, "Mujeres que no se dejan"; Musset, "León/Sutiaba [Nicaragua]").

15. Gould, *To Lead as Equals*; McMichael, "Land Grab and Corporate Food"; Li, "Centering Labor in the Land Grab Debate"; Hollander, "Power Is Sweet."

16. Woods and Narlikar, "Governance and the Limits of Accountability," 576.

17. CAO, "Guide to Designing and Implementing Grievance Mechanisms" (emphasis added).

18. For more on how such evidence falters in legal and regulatory contexts, see Fortun, *Advocacy after Bhopal*; Little, *Toxic Town*; Wylie, *Fractivism.* The CAO's description of itself reflects an "instrumentalism" that dominates in international law, where the law is sometimes seen as a neutral tool for solving problems, irrespective of context (Riles, "Anthropology, Human Rights, and Legal Knowledge," 54).

19. Hedström and Ylikoski, "Causal Mechanisms in the Social Sciences"; Krieger, "Proximal, Distal, and the Politics of Causation"; Yates-Doerr, "Reworking the Social Determinants of Health"; Hansson et al., "Pathophysiological Mechanisms."

20. See, for example, Fiske, *Reckoning with Harm*; Little, "Corporate Mortality Files"; Ottinger, *Refining Expertise*; Sawyer, *Crude Chronicles.*

21. Hetherington, *Guerrilla Auditors*; Povinelli, *Economies of Abandonment.*

22. Dolan and Rajak, *Anthropology of Corporate Social Responsibility*.

23. Center for International Environmental Law, "People of León and Chinandega's Complaint," 2.

24. Center for International Environmental Law, "People of León and Chinandega's Complaint," 2.

25. Hetherington, *Guerrilla Auditors*; Kearney, *Reconceptualizing the Peasantry*; Perry, *Black Women against the Land Grab*.

26. Brooks and McClean, "Summary Report."

27. Proparco, "Loan to Support Responsible Sugar Production in Nicaragua," accessed January 13, 2024, https://www.proparco.fr/en/carte-des-projets/suganc.

28. Carruthers, "Flor de Caña Gains Fairtrade Certification." Sarah Besky, in "Agricultural Justice, Abnormal Justice," notes that by comparison to other ethical trade certifiers such as Equal Exchange, the certifier of the rum, Fair Trade USA, has taken a broader view of what kinds of economic justice projects qualify for fair trade status, permitting corporate plantations to gain the value-added label in addition to the small farmer cooperatives that had been fair trade's historic subjects, including in Nicaragua, where the fair trade movement arguably began.

29. Chavkin, "World Bank Approves Loan."

30. International Finance Corporation, "Disclosure—Ingenio Montelimar."

31. CAO, "Complaint of CFI Project 32253," 6. The complaint, originally written in Spanish, was translated into English for the CAO, but the name Asociación Montelimar Bendición de Dios was not.

32. This tendency to partition religion from science and politics runs across both activism and anthropology, perhaps particularly medical anthropology. See Boon, "Accenting Hybridity"; Whitmarsh and Roberts, "Nonsecular Medical Anthropology."

33. O'Connor, *Mystery and Manners*, 44–45.

34. O'Connor, *Mystery and Manners*, 44–45.

35. These categories, as Jackson points out, are the result of what anthropologists see as our unique ability to deconstruct the actions of those we "anthropologize." Too narrowly conceptualizing our interlocutors as "political" or "religious" actors is what Jackson calls a "quietist act." What would it mean, Jackson asks, to dwell on the question of "sincerity," to ask "how decidedly deconstructed identities continue to structure people's lives and life chances"? (Jackson, *Thin Description*, 275–77).

36. Within anthropology, much ink has been spilled in the effort to integrate what Anna Tsing, Andrew Mathews, and Nils Bubandt call "nonsecular cosmologies" into analyses of the causes and consequences of climate crisis: to refuse to reduce the lived experience of irreversible ecological and biological change to the universalizing terms already familiar to global, Western science. The challenge in doing this is that planetary change is still planetary, so any attempt to "provincialize" the Anthropocene must, as Tsing, Mathews, and Bubandt put it, "[attend] to specificity without being parochial" (Tsing, Mathews, and Bubandt, "Patchy Anthropocene," s191). Elsewhere, the medical anthropologists Ian Whitmarsh and Elizabeth Roberts have advocated a "nonsecular" approach that acknowledges the ways in which spirits, gods, demons, and other "irrational" entities persistently creep into purportedly secular and universal biomedical models

of the body and the psyche. Concepts like Marisol de la Cadena's ethnographically informed reformulation of Isabelle Stengers's "cosmopolitics," Alyssa Paredes's "in vivo experiments," Bruno Latour's inquiries into the modes of existence, and Kim Fortun and others' notion of the "quotidian Anthropocene" all point to these nontotalizing, nonsecular forms of acting in and on the environment (Whitmarsh and Roberts, "Nonsecular Medical Anthropology"; Cadena, *Earth Beings*; Stengers, "Cosmopolitical Proposal"; Paredes, "Experimental Science for the 'Bananapocalypse'"; Latour, *Inquiry into Modes of Existence*; Fortun et al., "Knowledge Infrastructure and Research Agendas").

37. Kockelman, "Grading, Gradients, Degradation, Grace," 356.

38. Haynes, "Benefit of the Doubt"; Reichman, *Broken Village*; O'Neill, *City of God*; Zigon, *"HIV Is God's Blessing."*

39. CAO, "Dispute Resolution Conclusion Report."

40. Petryna, *Life Exposed*; Nguyen, *Republic of Therapy*.

41. Wool and Livingston, "Collateral Afterworlds," 2.

42. CAO, "Agreement," 6.

43. CAO, "Agreement," 5.

44. Kirsch, *Mining Capitalism*; Welker, *Enacting the Corporation*.

45. CAO, "Agreement," 12.

46. CAO, "Agreement," 13.

47. Hetherington, *Guerrilla Auditors*, 9.

48. Shapiro, Zakariya, and Roberts, "Wary Alliance," 586.

49. Fortun, "Poststructuralism, Technoscience."

50. Fortun, "Ethnography in Late Industrialism."

51. Yusoff, "Indeterminate Subjects," 91.

52. Kockelman, *Anthropology of Intensity*.

53. Cross, "Coming of the Corporate Gift."

54. Povinelli, *Between Gaia and Ground*.

55. None of this seems particularly unusual when one looks at the dynamics of community organization in rural Latin America, where Gabriela Vargas-Centina has argued that temporary, contingent "ephemeral associations" have become much more common than the ideal-typical cooperative, political party, or stakeholder group (Vargas-Centina, "Anthropology and Cooperatives").

CHAPTER 2. ATMOSPHERIC FIXES

Portions of this chapter were published in Nading, "The Plantation as Hotspot."

1. Johnson et al., "Climate Change and the Kidney."

2. Hulme, "Better Weather?," 239; see also Choy and Zee, "Condition—Suspension"; Choy, *Ecologies of Comparison*; Ahmann and Kenner, "Breathing Late Industrialism."

3. Blanchette, *Porkopolis*; Harrison, *Pesticide Drift*; Hetherington, *Government of Beans*.

4. Masco, "End of Ends," 1108; see also Daggett, *Birth of Energy*.

5. These fixes tend to treat both workers and those who support them by doing the reproductive labor of cleaning, cooking, and maintaining homes not as people but as "bodies" (Guthman, *Wilted*, 147).

6. World Bank, "Nicaragua—Climatology."

7. Here I draw on Donna Haraway's rereading of Richard Gordon's idea of the "home-work economy," the late capitalist formation in which all labor has become feminized. As Haraway puts it, "To be feminized means to be made extremely vulnerable; able to be disassembled, reassembled, exploited as a reserve labor force; seen less as workers than as servers; subjected to time arrangements on and off the paid job that make a mockery of a limited workday; leading an existence that always borders on being obscene, out of place" (Haraway, "Cyborg Manifesto," 38). In his research on how people in the town of Puchuncaví, Chile, endure amid ongoing toxic harm, Manuel Tironi suggests that atten-tion to how reproductive work produces solidarities can widen the scope of what scholars typically understand as political (Tironi, "Hypo-interventions," 443).

8. The anthropologist Eli Elinoff and the sociologist Tyson Vaughan have called attention to the diverse ways in which planetary change is experienced and understood in situated locales, how "microscale quotidian practices and macroscale environmental changes mutually produce and influence each other" (Elinoff and Vaughan, *Disastrous Times*, 3). I first became aware of Elinoff and Vaughan's idea through its application in the Anthropocene Field Campus Project (see Fortun et al., "Knowledge Infrastructure and Research Agendas").

9. Cardenal, *Zero Hour*; Faber, "Sea of Poison"; Francis, "'Point Four Does Not Exist.'"

10. Striffler and Moberg, *Banana Wars*; Gobat, *Confronting the American Dream*.

11. Pérez-Baltodano, *Entre el Estado Conquistador*; Gould, *To Lead as Equals*.

12. Francis, "'Point Four Does Not Exist,'" 132.

13. Francis, "'Point Four Does Not Exist,'" 130.

14. Francis, "'Point Four Does Not Exist,'" 130, 132.

15. Gobat, *Confronting the American Dream*; Quesada, "Brief History of Violence."

16. Faber, "Sea of Poison."

17. Citing the key role played by militaries in the Kennedy-era development strategy, the historian Greg Grandin has called the Alliance for Progress "nation building by death squad." See Grandin, "Beyond the Four Freedoms."

18. Faber, "Sea of Poison," 32.

19. Faber, "Imperialism, Revolution, and the Ecological Crisis," 19.

20. Walker and Wade, *Nicaragua*; Gould, *To Lead as Equals*.

21. Gould, *To Lead as Equals*, 15.

22. Recounting the anticipatory climate of the 1950s, Francis quotes a headline in the Nicaraguan newspaper *La Prensa*, a fount of anti-Somoza sentiment, which mockingly celebrated the arrival of the first crop-dusting aircraft in Central America. "Not here," the headline clarified, "in Guatemala." Before pesticides became affectively associated with "the smell of Nicaragua," they were invoked as the missing piece of Somoza's promised agricultural boom (Francis, "'Point Four Does Not Exist,'" 132).

23. Faber, "Sea of Poison," 33.

24. The sociologist Douglas Murray can be credited with popularizing the treadmill concept, in part through his study of the impact of Somoza-era agricultural industrialism and his subsequent work with the revolutionary regime in the 1980s to roll back its worst environmental excesses. See Murray, *Cultivating Crisis*.

25. Faber, "Sea of Poison," 36.

26. Faber, "La Liberación del Medio Ambiente."

27. Murray, *Cultivating Crisis.*

28. Wilson, "Breaking the Chains."

29. Envío Team, "Environment."

30. Bohme, *Toxic Injustice.*

31. Boix and Bohme, "Secrecy and Justice," 155; INCAE, "INCAE nombró a Enrique Bolaños"; Machuca, "Empresa de Bolaños acusada." President Bolaños's son, Enrique Bolaños Abaunza, was the head of Monsanto Latin America from 1991 to 1995, and during the period of the Nemagon case, the elder Bolaños was in the process of bringing charges of corruption against his predecessor as president (and fellow Liberal Party member), Arnoldo Alemán. In retaliation, Alemán's backers accused the Bolaños family of profiting from the harm done to workers by the pesticide industry (Sandoval, "Politizan caso Nemagón").

32. Decreto no. 42-2006, *La Gaceta*, October 7, 2006, 133.

33. Tittor, "Changing Drivers of Oil Palm Cultivation"; Decreto no. 42-2006, *La Gaceta*, October 7, 2006, 133.

34. Deininger et al., *Rising Global Interest in Farmland*; Li, "Centering Labor in the Land Grab Debate."

35. McMichael, "Land Grab and Corporate Food," 687; Hollander, "Power Is Sweet."

36. Wesseling, "Is an Environmental Nephrotoxin the Primary Cause of CKDu," 599.

37. Daggett, *Birth of Energy*, 136–37.

38. Mintz, *Sweetness and Power.*

39. Rabinbach, *Human Motor*, 7.

40. Rabinbach, *Human Motor*, 63.

41. Here, I draw on Nicole Starosielski's argument that "[crop] growth is not simply a gift or effect of the sun, but is also mediated labor" (Starosielski, "Beyond the Sun," 15).

42. Johnson et al., "Climate Change and the Kidney."

43. Wei, "Silent Epidemic"; Hoebink, "Sugar from Nicaragua."

44. Wei, "Climate Change Is Already Killing Farm Workers"; Nading and Lowe, "Social Justice as Epidemic Control."

45. Kjellstrom et al., "Heat, Human Performance, and Occupational Health," 98.

46. Verisk Maplecroft, "Heat Stress Threatens to Cut Labor Productivity."

47. Horton, *They Leave Their Kidneys in the Fields*, 2–4.

48. Glaser et al., "Preventing Kidney Injury among Sugarcane Workers"; Hansson et al., "Pathophysiological Mechanisms."

49. Prince, "Measure of the Return on Ingenio San Antonio's Investment."

50. Sullivan, "Adelante Initiative Receives Major Funding"; Glaser et al., "Preventing Kidney Injury among Sugarcane Workers."

51. Glaser et al., "Preventing Kidney Injury among Sugarcane Workers," 3.

52. The subject of the Adelante experiments is not just the body of the worker, then, but the water-rest-shade apparatus itself. In this sense, they are excellent examples of

what Hans-Jorg Reinberger calls "experimental systems" (Reinberger, "Experimental Systems"). Reinberger's work in laboratory contexts can be extrapolated to the context of agricultural systems more broadly. For example, thermal and atmospheric experimentation formed the bedrock of modern medicine's understandings of race. The historian Lundy Braun quotes Thomas Jefferson's claim in *Notes on the State of Virginia* that one of the key differences between Black and white bodies was in "the pulmonary apparatus . . . the principal regulator of animal heat" (Braun, *Breathing Race into the Machine*, 28). A few decades later, the physician Samuel Cartwright used the spirometer to "prove" that Blacks had inferior lung capacity and to justify forced labor as the only means of "vitalizing" or oxygenating their blood (Braun, *Breathing Race into the Machine*, 28).

53. Rottenburg, "Social and Public Experiments," 425–26; Adams, *Metrics*. Adelante's work in isolated sectors of large plantations will be familiar to those who have followed global health interventions elsewhere: what Richard Rottenburg, in his work on AIDS research in sub-Saharan Africa, calls an "archipelago" of experimental sites that are territorially diffuse rather than corresponding to national or even regional borders.

54. CAO, "Dispute Resolution Conclusion Report."

55. Olson, "Ecobiopolitics of Space Biomedicine," 172.

56. Olson, "Ecobiopolitics of Space Biomedicine," 172.

57. Günel, *Spaceship in the Desert*, 10.

58. WE-Adelante Research Team, "Adelante Initiative," 3.

59. Hecht, "Interscalar Vehicles," 130–31.

60. Hecht, "Interscalar Vehicles," 131.

61. Pacheco-Zenteno et al., "Prevention of Occupational Heat Stress," 7.

62. Prince, "Measure of the Return on Ingenio San Antonio's Investment," 2.

63. Scott-Smith, "Beyond the Boxes"; Collier et al., "Preface"; Redfield, "Bioexpectations."

64. Pacheco-Zenteno et al., "Prevention of Occupational Heat Stress," 7. As one manager told the researchers in this study, "We say here that the guys are like kids that you have to be telling every day: 'Hey, put the clothes in the laundry basket!' 'Hey, brush your teeth!' 'Hey, put your shoes on!'"

65. Murphy, *Economization of Life*, 53.

66. Wynter, "Unsettling the Coloniality of Being," 329. Daggett draws on Wynter's work to show how notions of Western (white) racial superiority were validated energetically, through the cultivation of "a superior work ethic, imbued with an energetic disposition that sought efficiency and productivity above all other measures of value" (Daggett, *Birth of Energy*, 135).

67. King, "Labor of (Re)reading Plantation Landscapes."

68. Appel, "Walls and White Elephants," 442.

69. Again, see Wesseling, "Is an Environmental Nephrotoxin the Primary Cause of CKDu."

70. Campese, "Con: Mesoamerican Nephropathy," 605.

71. Guevara Jerez, "Thirsty Country with Lots of Water."

72. Herrera, "How Much Longer."

73. Elinoff and Vaughan, *Disastrous Times*.

74. This is a point reflected in Nari Senanayake's research on CKDnt in Sri Lanka, where "diagnosis and dialysis divert household labour from activities that secure livelihoods to unpaid care work" (Senanayake, "'We Are the Living Dead,'" 1976).

75. Adams, *Glyphosate and the Swirl*.

76. Keck, *Avian Reservoirs*; Murphy, "Chemical Infrastructures"; Spackman, "In Smell's Shadow."

77. Nading, "Local Biologies, Leaky Things."

78. The application of bleach was less a technical fix than what Tironi calls a "hypo-intervention," a small, individually inconsequential action that "grants an ecological emplacement crucial for those who have to persevere in toxic environments" (Tironi, "Hypo-interventions," 450). See also Kenner, *Breathtaking*; Shapiro, "Attuning to the Chemosphere."

79. Tironi, "Hypo-interventions," 450.

80. Duclos and Criado, "Care in Trouble"; Murphy, "Unsettling Care."

CHAPTER 3. RENAL ENVIRONMENTS

1. Mishra, "Gender and Sanitation"; Wells and Whiteford, "Medical Anthropology of Water and Sanitation"; Morales, Harris, and Oberg, "Citizenshit."

2. Lamoreaux, "What If the Environment Is a Person?" A reassessment of human wastes as relational and lively has been ongoing for some time in discussions of the fecal microbiome. The ideal stool is a more-than-human community. To think of it as just waste would be both incorrect and dangerous, or so a veritable cascade of recent scientific and social research has claimed. Healthy stools are teeming with microbial life, and the presence of a healthy community of microbiota in the digestive tract has become a proxy for a healthy human body and a healthy environment (see Lorimer, *Probiotic Planet*; Benezra, *Gut Anthro*; Benezra, DeStefano, and Gordon, "Anthropology of Microbes").

3. Wesseling et al., "Chronic Kidney Disease"; Zelaya, "Causas de la Enfermedad Renal Crónica."

4. Brooks, "Final Scoping Study Report," 144; Haber, "Pisse Prophecy." When you think about it, it shouldn't be too surprising to hear that urination was such a key element in sugarcane labor relations. Urinalysis is fully baked into human resource management, especially in heavy industry. In the United States, if you have ever worked in a factory, driven a truck, or operated machinery, you have likely been asked to submit a urine sample before starting your job, and probably again periodically or randomly thereafter. That sample would have been scanned for the residues of certain kinds of substances (cocaine, cannabis, opiates). Even if you had been doing a good job, your employer might use the presence of these "toxins" in your urine as a justification for termination. This kind of analysis turns urine into a material proxy for legal risk, industrial efficiency, and a racial and class hierarchy masked as a uniform and neutral code of moral behavior. White-collar workers (stockbrokers, accountants, college professors) are not usually asked to have their urine sampled. They are free to snort, smoke, slam, and flush.

5. Little, "Corporate Mortality Files"; see also Ottinger, "Refining Expertise"; Balshem, *Cancer in the Community*.

6. CAO, "Complaint of CFI Project 32253," 1.

7. Jamie Cross's examination of how dust became an object of concern for management, occupational physicians, and workers illustrates the complex networks of knowledge that must be aligned in order for occupational exposure to be actionable. Cross ("Occupational Health, Risk and Science"), Linda Nash (*Inescapable Ecologies*), Lochlann Jain (*Injury*), and Dvera Saxton (*Devil's Fruit*) have each examined how industrial farmworkers in the United States succeeded in making exposure a legally actionable category. And Marx, in his analysis of the working day in *Capital*, noted that both early factory workers and capitalists realized the limits of both human endurance and machinery. Marx famously called factory machinery "dead labor, that, vampire-like, only lives by sucking living labour, and lives the more, the more labour it sucks" (Marx, *Capital*, 342). If you're the manager of a factory or a plantation, you end up being very concerned with the sleep habits, sexual appetites, and, of course, food intake of your workers (see Besky, "Fixity"; Daggett, *Birth of Energy*). In the colonial plantation economy of Latin America and the Caribbean, sugar—what Sidney Mintz (*Sweetness and Power*) called a "proletarian hunger-killer"—became a mechanism for doing this. Sugar carried cheap calories, but it also carried a latent contradiction. The acceleration of capitalist accumulation (and sugar consumption) over the decades of the nineteenth and the twentieth century fueled the slow-moving metabolic epidemics of diabetes and obesity (Moran-Thomas, *Traveling with Sugar*).

8. Povinelli, *Between Gaia and Ground*, 127.

9. Povinelli, *Between Gaia and Ground*, 127.

10. By making the fragility of watercourses a matter of concern, and by insisting that the Montelimar Corporation should also think of them that way, AMBED enacted a form of politics in which relations would be premised on a meeting between different forms of weakness, rather than strength versus weakness (see Livingston, *Debility*.)

11. Scaramelli, in work on wetlands in Turkey, outlines a "moral ecology of infrastructure," in which infrastructure and ecology become inseparable, and in which the "moral" points to "people's notions of just relations between people, land, water, nonhuman animals, plants, buildings, technologies, and infrastructures" (Scaramelli, "Delta Is Dead," 389). As Julie Livingston has suggested, even heavily engineered landscapes like that of Montelimar might be usefully understood as "animated ecologies," infrastructures that are also environments. "In an animated ecology," Livingston writes, "water has value in how it condenses (literally) the success or failure of moral relationships, of political vision, of collective self-agreement, however hierarchical the collective" (Livingston, *Self-Devouring Growth*, 33).

12. The issue at the heart of this grievance was laundry, but it was also one of what Murphy calls "distributed reproduction," "the extensive sense of existing over time that stretches beyond bodies to include the uneven relations and infrastructures that shape what forms of life are supported to persist, thrive, and alter, and what forms of life are destroyed, injured, and constrained" (Murphy, *Economization of Life*, 141–42). For an example of how plantations might be reframed as tools for the management of reproduction in this way, see Besky, "Plantation's Outsides."

13. Nading, *Mosquito Trails*; Nading, "Local Biologies, Leaky Things."

14. Laundry was an act of reproduction not in a minimalist sense but in a fully humanizing one. This kind of reproductive labor and the capacity for it have been extracted from Black women in particular since the dawn of the transatlantic slave-plantation system. Women's capacity for both biological and social care became, as Hortense Spillers and others have noted, a fungible resource in itself (Spillers, "Mama's Baby, Papa's Maybe"; Hartman, *Scenes of Subjection*; McKittrick, *Demonic Grounds*).

15. Livingston, *Self-Devouring Growth*; Povinelli, *Between Gaia and Ground*.

16. For a keen analysis of the shortcomings of this logic of equivalences, see Fabiana Li's work on corporate responsibility in Andean mining contexts (Li, *Unearthing Conflict*) or Ashley Carse's study of the biopolitics of environmental mitigation in infrastructure development projects in the United States (Carse, "Ecobiopolitics of Environmental Mitigation"). And again, one thinks in this case of Yusoff's identification of the failures of the "recuperative logic" of late capitalism (Yusoff, "Indeterminate Subjects").

17. As Fortun argues, double binds are not deterministic. Rather, "they set up search spaces that people must wander within. Ethnographic observation of these wanderings (and processes of figuring out workable even if imperfect solutions) often yields material that can operate as cultural critique" (Fortun, "Figuring Out Ethnography," 178).

18. Tironi, "Hypo-interventions."

19. Li, *Unearthing Conflict*, 21–22.

20. Li, *Unearthing Conflict*, 171.

21. Water politics are a lively element of Nicaraguan public intellectual life. See, for example, Herrera, "How Much Longer"; Elizondo, "State Is Mainly Responsible."

22. Livingston, *Self-Devouring Growth*, 21.

23. Scaramelli, "Delta Is Dead."

24. Here, it helps to think of the CDKnt epidemic, then, not as a crisis of work but as what Cynthia Morinville and Nicole Van Lier call "a crisis of life-making" (Morinville and Van Lier, "On Nature, Degradation, and Life-Making").

25. Povinelli, *Between Gaia and Ground*.

26. To give two classic examples, it is one that Don Taso, the protagonist of Sidney Mintz's *Worker in the Cane*, experienced almost verbatim, and one that formed the backstory of Nancy Scheper-Hughes's *Death without Weeping*.

27. Vaughn, "Political Economy of Regions," 108.

28. White, *Organic Machine*, 58.

29. Morgan, *American Beaver and His Works*; Feeley-Harnik ("Ethnography of Creation") notes how Lewis Henry Morgan's beaver work directly informed his understandings of kinship.

30. This is a mantra of the beaver conservation world. See, for example, Beaver Solutions, "Beaver Facts." Thanks to Jamie Lorimer for bringing this to my attention.

31. Weston, *Animate Planet*, 33. Struggles over water—both its availability and its contents—in Nicaragua's sugarcane zone reflect the ways in which, as Veena Das and Clara Han put it, the fragility of the natural and the fragility of the social are absorbed into one another (Das and Han, "Introduction," 4).

32. Solomon, *Metabolic Living*.

33. Povinelli, *Between Gaia and Ground*, 51.

34. Tironi, "Hypo-interventions."

CHAPTER 4. TOXIC MEDIATION

1. Griffin, "Protest Practice"; Hetherington, *Government of Beans*; Guthman, *Wilted*. For more on the ways that plants underwrite territorial claims, see Besky and Padwe, "Placing Plants in Territory."

2. Hetherington, *Government of Beans*, 61.

3. Theorists of language and politics have argued the discourse of crisis—whether applied to the prevalence of obesity in low-income children, to the warming of the planet, or to financial markets—tends to make chronic conditions appear as if they are sudden, singular events. In the near term, talk of crisis can help marshal resources and attention, but in the long term, talk of crisis can occlude our appreciation of slower forms of violence. Prominent critics of crisis talk Lauren Berlant ("Cruel Optimism") and Joe Masco ("Crisis in Crisis") engage the blended questions of health, embodiment, and the environment. Though they each heavily focus on the discourse of crisis in North America, and mostly the United States, both authors seem to share with scholars more focused on the Global South (e.g., Nixon, *Slow Violence*; Barrios, "What Does Catastrophe Reveal") a concern that the constant refrain of crisis precludes attention to ordinary, quotidian forms of violence.

4. The key contribution here has been to rethink exposure as more than just a technically measurable event and to see it as something ongoing. The essays in Mitman et al.'s *Landscapes of Exposure* illustrate this approach quite well, as do key works on pesticide and petrochemical harm by Liboiron (*Pollution Is Colonialism*); Murphy ("Chemical Infrastructures"; *Sick Building Syndrome*); Nash (*Inescapable Ecologies*); Sawyer (*Small Matter of Suing Chevron*); Langston (*Toxic Bodies*); and Harrison (*Pesticide Drift*).

5. Masco, "Optics of Exposure"; see also Alaimo, *Exposed*.

6. Kohn, *How Forests Think*; Goldstein and Hall, "Mass Hysteria in Le Roy, New York"; Silver, "Tear Gas in Orbit."

7. As Hanks explains, drawing on the work of Charles Sanders Peirce, "an indexical sign stands in a relation of 'dynamical coexistence' with its object. In other words, the indexical and what it stands for are in a sense copresent in the context of utterance" (Hanks, "Indexicality," 124).

8. Kohn, "Runa Realism," 187.

9. Alaimo, *Bodily Natures*, 115.

10. Here, I am adapting linguistic anthropologist Constantine Nakassis's observation that indexical signs are ambivalent: they offer both direct experience of the world and a mediated representation of the world. See Nakassis, "Indexicality's Ambivalent Ground."

11. Tousignant, *Edges of Exposure*.

12. Forensic Architecture, "Herbicidal Warfare in Gaza."

13. I would call toxic mediation a subgenre of what Mel Chen (*Animacies*, 196) calls "toxic worlding." Toxicity is one of those concepts that, following Povinelli, "aren't merely situated in the social world. They are the social world" (Povinelli, *Between Gaia*

and Ground, 129). For more on worlding toxic landscapes, see Nading, "Living in a Toxic World."

14. Chen, *Animacies*, 196.

15. Tousignant, *Edges of Exposure*, 4.

16. Moyer and Nguyen, "Edgework in Medical Anthropology." Thanks to Kregg Hetherington for pointing this out.

17. Wesseling, Corriols, and Bravo, "Acute Pesticide Poisoning"; Corriols, "Pesticide Poisoning in Nicaragua"; Wesseling et al., "Hazardous Pesticides in Central America." The problem is, of course, not unique to Nicaragua's sugarcane zone (see Lyons, *Vital Decomposition*; Hetherington, "Beans before the Law").

18. Glaser and Lopez, *Banana Land;* Gardner, "The Filmmaker Who Became a Legal Spy." Nicaraguan banana workers were exposed to the nematicide Nemagon, or dibromochloropropane (DBCP); see chapter 2.

19. La Isla Network, "About Us," accessed January 7, 2022, https://laislanetwork.org /about-us/.

20. Hodal, "Mystery Epidemic."

21. La Isla Network, "About CKDu," accessed January 17, 2022, https://laislanetwork .org/about-ckdu/.

22. Benton, "Risky Business"; see also Prince, "Diseased Body and the Global Subject."

23. My use of the term *genre* is quite deliberate. A genre is a classificatory type, akin to a biological taxon or a chemical signature. If you are studying an animal or a plant, you are interested not in one particular individual (though its movements and behavior may be illuminating) but in the type. As the historian Luise White explains, "It is the pattern of the tale, not the circumstances of the telling, that makes a story recognizable as belonging to a genre" (White, *Speaking with Vampires*, 6).

24. Benjamin, *Race after Technology*, 2.

25. Canon Europe, "'They Die within Six to 24 Months.'"

26. Kashi, *Curse of the Black Gold*. For examples, see work by Gabrielle Hecht (*Residual Governance*), Jason de León (*Land of Open Graves*), Philippe Bourgois and Jeff Schoenberg (*Righteous Dopefiend*), and Danny Hoffman (*Monrovia Modern*).

27. De León, "The Indecisive Moment"; Moyer and Nguyen, "(Re)framing and the (Medical) Anthropological Lens."

28. Fortun and Fortun, "Scientific Imaginaries and Ethical Plateaus."

29. Hanks, "Indexicality"; Kohn, *How Forests Think*.

30. In its many forms, imaginative testimony has the capacity to make visible what Nixon (*Slow Violence*, 13–14) calls "slow violence," the accretive harm done by extractive industry, militarism, colonialism, and agriculture. In her writing on nuclear toxicity in North America, the geographer Shiloh Krupar calls this invitation to apprehension "hotspotting," by which she means "identifying, making visible, and keeping open the possibility that more can be identified" (Krupar, *Hot Spotter's Report*, 281; see also Shapiro, Zakariya, and Roberts, "Wary Alliance").

31. Murphy, "Chemical Infrastructures"; Lyons, *Vital Decomposition*.

32. This is despite the known risks chemicals like glyphosate pose to renal health (Seneff and Orlando, "Is Glyphosate a Key Factor"; see also Guthman, *Wilted*, 91; Romero et al., "Chemical Geographies").

33. As I have discussed elsewhere (Nading, "Ethnography in a Grievance"), what tran-spired in my collaboration with AMBED was a deliberate and self-aware construction of a "context" for the epidemic. Context is not something that ethnography reveals but that it helps to create. This is an insight that Jackson (*Thin Description*; "Ethnographic Filmflam") has also unpacked in his visual documentary work both in Harlem and with the African Hebrew Israelites of Jerusalem. Jackson draws on Faye Ginsburg's ("Culture/ Media") observation that the democratization of digital film and photo technology has created a "parallax effect," whereby the visual productions of anthropologists and others spark collaborative conversation. The methodological difference in my case is that I am not a filmmaker and never set out to do anything other than supplement field notes with photos and videos.

34. Chemicals, as many critical scholars have noted, have become useful devices for marking time, but since their effects can often be slow, they invite apprehension of time in unexpected ways (Boudia and Jas, *Powerless Science?*; Murphy, "Chemical Infrastructures").

35. Peters, *Marvelous Clouds*, 2.

36. Peters, *Marvelous Clouds*, 11.

37. Plantation agriculture can, in this sense, be considered a form of aerial occupation (Li and Semedi, *Plantation Life*). Again, Weizman's work on the role of aircraft and chemicals in the Israeli occupation of Palestinian territory is pertinent. In *Hollow Land*, he has shown how contemporary military and economic power operates in a three-dimensional, volumetric manner, and sugarcane production operates in a similar fashion (see Nading, "Filtration").

38. Rosenberg, "What Is an Epidemic?," 3.

39. As Bishnupriya Ghosh has written, "The epidemic episteme reconfigures life as form, process, and relation, and, perhaps most crucially, as mediation. . . . To analyze epidemic media is to grapple with how we capture, manipulate, and sometimes fabricate life at its most exigent" (Ghosh, *Virus Touch*, 8).

40. Steingraber, *Living Downstream*.

41. Wylie, *Fractivism*; Pulido, "Flint, Environmental Racism"; Brown, Morello-Frosch, and Zavestoski, *Contested Illnesses*.

42. Rosenberg, "What Is an Epidemic?" A classic example is Phil Brown's account of a cancer cluster in Woburn, Massachusetts (Brown, "Popular Epidemiology and Toxic Waste").

43. Moments in toxic narratives like the dog's death are what Elizabeth Povinelli (*Economies of Abandonment*) might call "quasi-events," or what Sylvia Wynter ("Novel and History") might call "adjuncts" to epidemic narratives (see also Shapiro, "Attuning to the Chemosphere").

44. Jackson, *Thin Description*. Importantly, they are also not what Murphy ("Alterlife and Decolonial Chemical Relations," 496) calls "body centric damage narratives," in that they are less apt to invite sympathy or pity on the part of outside observers (see Tuck, "Suspending Damage"). Thinness of description, like the kind found in fragmentary stories and pixelated images, as Benjamin explains, does not speak to "an analytic *failure*, but an acceptance of *fragility*" (Benjamin, *Race after Technology*, 46).

45. The notion that "science" (seen here as the search for causal drivers) operates in a frame called "context" is worth contesting. For example, ecosocial epidemiologists have long argued that context is far from an external frame. As Nancy Krieger and George Davey Smith put it, "People literally embody, biologically, their societal and ecological context" (Krieger and Davey Smith, "Tale Wagged by the DAG," 1802).

46. I take this rendering of the relationship between figure and ground from Fortun ("Figuring Out Ethnography"), who suggests that anthropology is partly distinguished by its acknowledgment that people do not just work within context but actively construct it.

47. The hype around this has been critiqued by medical anthropologists, including me (Nading, *Mosquito Trails*). As Susan Erikson ("Cell Phones ≠ Self") has noted, much of the promise of digital media has been located in its potential as a source of "big data" about individual users. The problem with the expectation that cell phone data, for example, might say something about the spread of an epidemic is that it overestimates the extent to which individual people are attached, figuratively and materially, to individual phones. Erikson found that cell phone use in Sierra Leone was much more embedded in extraindividual networks of social and economic exchange than models produced by computational epidemiologists predicted. This limited the predictive value of cell phone data for tracking the epidemic's trajectory.

48. White, *Speaking with Vampires*, 8.

49. Here, I draw on the work of Yarimar Bonilla and Jonathan Rosa, who suggest that statements made on social media possess an "interdiscursive capacity to lasso accompanying texts and their indexical meanings as part of a frame" (Bonilla and Rosa, "#Ferguson," 6).

50. Bonilla and Rosa, "#Ferguson," 7.

51. Thomas, "Time and the Otherwise."

52. White, "'They Could Make Their Victims Dull.'"

53. Thomas, "Time and the Otherwise."

54. Wolf, "Specific Aspects of Plantation Systems."

55. Wynter, "Novel and History."

56. Wynter, "Novel and History." For Wynter, what is problematic about these dominant narratives is that enslaved persons may not be portrayed as "characters" at all. Such narratives call their humanity into question.

57. Thomas, "Time and the Otherwise," 188.

58. Stacey Langwick has found a similar role for toxicity in contemporary Tanzania, where toxicity is both "a condition of modern life and the substance of ethical engagement" (Langwick, "Politics of Habitability," 420).

59. See, for example, Shapiro, "Attuning to the Chemosphere."

60. Shapiro, Zakariya, and Roberts, "Wary Alliance," 587–88.

61. To me, at least, they seemed like perfect examples of "little development devices" or "humanitarian goods" (see Collier et al., "Preface").

Portions of this chapter were published in Nading, "Disposability, Social Security, and the Facts of Work in Nicaragua's Sugarcane Zone."

1. Fisher and Nading, "End of the Cooperative Model."

2. As Gould explains, Nicaraguans in the sugarcane zone sometimes identify as Indigenous, or as day laborers, or as farmers, but they use the term *campesino* "to describe their common condition of residence in small, poverty-stricken villages" (Gould, *To Lead as Equals*, 7).

3. Wells, *Strawberry Fields*; Holmes, *Fresh Fruit, Broken Bodies*; Horton, *They Leave Their Kidneys in the Fields*.

4. Guthman, *Wilted*, 147.

5. Horton, *They Leave Their Kidneys in the Fields*; Mulligan and Castañeda, *Unequal Coverage*.

6. Ruiz Arias quotes Bolívar as saying, "The most perfect system of government is that which produces the greatest amount of happiness possible, the greatest amount of political stability and the greatest amount of social security" (Ruiz Arias, "On Social Security").

7. Mauss, *The Gift*, 86; Douglas, "Foreword," xiii. The capacity of social insurance to create solidarity is weak, according to Douglas, and this observation is borne out in more recent anthropological studies of health insurance (see, e.g., Mulligan, *Unmanageable Care*; Mulligan and Castañeda, *Unequal Coverage*).

8. Graeber, "Dead Zones of the Imagination"; Gupta, *Red Tape*; Biehl, "Judicialization of Biopolitics"; Abadía-Barrero, "Neoliberal Justice."

9. Scott, *Moral Economy of the Peasant*; Edelman, "Bringing the Moral Economy Back In"; Wolford, *This Land Is Ours Now*; Winchell, *After Servitude*.

10. Welker, *Enacting the Corporation*.

11. Queiroz and Vanderstraeten, "Unintended Consequences," 129.

12. Francis, "'Point Four Does Not Exist'"; Gould, *To Lead as Equals*; Faber, "La Liberación del Medio Ambiente."

13. The Nicaraguan historian Andrés Pérez-Baltodano (*Entre el Estado Conquistador*) identifies the push to turn campesinos into workers as rooted in creole elites' long-standing anxieties about the country's failure to emulate a European model of liberal development. See also Silva, "History of the Nicaraguan Social Security Institute."

14. Gould, *To Lead as Equals*, 15.

15. Ripoll, "Moral Economy of Labour and Resistance"; Walker and Wade, *Nicaragua*. As Ruiz Arias explains, "Between 1957 and 1979, social security was geographically very restricted and functionally limited, based essentially on labor relations. It existed in Managua; San Rafael del Sur and Tipitapa [all areas where Somoza's sugar operations were located]; in León, only in the city; and in Chinandega only in the urban area, the municipalities of Chichigalpa, around the San Antonio sugar refinery, and Puerto Corinto. It also existed in the mining triangle municipalities of Siuna, Bonanza and Rosita. Nowhere else. Due to its limited form, barely 120,000 people were covered (only 10% of them women) and the insurance only covered 9,000 pensions" (Ruiz Arias, "On Social Security").

16. Those who started their careers in the cane as cabras recognized work in the cane as an activity that was entangled in what the feminist geographer J. K. Gibson-Graham calls a "diverse economy" (Gibson-Graham, *End of Capitalism*). Gibson-Graham's notion of the diverse economy adds complexity to the familiar anthropological dyad of "embedded" reciprocity and "disembedded" capital accumulation (see Polanyi, *Great Transformation*).

17. This framing of entanglement and autonomy comes in part from Povinelli's work on liberalism, and in part from the debates in peasant studies about commoditization and resistance to it (Povinelli, *Economies of Abandonment*; Edelman, "Bringing the Moral Economy Back In"; Scott, *Moral Economy of the Peasant*). In the early in the days of the CKDnt epidemic, there was a lot of attention to the problem of "child labor" and what it might have to do with early-onset kidney disease, but such discussion has since receded. The cabra system is less evident today but has not gone away, but the linkage between children working in fields and CKDnt has not been established, partly because the question of child labor itself occludes the broader health concern at hand.

18. Walker and Wade, *Nicaragua*; Pérez-Baltodano, *Entre el Estado Conquistador*.

19. Swezey and Faber, "Disarticulated Accumulation."

20. Ruiz Arias, "On Social Security."

21. Ripoll, "Moral Economy of Labour and Resistance," 1558; Wheelock, *Imperialismo y dictadura*; Deere, Marchetti, and Reinhardt, "Peasantry and the Development of Sandinista Agrarian Policy."

22. Ruiz Arias, "On Social Security."

23. Ripoll, "Moral Economy of Labour and Resistance," 1559.

24. Faber, "La Liberación del Medio Ambiente."

25. Houtart, "Los Trabajadores de la Caña Piensan Así."

26. *La Prensa*, "Indemnizan a excañeros."

27. Ruiz Arias, "On Social Security."

28. Queiroz and Vanderstraeten, "Unintended Consequences."

29. Ballestero, *Future History of Water*; Strathern, *Property, Substance, and Effect*.

30. As Anna Tsing has argued, plantation economies also depend on the condensation and simplification of life, including exchange relationships (Tsing, *Mushroom at the End of the World*).

31. Gupta, *Red Tape*; Graeber, "Dead Zones of the Imagination."

32. Jain, *Injury*.

33. Ballestero, *Future History of Water*. I thank James Slotta for pushing me to consider this point.

34. Jain, *Injury*; Cross, "Occupational Health, Risk and Science"; Nash, *Inescapable Ecologies*.

35. Ruiz Arias, "On Social Security."

36. International Monetary Fund, "Nicaragua."

37. Envío Team, "Three Economic Storm Clouds"; Envío Team, "April 2018."

38. Klein, Cuesta, and Chagalj, "Nicaragua Protest Crisis"; Cruz-Feliciano, "Whither Nicaragua"; Martí i Puig and Serra, "Nicaragua"; Bran Aragón and Goett, "¡Matria Libre y Vivir!"; Goett, "Beyond Left and Right"; Chamorro and Yang, "Movilización social y tácticas de control"; Buben et al., "Nicaragua en 2020."

39. Gobierno de Nicaragua, ley no. 815; INSS, "Seguro de Riesgos Profesionales," accessed January 13, 2024, https://inss-princ.inss.gob.ni/index.php/sergurosinss-2/8-seguro-de-riesgos-profesionales-rp.

40. Ruiz Arias, "On Social Security."

41. Biehl, "Juridical Hospital."

42. Strathern, *Property, Substance, and Effect.*

43. Alaimo, *Bodily Natures,* 31; Horton, *They Leave Their Kidneys in the Fields.*

44. Crowley-Matoka and Hamdy, "Gendering the Gift of Life."

45. International Monetary Fund, "Nicaragua."

46. Graeber, "Dead Zones of the Imagination," 111; see also Gupta, *Red Tape;* Mathews, *Instituting Nature.*

47. Graeber, "Dead Zones of the Imagination," 115.

48. McKittrick, "Plantation Futures"; King, "The Labor of (Re)reading Plantation Landscapes"; Li and Semedi, *Plantation Life.* This core insight from plantation studies is worth placing alongside Graeber's ideas about violence. Consider the status of diagnostic figures like eGFR and creatinine counts. What people like Doña Cynthia seemed to be saying is that these numbers were as much a product of plantation production as was sugarcane itself. The Hungarian philosopher Georg Luckacs used the term *reification* to describe the process whereby the world under commodity capitalism appears to look like a collection of discrete bounded things. He understood commodity capitalism to be the achievement of a certain state of affairs, in which "a relation between people takes on the character of a thing and thus acquires a 'phantom objectivity,' an autonomy that seems so strictly rational and all-embracing as to conceal every trace of its fundamental nature: the relation between people" (quoted in Taussig, "Reification and the Consciousness of the Patient"). Michael Taussig extends Lukacs's thesis to argue that medical diagnoses, too, were possessed of this phantom objectivity. The diagnosis of a disease, or the reduction of bodily conditions to diagnostic numbers, says nothing about the (violent) social relations that caused those conditions.

49. Jain, "Injury Fields," 154.

50. Widger, "Anti-hesitation."

51. This makes CKDnt similar to other ontologically indeterminate occupational conditions, particularly sick building syndrome (see Murphy, *Sick Building Syndrome*).

52. Graeber, "Dead Zones of the Imagination." In her reading of Sarah Besky's Indian tea plantation research, Guthman (*Wilted,* 210n22) uses the term "social security" to describe workers' sense of attachment to plantations, and she argues that California farmworkers, like Indian tea workers, are existentially invested in the well-being of the monocultures they help produce.

53. Tsing, *Mushroom at the End of the World.*

54. Li and Semedi, *Plantation Life.*

55. Guthman, *Wilted;* Horton, *They Leave Their Kidneys in the Fields;* Mitchell, *They Saved the Crops;* Wells, *Strawberry Fields.*

56. Fortun, "Ethnography in Late Industrialism."

57. Whitmarsh and Roberts, "Nonsecular Medical Anthropology"; Roberts, "What Gets Inside."

CHAPTER 6. PLANTATION PATIENTHOOD

1. Hamdy, "When the State and Your Kidneys Fail"; Moran-Thomas, *Traveling with Sugar*; Crowley-Matoka, *Domesticating Organ Transplant*; Solomon, *Metabolic Living*.

2. Rabinow, *Essays*. For a discussion of biosociality and treatment regimes in the context of HIV/AIDS, see Nguyen, *Republic of Therapy*; Marsland, "(Bio)sociality and HIV in Tanzania."

3. Kline, "Life, Death, and Dialysis"; Melo, "Stratified Access"; Moran-Thomas, *Traveling with Sugar*.

4. To tell the story of plantation patienthood is to explore how plantations and the people whose labor they extract work through what Michelle Murphy calls "an entrapment in and a response to each other's life supports and conditions" (Murphy, "Alterlife," 498).

5. Kaufman, *Ordinary Medicine*.

6. Hunt et al., "Corporate Logic in Clinical Care"; Little, "Corporate Mortality Files."

7. Here, again, Guthman's thoughts on the propensity of monocultures for "iatrogenic harm" are salient (Guthman, *Wilted*).

8. For a similar case of patient-driven etiological theories around kidney disease, see Hamdy, "When the State and Your Kidneys Fail."

9. Hetherington, *Government of Beans*.

10. Mbembe, "Necropolitics," 39.

11. Tsing, "On Nonscalability"; Spillers, "Mama's Baby, Papa's Maybe"; Scheper-Hughes, *Death without Weeping*.

12. King, "The Labor of (Re)reading Plantation Landscapes."

13. Marshall, "Political Life of Fungibility"; Hartman, *Scenes of Subjection*.

14. Mbembe, "Necropolitics," 21. In *Death without Weeping*, Nancy Scheper-Hughes portrayed the environs of industrial sugar plantations, long after the formal end of slavery, as a place where life was so exhausting that grief met its limits. In some cases, for a mother to mourn the loss of her baby became illogical. Life on plantations, in Scheper-Hughes's telling, was too cheap to lament.

15. Whyte et al., "Therapeutic Clientship."

16. Scott, *Moral Economy of the Peasant*, 174; Thompson, "Moral Economy of the English Crowd"; Winchell, "Economies of Obligation."

17. As Tania Li argues based on her observations of changing plantation labor patterns in Indonesia, appeals to "freedom" by workers can be understandable attempts to get out from under the yoke of hierarchical systems of patronage, yet "ineffective labor laws and weak worker mobilization enable employers to avoid the costs of sustaining and reproducing workers daily or intergenerationally. Employers can buy labor power at will, treating it as a commodity like any other. Employers, in short, are too free" (Li, "Price of Un/Freedom," 246).

18. Solomon, "Living on Borrowed Breath," 116.

19. Solomon, "Living on Borrowed Breath," 116.

20. Jain, "Living in Prognosis," 90.

21. As Amy Moran-Thomas advises, adapting the work of Georges Canguilhem, a disease is nothing more than the material limit of one's tolerance for "the inconsistencies of the environment" (Moran-Thomas, *Traveling with Sugar*, 91).

22. For an analysis of how "patience" is leveraged politically in Latin America, see Auyero, *Patients of the State*.

23. Biehl, "Juridical Hospital," 265–66.

24. Li and Semedi, *Plantation Life*, 4.

25. This phrase comes from a lyric by the songwriter Townes Van Zandt. His song "Waitin' Around to Die" tells the story of a character who spends a lifetime running from abuse, the law, and bad relationships because, as the refrain goes, "it's easier than just waitin' around to die." The song ends on what looks like a resigned note:

> I got me a friend at last.
> He don't drink or steal or cheat or lie.
> His name's Codeine.
> He's the nicest thing I've seen.
> Together we're gonna wait around and die.

The song is about addiction, maybe, but I think it's also about a kind of chosen endurance. Codeine is a palliative not just for bodily aches but for emotional weariness. I hear the song as an autobiographical eulogy, an expression of grief rather than of nihilism.

26. Russ, Shim, and Kaufman, "Is There Life on Dialysis?," 299 (emphasis in original).

27. For more on patient movements for dialysis access, see Moran-Thomas, *Traveling with Sugar*.

28. Biehl, *Will to Live*; Nguyen, *Republic of Therapy*.

29. Jain, "Living in Prognosis."

30. Allewaert, "Swamp Sublime," 343.

31. Sharpe, *In the Wake*; Hartman, *Scenes of Subjection*; Lennon, "Postcarbon Amnesia."

32. Povinelli, *Economies of Abandonment*, 125–29. For Povinelli, endurance should not be interpreted as the opposite of exhaustion. Endurance is neither "a means of avoiding the nature of the given world," nor a striving to overcome its generalized decay, nor, still, a means of returning that world to some state of normalcy. See also Besky, "Exhaustion and Endurance."

33. Winchell, "Economies of Obligation," 163.

34. Rajak, *In Good Company*; Cross, *Dream Zones*; Welker, *Enacting the Corporation*; Li, *Unearthing Conflict*.

35. Russ, Shim, and Kaufman, "The Value of 'Life at Any Cost'"; Kaufman, *Ordinary Medicine*.

36. Nguyen, *Republic of Therapy*; Whitmarsh, "Medical Schismogenics"; Farmer, "Consumption of the Poor"; see also Berlant, "Cruel Optimism."

37. Hartman, *Scenes of Subjection*.

38. Senanayake, "'We Are the Living Dead.'"

39. In this way, they wrestled with what Wool and Livingston call "the uncertain temporalities and patterns . . . created by liberal yearning toward the good life" (Wool and Livingston, "Collateral Afterworlds," 7).

40. Lancaster, *Life Is Hard*.

41. Nixon, *Slow Violence*.

42. Mbembe, "Necropolitics," 22. See also Wynter, "Novel and History"; Hartman, *Scenes of Subjection*.

43. Wynter, "Unsettling the Coloniality of Being."

CONCLUSION

1. Sorensen and Garcia-Trabanino, "New Era of Climate Medicine."

2. Guthman, *Wilted*, 210n22; Faber, "Sea of Poison"; Corriols, "Pesticide Poisoning in Nicaragua"; Dore, *Myths of Modernity*; Gould, *To Lead as Equals*.

3. Guevara Jerez, "Thirsty Country with Lots of Water."

4. For a moving discussion of Pasos's life and work, see Shook, "Chasing Pasos."

5. Livingston, *Self-Devouring Growth*.

6. Dunk and Anderson, "Assembling Planetary Health," 31.

7. Dunk and Anderson, "Assembling Planetary Health," 31.

8. Blanchette, "Living Waste," 96.

9. Canguilhem, *Writings on Medicine*, 70.

10. Dunk and Anderson, "Assembling Planetary Health."

11. Raffles, *Book of Unconformities*.

12. Besky and Blanchette, "Introduction," 6–7. As they add, "While there are copious critiques of conditions of work in journalism and scholarship, and many efforts to realize a world where work is justly remunerated and carried on with dignity, few question the institution of work itself, or the logic of a society where work disproportionately shapes everyday hierarchies and environments" (7). Too few, for example, question the deep historical linkages between the rights that accrue to workers and the right to health.

13. Puar, *Right to Maim*, xviii.

14. Nash, *Inescapable Ecologies*, 210.

15. Murphy, "Toward Non-innocent Reassemblies"; Sedgwick, "Paranoid Reading and Reparative Reading."

Bibliography

Abadía-Barrero, César Ernesto. "Neoliberal Justice and the Transformation of the Moral: The Privatization of the Right to Health Care in Colombia." *Medical Anthropology Quarterly* 30, no. 1 (2016): 62–79. https://doi.org/10.1111/maq.12161.

Adams, Vincanne. *Glyphosate and the Swirl: An Agroindustrial Chemical on the Move.* Durham, NC: Duke University Press, 2022.

Adams, Vincanne, ed. *Metrics: What Counts in Global Health.* Durham, NC: Duke University Press, 2016.

Agard-Jones, Vanessa. "Bodies in the System." *Small Axe* 17, no. 3 (2013): 182–92.

Ahmann, Chloe, and Alison Kenner. "Breathing Late Industrialism." *Engaging Science, Technology, and Society* 6 (2020): 416–38. https://doi.org/10.17351/ests2020.673.

Alaimo, Stacy. *Bodily Natures: Science, Environment, and the Material Self.* Bloomington: Indiana University Press, 2010.

Alaimo, Stacy. *Exposed: Environmental Politics and Pleasures in Posthuman Times.* Minneapolis: University of Minnesota Press, 2016.

Allewaert, M. "Swamp Sublime: Ecologies of Resistance in the American Plantation Zone." *PMLA* 123, no. 2 (2008): 340–57. https://doi.org/10.1632/pmla.2008.123.2.340.

Anand, Nikhil. *Hydraulic City: Water and the Infrastructures of Citizenship in Mumbai.* Durham, NC: Duke University Press, 2017.

Anderson, Warwick, and James Dunk. "Planetary Health Histories: Toward New Ecologies of Epidemiology?" *Isis* 113, no. 4 (2022): 767–88. https://doi.org/10.1086/722308.

Appel, Hannah C. "Walls and White Elephants: Oil Extraction, Responsibility, and Infrastructural Violence in Equatorial Guinea." *Ethnography* 13, no. 4 (2012): 439–65. https://doi.org/10.1177/1466138111435741.

Auyero, Javier. *Patients of the State: The Politics of Waiting in Argentina.* Durham, NC: Duke University Press, 2012.

Auyero, Javier, and Debra Swistun. *Flammable: Environmental Suffering in an Argentine Shantytown.* Oxford: Oxford University Press, 2009.

Baker, Aryn. "Chronic Kidney Disease Is Poised to Become the Black Lung of Climate Change." *Time* (blog). August 9, 2023. https://time.com/6303020/chronic-kidney-disease-climate-change/.

Ballestero, Andrea. *A Future History of Water*. Durham, NC: Duke University Press, 2019.

Balshem, Martha. *Cancer in the Community: Class and Medical Authority*. Washington, DC: Smithsonian Books, 2013.

Barrios, Roberto E. "What Does Catastrophe Reveal for Whom? The Anthropology of Crises and Disasters at the Onset of the Anthropocene." *Annual Review of Anthropology* 46, no. 1 (2017): 151–66. https://doi.org/10.1146/annurev-anthro-102116-041635.

Beaver Solutions. "Beaver Facts: What Good Are Beavers?" 2023. https://www.beaversolutions.com/beaver-facts-education/what-good-are-beavers.

Benezra, Amber. *Gut Anthro: An Experiment in Thinking with Microbes*. Minneapolis: University of Minnesota Press, 2023.

Benezra, Amber, Joseph DeStefano, and Jeffrey I. Gordon. "Anthropology of Microbes." *Proceedings of the National Academy of Sciences* 109, no. 17 (2012): 6378–81. https://doi.org/10.1073/pnas.1200515109.

Benjamin, Ruha. *Race after Technology: Abolitionist Tools for the New Jim Code*. New York: Wiley, 2019.

Benton, Adia. "Risky Business: Race, Nonequivalence and the Humanitarian Politics of Life." *Visual Anthropology* 29, no. 2 (2016): 187–203. https://doi.org/10.1080/08949468.2016.1131523.

Berlant, Lauren. "Cruel Optimism: On Marx, Loss and the Senses." *New Formations*, December 2007.

Besky, Sarah. "Agricultural Justice, Abnormal Justice? An Analysis of Fair Trade's Plantation Problem." *Antipode* 47, no. 5 (2015): 1141–60. https://doi.org/10.1111/anti.12159.

Besky, Sarah. *The Darjeeling Distinction: Labor and Justice on Fair-Trade Tea Plantations in India*. Berkeley: University of California Press, 2014.

Besky, Sarah. "Exhaustion and Endurance in Sick Landscapes: Cheap Tea and the Work of Monoculture in the Dooars, India." In *How Nature Works: Rethinking Labor on a Troubled Planet*, edited by Sarah Besky and Alex Blanchette, 23–40. Santa Fe, NM: School for Advanced Research Press, 2019.

Besky, Sarah. "Fixity: On the Inheritance and Maintenance of Tea Plantation Houses in Darjeeling, India." *American Ethnologist* 44, no. 4 (2017): 617–31. https://doi.org/10.1111/amet.12561.

Besky, Sarah. "The Plantation's Outsides: The Work of Settlement in Kalimpong, India." *Comparative Studies in Society and History* 63, no. 2 (2021): 433–63. https://doi.org/10.1017/S0010417521000104.

Besky, Sarah, and Alex Blanchette, eds. *How Nature Works: Rethinking Labor on a Troubled Planet*. Santa Fe, NM: School for Advanced Research Press, 2019.

Besky, Sarah, and Alex Blanchette. "Introduction: The Fragility of Work." In *How Nature Works: Rethinking Labor on a Troubled Planet*, 1–20. Santa Fe, NM: School for Advanced Research Press, 2019.

Besky, Sarah, and Jonathan Padwe. "Placing Plants in Territory." *Environment and Society* 7, no. 1 (2016): 9–28. https://doi.org/10.3167/ares.2016.070102.

Biehl, João. "The Judicialization of Biopolitics: Claiming the Right to Pharmaceuticals in Brazilian Courts." *American Ethnologist* 40, no. 3 (2013): 419–36. https://doi.org/10.1111/amet.12030.

Biehl, João. "The Juridical Hospital." In *Living and Dying in the Contemporary World: A Compendium*, edited by Veena Das and Clara Han, 251–69. Oakland: University of California Press, 2015.

Biehl, João. *Will to Live: AIDS Therapies and the Politics of Survival*. Princeton, NJ: Princeton University Press, 2007. https://doi.org/10.1515/9781400832798.

Biehl, João, and Vincanne Adams, eds. *Arc of Interference: Medical Anthropology for Worlds on Edge*. Durham, NC: Duke University Press, 2023.

Biruk, Cal. *Cooking Data: Culture and Politics in an African Research World*. Durham, NC: Duke University Press, 2018.

Biruk, Cal. "Ebola and Emergency Anthropology: The View from the 'Global Health Slot.'" *Somatosphere* (blog). 2014. http://somatosphere.net/2014/ebola-and -emergency-anthropology-the-view-from-the-global-health-slot.html/.

Blanchette, Alex. "Living Waste and the Labor of Toxic Health on American Factory Farms." *Medical Anthropology Quarterly* 33, no. 1 (2019): 80–100. https://doi.org/10 .1111/maq.12491.

Blanchette, Alex. *Porkopolis: American Animality, Standardized Life, and the Factory Farm*. Durham, NC: Duke University Press, 2020.

Bohme, Susanna Rankin. *Toxic Injustice: A Transnational History of Exposure and Struggle*. Oakland: University of California Press, 2015.

Boix, Vicent, and Susanna R. Bohme. "Secrecy and Justice in the Ongoing Saga of DBCP Litigation." *International Journal of Occupational and Environmental Health* 18, no. 2 (2012): 154–61. https://doi.org/10.1179/1077352512Z.00000000010.

Bonilla, Yarimar, and Jonathan Rosa. "#Ferguson: Digital Protest, Hashtag Ethnography, and the Racial Politics of Social Media in the United States." *American Ethnologist* 42, no. 1 (2015): 4–17. https://doi.org/10.1111/amet.12112.

Boon, James. "Accenting Hybridity: Postcolonial Cultural Studies, a Boasian Anthropologist, and I." In *"Culture" and the Problem of the Disciplines*, edited by John Carlos Rowe, 141–70. New York: Columbia University Press, 1998.

Boudia, Soraya, and Nathalie Jas. *Powerless Science? Science and Politics in a Toxic World*. New York: Berghahn, 2014.

Bourgois, Philippe, and Jeff Schonberg. *Righteous Dopefiend*. Berkeley: University of California Press, 2009.

Bran Aragón, Fiore Stella, and Jennifer Goett. "¡Matria Libre y Vivir! Youth Activism and Nicaragua's 2018 Insurrection." *Journal of Latin American and Caribbean Anthropology* 25, no. 4 (2020): 532–51. https://doi.org/10.1111/jlca.12531.

Braun, Lundy. *Breathing Race into the Machine: The Surprising Career of the Spirometer from Plantation to Genetics*. Minneapolis: University of Minnesota Press, 2014.

Briggs, Charles L., and Clara Mantini-Briggs. *Tell Me Why My Children Died: Rabies, Indigenous Knowledge, and Communicative Justice*. Durham, NC: Duke University Press, 2016.

Brooks, Daniel. "Final Scoping Study Report: Epidemiology of Chronic Kidney Disease in Nicaragua." Washington, DC: Office of the Compliance Advisor/Ombudsman International Finance Corporation Multilateral Investment Guarantee Agency, 2009.

Brooks, Daniel, and Michael McLean. "Summary Report: Boston University Investigation of Chronic Kidney Disease in Western Nicaragua, 2009–2012." Washington,

DC: Compliance Advisor Ombudsman, 2012. https://www.cao-ombudsman.org/sites /default/files/downloads/BU_SummaryReport_August122012.pdf.

Brown, Hannah, and Ann H. Kelly. "Material Proximities and Hotspots: Toward an Anthropology of Viral Hemorrhagic Fevers." *Medical Anthropology Quarterly* 28, no. 2 (2014): 280–303. https://doi.org/10.1111/maq.12092.

Brown, Hannah, and Alex M. Nading. "Introduction: Human Animal Health in Medical Anthropology." *Medical Anthropology Quarterly* 33, no. 1 (2019): 5–23. https://doi.org /10.1111/maq.12488.

Brown, Phil. "Popular Epidemiology and Toxic Waste Contamination: Lay and Profes- sional Ways of Knowing." *Journal of Health and Social Behavior* 33, no. 3 (1992): 267–81.

Brown, Phil, Rachel Morello-Frosch, and Stephen Zavestoski. *Contested Illnesses: Cit- izens, Science, and Health Social Movements*. Berkeley: University of California Press, 2011.

Brown, Theodore M., Marcos Cueto, and Elizabeth Fee. "The World Health Organization and the Transition from 'International' to 'Global' Public Health." *American Journal of Public Health* 96, no. 1 (2006): 62–72. https://doi.org/10.2105 /AJPH.2004.050831.

Brown, Wendy. *Edgework: Critical Essays on Knowledge and Politics*. Princeton, NJ: Princeton University Press, 2005.

Buben, Radek, and Karel Kouba. "Nicaragua en 2019: La sorprendente solidez del autoritarismo tras la crisis del régimen." *Revista de Ciencia Política (Santiago)* 40, no. 2 (2020): 431–55. https://doi.org/10.4067/S0718-090X2020005000114.

Butler, Rhett. "Nicaragua Forest Information and Data." World Rainforests, 2023. https://rainforests.mongabay.com/deforestation/2000/Nicaragua.htm.

Butt, Leslie. "The Suffering Stranger: Medical Anthropology and International Morality." *Medical Anthropology* 21, no. 1 (2002): 1–24. https://doi.org/10.1080/01459740210619.

Campese, Vito M. "Con: Mesoamerican Nephropathy: Is the Problem Dehydration or Rehydration?" *Nephrology, Dialysis, Transplantation: Official Publication of the European Dialysis and Transplant Association—European Renal Association* 32, no. 4 (2017): 603–6. https://doi.org/10.1093/ndt/gfx033.

Canguilhem, Georges. *Writings on Medicine*. New York: Fordham University Press, 2012.

Canon Europe. "'They Die within Six to 24 Months': Ed Kashi Documents a Deadly Epidemic." Accessed February 27, 2023. https://www.canon-europe.com/pro/stories /ed-kashi-ckdu.

CAO. "Agreement between Corporación Montelimar and Asociación Montelimar Bendi- ción de Diós." Washington, DC: Compliance Advisor Ombudsman, 2017.

CAO. "Complaint of CFI Project 32253." Washington, DC: Compliance Advisor Ombudsman, 2015. https://www.cao-ombudsman.org/sites/default/files/downloads /ComplaintforwebEnglish.pdf.

CAO. "Dispute Resolution Conclusion Report Regarding Complaint Received in Rela- tion to IFC's Investment in Montelimar Sugar Mill (#32253) in Nicaragua." Washing- ton, DC: Compliance Advisor Ombudsman, 2023. https://www.cao-ombudsman.org /sites/default/files/downloads/CAO%20DR%20Conclusion%20Report%20-%20 Nicaragua%20Montelimar%20-%20ENG.pdf.

CAO. "A Guide to Designing and Implementing Grievance Mechanisms for Development Projects | Office of the Compliance Advisor/Ombudsman." Washington, DC: World Bank, 2008. https://www.cao-ombudsman.org/resources/guide-designing-and-implementing-grievance-mechanisms-development-projects.

Cardenal, Ernesto. *Zero Hour and Other Documentary Poems*. Translated by Jonathan Cohen. New York: New Directions, 1980.

Carruthers, Nicola. "Flor de Caña Gains Fairtrade Certification." *Spirits Business*, 2018. https://www.thespiritsbusiness.com/2018/05/flor-de-cana-gains-fair-trade-certification.

Carse, Ashley. "The Ecobiopolitics of Environmental Mitigation: Remaking Fish Habitat through the Savannah Harbor Expansion Project." *Social Studies of Science* 51, no. 2 (2021): 512–37. https://doi.org/10.1177/0306312721992541.

Center for International Environmental Law. "People of León and Chinandega's Complaint Regarding the Operations of Nicaragua Sugar Estates Limited S.A., International Finance Corporation Project 25331." 2008. https://www.ciel.org/Publications/NSEL_Complaint_31Mar08.pdf.

Chabrol, Fanny, and Jean-Paul Gaudillère. *Introduction à la santé globale*. Paris: Éditions La Découverte, 2023.

Chamorro, Luciana, and Emilia Yang. "Movilización social y tácticas de control en el neosandinismo: El caso de #OcupaINSS." *Cahiers des Amériques latines*, no. 87 (September 2018): 91–115. https://doi.org/10.4000/cal.8546.

Chavkin, Sasha. "World Bank Approves Loan to Sugar Plantation amid Concerns about Kidney Disease." Center for Public Integrity, August 28, 2013. http://publicintegrity.org/health/world-bank-approves-loan-to-sugar-plantation-amid-concerns-about-kidney-disease.

Chen, Mel Y. *Animacies: Biopolitics, Racial Mattering, and Queer Affect*. Durham, NC: Duke University Press, 2012.

Choy, Timothy. *Ecologies of Comparison: An Ethnography of Endangerment in Hong Kong*. Durham, NC: Duke University Press, 2011.

Choy, Timothy, and Jerry Zee. "Condition—Suspension." *Cultural Anthropology* 30, no. 2 (2015): 210–23. https://doi.org/10.14506/ca30.2.04.

Clare, Eli. *Brilliant Imperfection: Grappling with Cure*. Durham, NC: Duke University Press, 2017.

Collier, Stephen J., Jamie Cross, Peter Redfield, and Alice Street. "Preface: Little Development Devices / Humanitarian Goods." *Limn*, no. 9 (April 2018). https://limn.it/articles/precis-little-development-devices-humanitarian-goods.

Cooper Owens, Deirdre. *Medical Bondage: Race, Gender, and the Origins of American Gynecology*. Athens: University of Georgia Press, 2017. https://doi.org/10.2307/j.ctt1pwt69x.

Corriols, M. "Pesticide Poisoning in Nicaragua—Five Decades of Evidence." *Pesticide News*, no. 89 (2010): 3–6.

Craddock, Susan, and Steve Hinchliffe. "One World, One Health? Social Science Engagements with the One Health Agenda." *Social Science and Medicine* 129 (March 2015): 1–4. https://doi.org/10.1016/j.socscimed.2014.11.016.

Cross, Jamie. "The Coming of the Corporate Gift." *Theory, Culture and Society* 31, no. 2–3 (2014): 121–45. https://doi.org/10.1177/0263276413499191.

Cross, Jamie. "Detachment as a Corporate Ethic: Materializing CSR in the Diamond Supply Chain." *Focaal* 2011, no. 60 (2011): 34–46. https://doi.org/10.3167/fcl.2011.600104.

Cross, Jamie. *Dream Zones: Anticipating Capitalism and Development in India*. London: Pluto Press, 2014.

Cross, Jamie. "Occupational Health, Risk and Science in India's Global Factories." *South Asian History and Culture* 1, no. 2 (2010): 224–38. https://doi.org/10.1080/19472491003592912.

Crowley-Matoka, Megan. *Domesticating Organ Transplant: Familial Sacrifice and National Aspiration in Mexico*. Durham, NC: Duke University Press, 2016. https://doi.org/10.1215/9780822374633.

Crowley-Matoka, Megan, and Sherine F. Hamdy. "Gendering the Gift of Life: Family Politics and Kidney Donation in Egypt and Mexico." *Medical Anthropology* 35, no. 1 (2016): 31–44. https://doi.org/10.1080/01459740.2015.1051181.

Crutzen, Paul J. "The Effects of Industrial and Agricultural Practices on Atmospheric Chemistry and Climate during the Anthropocene." *Journal of Environmental Science and Health, Part A* 37, no. 4 (2002): 423–24. https://doi.org/10.1081/ESE-120003224.

Cruz-Feliciano, Héctor M. "Whither Nicaragua Three Years On?" *Latin American Perspectives* 48, no. 6 (2021): 9–20. https://doi.org/10.1177/0094582X211041065.

Daggett, Cara New. *The Birth of Energy: Fossil Fuels, Thermodynamics, and the Politics of Work*. Durham, NC: Duke University Press, 2019. https://doi.org/10.1215/9781478005346.

Das, Veena, and Clara Han. "Introduction: A Concept Note." In *Living and Dying in the Contemporary World: A Compendium*, edited by Veena Das and Clara Han, 1–38. Oakland: University of California Press, 2015.

Davis, Janae, Alex A. Moulton, Levi Van Sant, and Brian Williams. "Anthropocene, Capitalocene, . . . Plantationocene? A Manifesto for Ecological Justice in an Age of Global Crises." *Geography Compass* 13, no. 5 (2019): E12438. https://doi.org/10.1111/gec3.12438.

Deere, Carmen Diana, Peter Marchetti, and Nola Reinhardt. "The Peasantry and the Development of Sandinista Agrarian Policy, 1979–1984." *Latin American Research Review* 20, no. 3 (1985): 75–109. https://doi.org/10.1017/S0023879100021701.

Deininger, Klaus, Derek Byerlee, Jonathan Lindsay, Andrew Norton, Harris Selod, and Mercedes Stickler. *Rising Global Interest in Farmland: Can It Yield Sustainable and Equitable Benefits?* World Bank Group, 2011. https://doi.org/10.1596/978-0-8213-8591-3.

de la Cadena, Marisol. *Earth Beings: Ecologies of Practice across Andean Worlds*. Durham, NC: Duke University Press, 2015.

de León, Jason. "The Indecisive Moment: Photoethnography on the Undocumented Migration Trail." In *Photography and Migration*, edited by Tanya Sheehan, 115–29. New York: Routledge, 2018.

de León, Jason. *The Land of Open Graves: Living and Dying on the Migrant Trail*. Oakland: University of California Press, 2015.

DeLoughrey, Elizabeth M. *Allegories of the Anthropocene*. Durham, NC: Duke University Press, 2019. https://doi.org/10.1215/9781478005582.

DeLoughrey, E. "Yam, Roots, and Rot: Allegories of the Provision Grounds." *Small Axe: A Caribbean Journal of Criticism* 15, no. 1 (2011): 58–75. https://doi.org/10.1215/07990537-1189530.

Derrida, Jacques. *Specters of Marx: The State of the Debt, the Work of Mourning and the New International*. London: Routledge, 2006.

Dolan, Catherine, and Dinah Rajak. *The Anthropology of Corporate Social Responsibility*. New York: Berghahn, 2016.

Dore, Elizabeth. *Myths of Modernity: Peonage and Patriarchy in Nicaragua*. Durham, NC: Duke University Press, 2006. https://doi.org/10.1215/9780822387626.

Douglas, Mary. "Foreword: No Free Gifts." In *The Gift: The Form and Reason for Exchange in Archaic Societies*, by Marcel Mauss, translated by W. D. Halls, ix–xxiii. New York: Routledge, 2002.

Duclos, Vincent, and Tomás Sánchez Criado. "Care in Trouble: Ecologies of Support from Below and Beyond." *Medical Anthropology Quarterly* 34, no. 2 (2020): 153–73. https://doi.org/10.1111/maq.12540.

Dunk, James, and Warwick Anderson. "Assembling Planetary Health: Histories of the Future." In *Planetary Health: Protecting Nature to Protect Ourselves*, edited by Samuel Myers and Howard Frumkin, 17–35. Washington, DC: Island, 2020.

Edelman, Marc. "Bringing the Moral Economy Back in . . . to the Study of 21st-Century Transnational Peasant Movements." *American Anthropologist* 107, no. 3 (2005): 331–45. https://doi.org/10.1525/aa.2005.107.3.331.

Elinoff, Eli, and Tyson Vaughan. *Disastrous Times: Beyond Environmental Crisis in Urbanizing Asia*. Philadelphia: University of Pennsylvania Press, 2020.

Elizondo, Desiree. "The State Is Mainly Responsible for the Country's Water Crisis." *Envío*, no. 430 (May 2017). https://www.revistaenvio.org/articulo/5357.

Envío Team. "April 2018: An Insurrection of the Nation's Consciousness." *Envío*, no. 449 (December 2018). https://www.envio.org.ni/articulo/5485.

Envío Team. "The Environment: Saving Nicaragua's Soils." *Envío*, no. 125 (December 1991). https://www.envio.org.ni/articulo/2852.

Envío Team. "Three Economic Storm Clouds Looming in Nicaragua's Skies." *Envío*, no. 431 (June 2017). https://www.envio.org.ni/articulo/5348.

Erikson, Susan L. "Cell Phones ≠ Self and Other Problems with Big Data Detection and Containment during Epidemics." *Medical Anthropology Quarterly* 32, no. 3 (2018): 315–39. https://doi.org/10.1111/maq.12440.

Faber, Daniel. "Imperialism, Revolution, and the Ecological Crisis of Central America." *Latin American Perspectives* 19, no. 1 (1992): 17–44. https://doi.org/10.1177/0094582X9201900102.

Faber, Daniel. "La Liberación del Medio Ambiente: The Rise and Fall of Revolutionary Ecology in Nicaragua, 1979–1999." *Capitalism Nature Socialism* 10, no. 1 (1999): 45–80. https://doi.org/10.1080/10455759909358848.

Faber, Daniel. "A Sea of Poison." *NACLA Report on the Americas* 25, no. 2 (1991): 31–40. https://doi.org/10.1080/10714839.1991.11723150.

Farman, Abou, and Richard Rottenburg. "Measures of Future Health, from the Nonhuman to the Planetary: An Introductory Essay." *Medicine Anthropology Theory* 6, no. 3 (2019). https://doi.org/10.17157/mat.6.3.659.

Farmer, Paul. *AIDS and Accusation: Haiti and the Geography of Blame*. 2nd ed. Berkeley: University of California Press, 2006.

Feeley-Harnik, Gillian. "The Ethnography of Creation: Lewis Henry Morgan and the American Beaver." In *Relative Values: Reconfiguring Kinship Studies*, edited by Sarah Franklin and Susan McKinnon, 54–84. Durham, NC: Duke University Press, 2002. https://doi.org/10.1515/9780822383222-005.

Ferry, Elizabeth Emma. "Geologies of Power: Value Transformations of Mineral Specimens from Guanajuato, Mexico." *American Ethnologist* 32, no. 3 (2005): 420–36.

Fisher, Joshua B., and Alex M. Nading. "The End of the Cooperative Model (as We Knew It): Commoning and Co-becoming in Two Nicaraguan Cooperatives." *Environment and Planning E: Nature and Space* 4, no. 4 (2021): 1232–54. https://doi.org/10.1177/2514848620901439.

Fiske, Amelia M. *Reckoning with Harm: The Toxic Relations of Oil in Amazonia*. Austin: University of Texas Press, 2023.

Forensic Architecture. "Herbicidal Warfare in Gaza." 2023. https://forensic-architecture.org/investigation/herbicidal-warfare-in-gaza.

Fortun, Kim. *Advocacy after Bhopal: Environmentalism, Disaster, New Global Orders*. Chicago: University of Chicago Press, 2001.

Fortun, Kim. "Ethnography in Late Industrialism." *Cultural Anthropology* 27, no. 3 (2012): 446–64. https://doi.org/10.1111/j.1548-1360.2012.01153.x.

Fortun, Kim. "Figuring Out Ethnography." In *Fieldwork Is Not What It Used to Be: Learning Anthropology's Method in a Time of Transition*, edited by James D. Faubion and George E. Marcus, 167–83. Ithaca, NY: Cornell University Press, 2009.

Fortun, Kim. "Poststructuralism, Technoscience, and the Promise of Public Anthropology." *India Review* 5, no. 3–4 (2006): 294–317. https://doi.org/10.1080/14736480600938993.

Fortun, Kim, James Adams, Tim Schütz, and Scott Gabriel Knowles. "Knowledge Infrastructure and Research Agendas for Quotidian Anthropocenes: Critical Localism with Planetary Scope." *Anthropocene Review* 8, no. 2 (2021): 169–82. https://doi.org/10.1177/20530196211031972.

Fortun, Kim, and Mike Fortun. "Scientific Imaginaries and Ethical Plateaus in Contemporary U.S. Toxicology." *American Anthropologist* 107, no. 1 (2005): 43–54.

Francis, Hilary. "'Point Four Does Not Exist': U.S. Expertise in 1950s Nicaragua." *Diplomatic History* 46, no. 1 (2022): 121–43. https://doi.org/10.1093/dh/dhab076.

Gardner, Eriq. "The Filmmaker Who Became a Legal Spy." *Hollywood Reporter*, December 21, 2010. https://www.hollywoodreporter.com/business/business-news/filmmaker-legal-spy-64060.

Ghosh, Amitav. "Embattled Earth: Commodities, Conflict and Climate Change in the Indian Ocean Region." O. P. Jindal Distinguished Lecture, Watson Institute for International and Public Affairs, Brown University, April 6, 2018.

Ghosh, Amitav. *The Great Derangement: Climate Change and the Unthinkable*. Chicago: University of Chicago Press, 2016.

Ghosh, Bishnupriya. *The Virus Touch: Theorizing Epidemic Media*. Durham, NC: Duke University Press, 2023.

Gibson-Graham, J. K. *The End of Capitalism (As We Knew It): A Feminist Critique of Political Economy*. Minneapolis, MN: University of Minnesota Press, 1996.

Ginsburg, Faye. "Culture/Media: A (Mild) Polemic." *Anthropology Today* 10, no. 2 (1994): 5–15. https://doi.org/10.2307/2783305.

Glaser, Jason, Erik Hansson, Ilana Weiss, Catharina Wesseling, Kristina Jakobsson, Ulf Ekström, Jenny Apelqvist, et al. "Preventing Kidney Injury among Sugarcane Workers: Promising Evidence from Enhanced Workplace Interventions." *Occupational and Environmental Medicine* 77, no. 8 (2020): 527–34. https://doi.org/10.1136/oemed-2020-106406.

Glaser, Jason, and Diego Lopez, dirs. *Banana Land: Blood, Bullets, and Poison*. La Isla Foundation, 2014. YouTube. https://www.youtube.com/watch?v=MoRmtQht8-E.

Gobat, Michel. *Confronting the American Dream: Nicaragua under U.S. Imperial Rule*. Durham, NC: Duke University Press, 2005.

Gobierno de Nicaragua. Ley no. 815: Código procesal del trabajo y de la seguridad social de Nicaragua. Managua, Nicaragua: Bitesca, 2012.

Goett, Jennifer. "Beyond Left and Right: Grassroots Social Movements and Nicaragua's Civic Insurrection." *LASA Forum* 49, no. 4 (2018): 25–31.

Goldstein, Donna M., and Kira Hall. "Mass Hysteria in Le Roy, New York: How Brain Experts Materialized Truth and Outscienced Environmental Inquiry." *American Ethnologist* 42, no. 4 (2015): 640–57. https://doi.org/10.1111/amet.12161.

Good, Byron J., Andrea Chiovenda, and Sadeq Rahimi. "The Anthropology of Being Haunted: On the Emergence of an Anthropological Hauntology." *Annual Review of Anthropology* 51, no. 1 (2022): 437–53. https://doi.org/10.1146/annurev-anthro-101819-110224.

Gould, Jeffrey L. *To Lead as Equals: Rural Protest and Political Consciousness in Chinandega, Nicaragua, 1912–1979*. Chapel Hill: University of North Carolina Press, 1990.

Gould, Jeffrey L. "'¡Vana Ilusión!' The Highlands Indians and the Myth of Nicaragua Mestiza, 1880–1925." *Hispanic American Historical Review* 73, no. 3 (1993): 393–429. https://doi.org/10.1215/00182168-73.3.393.

Graeber, David. "Dead Zones of the Imagination: On Violence, Bureaucracy, and Interpretive Labor: The Malinowski Memorial Lecture, 2006." *HAU: Journal of Ethnographic Theory* 2, no. 2 (2012): 105–28. https://doi.org/10.14318/hau2.2.007.

Graeter, Stefanie. "Infrastructural Incorporations: Toxic Storage, Corporate Indemnity, and Ethical Deferral in Peru's Neoextractive Era." *American Anthropologist* 122, no. 1 (2020): 21–36.

Grandin, Greg. "Beyond the Four Freedoms: Obama and Sovereignty." *NACLA Report on the Americas* 42, no. 1 (2009): 27–29. https://doi.org/10.1080/10714839.2009.11722249.

Griffin, Carl. "Protest Practice and (Tree) Cultures of Conflict: Understanding the Spaces of 'Tree Maiming' in Eighteenth- and Early Nineteenth-Century England." *Transactions of the Institute of British Geographers* 33, no. 1 (2008): 91–108.

Grossman, Richard. "The Nation Is Our Mother: Augusto Sandino and the Construction of a Peasant Nationalism in Nicaragua, 1927–1934." *Journal of Peasant Studies* 35, no. 1 (2008): 80–99. https://doi.org/10.1080/03066150801983337.

Grover, Natalie. "Too Hot to Handle: Can Our Bodies Withstand Global Heating?" *The Guardian*, October 20, 2021. https://www.theguardian.com/global-development/2021/oct/20/too-hot-to-handle-can-our-bodies-withstand-global-heating.

Guevara, Che. *Guerrilla Warfare*. New York: Rowman and Littlefield, 2002.

Guevara Jerez, Francisco A. "A Thirsty Country with Lots of Water." *Envío*, no. 310 (May 2007). https://www.envio.org.ni/articulo/3558.

Gunatilake, Sarath, Stephanie Seneff, and Laura Orlando. "Glyphosate's Synergistic Toxicity in Combination with Other Factors as a Cause of Chronic Kidney Disease of Unknown Origin." *International Journal of Environmental Research and Public Health* 16, no. 15 (2019): 2734. https://doi.org/10.3390/ijerph16152734.

Günel, Gökçe. *Spaceship in the Desert: Energy, Climate Change, and Urban Design in Abu Dhabi*. Durham, NC: Duke University Press, 2019.

Gupta, Akhil. *Red Tape: Bureaucracy, Structural Violence, and Poverty in India*. Durham, NC: Duke University Press, 2012.

Guthman, Julie. *Wilted: Pathogens, Chemicals, and the Fragile Future of the Strawberry Industry*. Oakland: University of California Press, 2019.

Haber, Meryl H. "Pisse Prophecy: A Brief History of Urinalysis." *Clinics in Laboratory Medicine* 8, no. 3 (1988): 415–30. https://doi.org/10.1016/S0272-712(18)30665-6.

Hamdy, Sherine. *Our Bodies Belong to God: Organ Transplants, Islam, and the Struggle for Human Dignity in Egypt*. Berkeley: University of California Press, 2012.

Hamdy, Sherine F. "When the State and Your Kidneys Fail: Political Etiologies in an Egyptian Dialysis Ward." *American Ethnologist* 35, no. 4 (2008): 553–69. https://doi.org/10.1111/j.1548-1425.2008.00098.x.

Hanks, William F. "Indexicality." *Journal of Linguistic Anthropology* 9, no. 2 (1999): 124–26. https://doi.org/10.1525/jlin.1999.9.1-2.124.

Hansson, Erik, Jason Glaser, Kristina Jakobsson, Ilana Weiss, Catarina Wesseling, Rebekah A. I. Lucas, Jason Lee Kai Wei, et al. "Pathophysiological Mechanisms by Which Heat Stress Potentially Induces Kidney Inflammation and Chronic Kidney Disease in Sugarcane Workers." *Nutrients* 12, no. 6 (2020): 1639. https://doi.org/10.3390/nu12061639.

Haraway, Donna. "Anthropocene, Capitalocene, Plantationocene, Chthulucene: Making Kin." *Environmental Humanities* 6, no. 1 (2015): 159–65. https://doi.org/10.1215/22011919-3615934.

Haraway, Donna J. "A Cyborg Manifesto: Science, Technology, and Socialist Feminism in the Late Twentieth Century." In *Manifestly Haraway*, 3–90. Minneapolis: University of Minnesota Press, 2016.

Harrison, Jill Lindsey. *Pesticide Drift and the Pursuit of Environmental Justice*. Cambridge, MA: MIT Press, 2011.

Hartman, Saidiya. *Scenes of Subjection: Terror, Slavery, and Self-Making in Nineteenth-Century America*. New York: W. W. Norton, 2022.

Haynes, Naomi. "The Benefit of the Doubt: On the Relationship between Doubt and Power." *Anthropological Quarterly* 92, no. 1 (2019): 35–57. https://doi.org/10.1353/anq.2019.0001.

Hecht, Gabrielle. "Interscalar Vehicles for an African Anthropocene: On Waste, Tempo-rality, and Violence." *Cultural Anthropology* 33, no. 1 (2018): 109–41. https://doi.org/10.14506/ca33.1.05.

Hecht, Gabrielle. *Residual Governance: How South Africa Foretells Planetary Futures.* Durham, NC: Duke University Press, 2023.

Hedström, Peter, and Petri Ylikoski. "Causal Mechanisms in the Social Sciences." *Annual Review of Sociology* 36, no. 1 (2010): 49–67. https://doi.org/10.1146/annurev.soc.012809.102632.

Herrera, Ruth Selma. "How Much Longer Will the Country's Water Last?" *Envío*, no. 397 (August 2014). https://www.envio.org.ni/articulo/4895.

Hetherington, Kregg. "Beans before the Law: Knowledge Practices, Responsibility, and the Paraguayan Soy Boom." *Cultural Anthropology* 28, no. 1 (2013): 65–85. https://doi.org/10.1111/j.1548-1360.2012.01173.x.

Hetherington, Kregg. "The Concentration of Killing." In *How Nature Works: Rethinking Labor on a Troubled Planet*, edited by Sarah Besky and Alex Blanchette, 41–58. Santa Fe, NM: School for Advanced Research Press, 2019.

Hetherington, Kregg. *The Government of Beans: Regulating Life in the Age of Monocrops.* Durham, NC: Duke University Press, 2020.

Hetherington, Kregg. *Guerrilla Auditors: The Politics of Transparency in Neoliberal Para-guay.* Durham, NC: Duke University Press, 2011.

Hinchliffe, Stephen, Lenore Manderson, and Martin Moore. "Planetary Healthy Publics after COVID-19." *Lancet Planetary Health* 5, no. 4 (2021): e230–e236. https://doi.org/10.1016/S2542-196(21)00050-4.

Hodal, Kate. "The Mystery Epidemic Striking Nicaragua's Sugar Cane Workers—A Photo Essay." *Guardian*, November 27, 2020. https://www.theguardian.com/global-development/2020/nov/27/the-mystery-epidemic-striking-nicaraguas-sugar-cane-workers-a-photo-essay.

Hoebink, Paul. "Sugar from Nicaragua: A Report for Fairfood International." Nijmegen, Netherlands: Centre for International Development Issues. Accessed May 14, 2023. https://www.business-humanrights.org/en/latest-news/pdf-sugar-from-nicaragua/.

Hoffman, Danny. *Monrovia Modern: Urban Form and Political Imagination in Liberia.* Durham, NC: Duke University Press, 2017.

Hollander, Gail. "Power Is Sweet: Sugarcane in the Global Ethanol Assemblage." *Journal of Peasant Studies* 37, no. 4 (2010): 699–721. https://doi.org/10.1080/03066150.2010.512455.

Holmes, Seth M. *Fresh Fruit, Broken Bodies: Migrant Farmworkers in the United States.* Berkeley: University of California Press, 2013.

Horton, Sarah Bronwen. *They Leave Their Kidneys in the Fields: Illness, Injury, and Ille-gality among U.S. Farmworkers.* Oakland: University of California Press, 2016.

Houtart, François. "Los Trabajadores de La Caña Piensan Así." *Envío*, no. 125 (April 1992). https://www.envio.org.ni/articulo/713.

Hulme, Mike. "Better Weather? The Cultivation of the Sky." *Cultural Anthropology* 30, no. 2 (2015): 236–44. https://doi.org/10.14506/ca30.2.06.

Hunt, Linda M., Hannah S. Bell, Anna C. Martinez-Hume, Funmi Odumosu, and Heather A. Howard. "Corporate Logic in Clinical Care: The Case of Diabetes Management." *Medical Anthropology Quarterly* 33, no. 4 (2019): 463–82. https://doi.org/10.1111/maq.12533.

IFC. "Disclosure—Ingenio Montelimar." 2013. https://disclosures.ifc.org/project-detail/ESRS/32253/ingenio-montelimar.

INCAE. "INCAE nombró a Enrique Bolaños Abaunza como vicepresidente ejecutivo." April 27, 2012. https://www.incae.edu/es/blog/2012/04/27/incae-nombro-enrique-bolanos-abaunza-como-vicepresidente-ejecutivo.html.

Instituo Nacional de Seguridad Social. "Seguro de Riesgos Profesionales (RP)." 2023. https://inss-princ.inss.gob.ni/index.php/sergurosinss-2/8-seguro-de-riesgos-profesionales-rp.

International Monetary Fund. "Nicaragua: Selected Issues." Washington, DC: International Monetary Fund, 2017. https://www.elibrary.imf.org/view/journals/002/2017/174/article-A001-en.xml.

Jackson, John L. "An Ethnographic Filmflam: Giving Gifts, Doing Research, and Videotaping the Native Subject/Object." *American Anthropologist* 106, no. 1: 32–42. https://doi.org/10.1525/aa.2004.106.1.32.

Jackson, John L. *Thin Description: Ethnography and the African Hebrew Israelites of Jerusalem*. Cambridge, MA: Harvard University Press, 2013.

Jain, S. Lochlann. "Injury Fields." In *Injury and Injustice: The Cultural Politics of Harm and Redress*, edited by Anne Bloom, David M. Engel, and Michael McCann, 154–84. Cambridge: Cambridge University Press, 2018.

Jain, S. Lochlann. *Injury: The Politics of Product Design and Safety Law in the United States*. Princeton, NJ: Princeton University Press, 2006.

Jain, S. Lochlann. "Living in Prognosis: Toward an Elegiac Politics." *Representations* 98, no. 1 (2007): 77–92. https://doi.org/10.1525/rep.2007.98.1.77.

Jegathesan, Mythri. "Black Feminist Plots before the Plantationocene and Anthropology's 'Regional Closets.'" *Feminist Anthropology* 2, no. 1 (2021): 78–93. https://doi.org/10.1002/fea2.12037.

Jegathesan, Mythri. *Tea and Solidarity: Tamil Women and Work in Postwar Sri Lanka*. Seattle: University of Washington Press, 2019.

Johnson, Richard J., Laura G. Sánchez-Lozada, Lee S. Newman, Miguel A. Lanaspa, Henry F. Diaz, Jay Lemery, Bernardo Rodriguez-Iturbe, et al. "Climate Change and the Kidney." *Annals of Nutrition and Metabolism* 74, supp. 3 (2019): 38–44. https://doi.org/10.1159/000500344.

Johnson, Tim. "Nicaragua's Latest Revolution: A Switch to Green Energy." *Seattle Times*, August 30, 2014. https://www.seattletimes.com/nation-world/nicaraguarsquos-latest-revolution-a-switch-to-green-energy/.

Kalofonos, Ippolytos. *All I Eat Is Medicine: Going Hungry in Mozambique's AIDS Economy*. Oakland: University of California Press, 2021.

Kashi, Ed. *Curse of the Black Gold*. Edited by Michael Watts. New York: Simon and Schuster, 2010.

Kaufman, Sharon R. *Ordinary Medicine: Extraordinary Treatments, Longer Lives, and Where to Draw the Line*. Durham, NC: Duke University Press, 2015.

Kearney, Michael. *Reconceptualizing the Peasantry: Anthropology in Global Perspective.* New York: Routledge, 1996.

Keck, Frédéric. *Avian Reservoirs: Virus Hunters and Birdwatchers in Chinese Sentinel Posts.* Durham, NC: Duke University Press, 2020.

Kenner, Alison. *Breathtaking: Asthma Care in a Time of Climate Change.* Minneapolis: University of Minnesota Press, 2018.

Kierans, Ciara. *Chronic Failures: Kidneys, Regimes of Care, and the Mexican State.* New Brunswick, NJ: Rutgers University Press, 2019.

Kierans, Ciara, and Cesar Padilla-Altamira. "Anthropological Perspectives on CKDnt in Mexico: Time for a Paradigm Shift on the Social Determinants of Health." *Frontiers in Nephrology* 3 (January 2023): 1155687. doi: 10.3389/fneph.2023.1155687.

King, Tiffany Lethabo. "The Labor of (Re)reading Plantation Landscapes Fungible(ly)." *Antipode* 48, no. 4 (2016): 1022–39. https://doi.org/10.1111/anti.12227.

Kirksey, Eben. *Emergent Ecologies.* Durham, NC: Duke University Press, 2015.

Kirsch, Stuart. *Engaged Anthropology: Politics beyond the Text.* Oakland: University of California Press, 2018.

Kirsch, Stuart. *Mining Capitalism: The Relationship between Corporations and Their Critics.* Oakland: University of California Press, 2014.

Kjellstrom, Tord, David Briggs, Chris Freyberg, Bruno Lemke, Matthias Otto, and Olivia Hyatt. "Heat, Human Performance, and Occupational Health: A Key Issue for the Assessment of Global Climate Change Impacts." *Annual Review of Public Health* 37, no. 1 (2016): 97–112. https://doi.org/10.1146/annurev-publhealth-032315-021740.

Klein, Graig R., José Cuesta, and Cristian Chagalj. "The Nicaragua Protest Crisis in 2018–2019: Assessing the Logic of Government Responses to Protests." *Journal of Politics in Latin America* 14, no. 1 (2022): 55–83. https://doi.org/10.1177/1866802X211024246.

Kline, Nolan. "Life, Death, and Dialysis: Medical Repatriation and Liminal Life among Undocumented Kidney Failure Patients in the United States." *PoLAR: Political and Legal Anthropology Review* 41, no. 2 (2018): 216–30. https://doi.org/10.1111/plar.12269.

Knowles, Scott Gabriel. "Learning from Disaster? The History of Technology and the Future of Disaster Research." *Technology and Culture* 55, no. 4 (2014): 773–84.

Kockelman, Paul. *The Anthropology of Intensity: Language, Culture, and Environment.* Cambridge: Cambridge University Press, 2022. https://doi.org/10.1017/9781009024235.

Kockelman, Paul. "Grading, Gradients, Degradation, Grace: Part 2: Phenomenology, Materiality, and Cosmology." *HAU: Journal of Ethnographic Theory* 6, no. 2 (2016): 337–65. https://doi.org/10.14318/hau6.3.022.

Kohn, Eduardo. *How Forests Think: Toward an Anthropology beyond the Human.* Berkeley: University of California Press, 2013.

Kohn, Eduardo O. "Runa Realism: Upper Amazonian Attitudes to Nature Knowing." *Ethnos* 70, no. 2 (2005): 171–96. https://doi.org/10.1080/00141840500141162.

Krieger, Nancy. "Proximal, Distal, and the Politics of Causation: What's Level Got to Do with It?" *American Journal of Public Health* 98, no. 2 (2008): 221–30. https://doi.org/10.2105/AJPH.2007.111278.

Krieger, Nancy, and George Davey Smith. "The Tale Wagged by the DAG: Broadening the Scope of Causal Inference and Explanation for Epidemiology." *International Journal of Epidemiology* 45, no. 6 (2016): 1787–808. https://doi.org/10.1093/ije/dyw114.

Krupar, Shiloh. *Hot Spotter's Report: Military Fables of Toxic Waste*. Minneapolis: University of Minnesota Press, 2013.

La Isla Network. "About Chronic Kidney Disease of Undetermined Causes (CKDnt) | La Isla." February 26, 2023. https://laislanetwork.org/about-ckdu/.

Lamoreaux, Janelle. *Infertile Environments: Epigenetic Toxicology and the Reproductive Health of Chinese Men*. Durham, NC: Duke University Press, 2023.

Lamoreaux, Janelle. "What If the Environment Is a Person? Lineages of Epigenetic Science in a Toxic China." *Cultural Anthropology* 31, no. 2 (2016): 188–214. https://doi.org/10.14506/ca31.2.03.

Lancaster, Roger N. *Life Is Hard: Machismo, Danger, and the Intimacy of Power in Nicaragua*. Berkeley: University of California Press, 1994.

Lancaster, Roger N. *Thanks to God and the Revolution: Popular Religion and Class Consciousness in the New Nicaragua*. New York: Columbia University Press, 1988.

Langston, Nancy. *Toxic Bodies: Hormone Disruptors and the Legacy of DES*. New Haven, CT: Yale University Press, 2010.

Langwick, Stacey Ann. "A Politics of Habitability: Plants, Healing, and Sovereignty in a Toxic World." *Cultural Anthropology* 33, no. 3 (2018): 415–43. https://doi.org/10.14506/ca33.3.06.

La Prensa. "Indemnizan a excañeros de ingenios privatizados." December 3, 2012. https://www.laprensani.com/2012/12/03/nacionales/126005-indemnizan-a-excaneros-de-ingenios-privatizados.

Latour, Bruno. *An Inquiry into Modes of Existence: An Anthropology of the Moderns*. Translated by Catherine Porter. Cambridge, MA: Harvard University Press, 2013.

Laveaga, Gabriela Soto. "Beyond Borlaug's Shadow: Octavio Paz, Indian Farmers, and the Challenge of Narrating the Green Revolution." *Agricultural History* 95, no. 4 (2021): 576–608. https://doi.org/10.3098/ah.2021.095.4.576.

Lennon, Myles. "Postcarbon Amnesia: Toward a Recognition of Racial Grief in Renewable Energy Futures." *Science, Technology, & Human Values* 45, no. 5 (2020): 934–62. https://doi.org/10.1177/0162243919900556.

Li, Fabiana. *Unearthing Conflict: Corporate Mining, Activism, and Expertise in Peru*. Durham, NC: Duke University Press, 2015.

Li, Tania Murray. "Centering Labor in the Land Grab Debate." *Journal of Peasant Studies* 38, no. 2 (2011): 281–98. https://doi.org/10.1080/03066150.2011.559009.

Li, Tania Murray. "The Price of Un/Freedom: Indonesia's Colonial and Contemporary Plantation Labor Regimes." *Comparative Studies in Society and History* 59, no. 2 (2017): 245–76. https://doi.org/10.1017/S0010417517000044.

Li, Tania Murray. *The Will to Improve: Governmentality, Development, and the Practice of Politics*. Durham, NC: Duke University Press, 2017.

Li, Tania Murray, and Pujo Semedi. *Plantation Life: Corporate Occupation in Indonesia's Oil Palm Zone*. Durham, NC: Duke University Press, 2021.

Liboiron, Max. *Pollution Is Colonialism*. Durham, NC: Duke University Press, 2021.

Little, Peter C. "Corporate Mortality Files and Late Industrial Necropolitics." *Medical Anthropology Quarterly* 32, no. 2 (2018): 161–76. https://doi.org/10.1111/maq.12417.

Little, Peter C. *Toxic Town: IBM, Pollution, and Industrial Risks*. New York: New York University Press, 2014.

Livingston, Julie. *Debility and the Moral Imagination in Botswana*. Bloomington: Indiana University Press, 2005.

Livingston, Julie. *Self-Devouring Growth: A Planetary Parable as Told from Southern Africa*. Durham, NC: Duke University Press, 2019.

Lock, Margaret. "Recovering the Body." *Annual Review of Anthropology* 46, no. 1 (2017): 1–14. https://doi.org/10.1146/annurev-anthro-102116-041253.

Lora-Wainwright, Anna. *Resigned Activism: Living with Pollution in Rural China*. Cambridge, MA: MIT Press, 2017.

Lorimer, Jamie. *The Probiotic Planet: Using Life to Manage Life*. Minneapolis: University of Minnesota Press, 2020.

Lyons, Kristina M. *Vital Decomposition: Soil Practitioners and Life Politics*. Durham, NC: Duke University Press, 2020.

Machuca, Leonardo. "Empresa de Bolaños acusada de distribuir pesticida nemagón." *Panamá América*, October 22, 2002. https://www.panamaamerica.com.pa/mundo/empresa-de-bolanos-acusada-de-distribuir-pesticida-nemagon-110887.

Marcus, George E. "Experimental Forms for the Expression of Norms in the Ethnography of the Contemporary." *HAU: Journal of Ethnographic Theory* 3, no. 2 (2013): 197–217. https://doi.org/10.14318/hau3.2.011.

Marshall, Stephen H. "The Political Life of Fungibility." *Theory and Event* 15, no. 2 (2012). https://muse.jhu.edu/pub/1/article/484457.

Marsland, Rebecca. "(Bio)Sociality and HIV in Tanzania: Finding a Living to Support a Life." *Medical Anthropology Quarterly* 26, no. 4 (2012): 470–85.

Martí i Puig, Salvador, and Macià Serra. "Nicaragua: De-democratization and Regime Crisis." *Latin American Politics and Society* 62, no. 2 (2020): 117–36. https://doi.org/10.1017/lap.2019.64.

Martínez, Ysabel Muñoz. "Gardening in Polluted Tropics: The Materiality of Waste and Toxicity in Olive Senior's Caribbean Poetry." *eTropic: Electronic Journal of Studies in the Tropics* 21, no. 2 (2022): 162–79. https://doi.org/10.25120/etropic.21.2.2022.3907.

Marx, Karl. *Capital: A Critique of Political Economy*. Vol. 1. Translated by Ben Fowkes. London: Penguin, 1990.

Marya, Rupa, and Raj Patel. *Inflamed: Deep Medicine and the Anatomy of Injustice*. New York: Farrar, Straus and Giroux, 2021.

Masco, Joseph. "The Crisis in Crisis." *Current Anthropology* 58, supp. 15 (2017): S65–S76. https://doi.org/10.1086/688695.

Masco, Joseph. "The End of Ends." *Anthropological Quarterly* 85, no. 4 (2012): 1107–24.

Masco, Joseph. "Optics of Exposure." In *Living in a Nuclear World: From Fukushima to Hiroshima*, edited by Bernadette Bensaude-Vincent, Soraya Boudia, and Kyoko Sato, 45–64. London: Routledge, 2022.

Mathews, Andrew S. *Instituting Nature: Authority, Expertise, and Power in Mexican Forests*. Cambridge, MA: MIT Press, 2021.

Mauss, Marcel. *The Gift: The Form and Reason for Exchange in Archaic Societies*. Edited by W. D. Halls. London: Routledge, 1990.

Mayblin, Maya. "The Way Blood Flows: The Sacrificial Value of Intravenous Drip Use in Northeast Brazil." *Journal of the Royal Anthropological Institute* 19, supp. 1 (2013): S42–S56. https://doi.org/10.1111/1467-9655.12015.

Mayer, Joshua L. "Conceptualizing Settler Colonialism in Nicaragua." *Urban Anthropology and Studies of Cultural Systems and World Economic Development* 49, no. 3/4 (2020): 195–245.

Mbembe, Achille. "Necropolitics." *Public Culture* 15, no. 1 (2003): 11–40.

McKay, Ramah. *Medicine in the Meantime: The Work of Care in Mozambique*. Durham, NC: Duke University Press, 2017.

McKittrick, Katherine. *Demonic Grounds: Black Women and the Cartographies of Struggle*. Minneapolis: University of Minnesota Press, 2006.

McKittrick, Katherine. "Plantation Futures." *Small Axe* 17, no. 3 (2013): 1–15.

McMichael, Philip. "The Land Grab and Corporate Food Regime Restructuring." *Journal of Peasant Studies* 39, no. 3–4 (2012): 681–701. https://doi.org/10.1080/03066150.2012.661369.

Melo, Milena Andrea. "Stratified Access: Seeking Dialysis Care in the Borderlands." In *Unequal Coverage: The Experience of Health Care Reform in the United States*, edited by Heide Castañeda and Jessica M. Mulligan, 59–78. New York: New York University Press, 2017. https://doi.org/10.18574/nyu/9781479897001.003.0007.

Millar, Kathleen M. "Garbage as Racialization." *Anthropology and Humanism* 45, no. 1 (2020): 4–24. https://doi.org/10.1111/anhu.12267.

Mintz, Sidney W. *Sweetness and Power: The Place of Sugar in Modern History*. New York: Penguin, 1986.

Mintz, Sidney W. *Worker in the Cane: A Puerto Rican Life History*. New York: W. W. Norton, 1974.

Mishra, Kriti. "Gender and Sanitation: Observations from North India." *Indian Anthropologist* 51, no. 2 (2021): 85–100.

Mitchell, Don. *They Saved the Crops: Labor, Landscape, and the Struggle over Industrial Farming in Bracero-Era California*. Athens: University of Georgia Press, 2012.

Mitman, Gregg. *Breathing Space: How Allergies Shape Our Lives and Landscapes*. New Haven, CT: Yale University Press, 2007.

Mitman, Gregg, M. Murphy, and Christopher Sellers, eds. *Landscapes of Exposure: Knowledge and Illness in Modern Environments*. Osiris, Volume 19. Chicago: University of Chicago Press, 2004.

Mol, Annemarie, and John Law. "Embodied Action, Enacted Bodies: The Example of Hypoglycaemia." *Body and Society* 10, no. 2–3 (2004): 43–62. https://doi.org/10.1177/1357034X04042932.

Moore, Amelia. *Destination Anthropocene: Science and Tourism in the Bahamas*. Oakland: University of California Press, 2019.

Moore, Jason W., ed. *Anthropocene or Capitalocene? Nature, History, and the Crisis of Capitalism*. Oakland, CA: PM, 2016.

Moore, Jason W. "Cheap Food and Bad Climate: From Surplus Value to Negative Value in the Capitalist World-Ecology." *Critical Historical Studies* 2, no. 1 (2015): 1–43. https://doi.org/10.1086/681007.

Morales, Margaret del Carmen, Leila Harris, and Gunilla Öberg. "Citizenshit: The Right to Flush and the Urban Sanitation Imaginary." *Environment and Planning A: Economy and Space* 46, no. 12 (2014): 2816–33. https://doi.org/10.1068/a130331p.

Moran-Thomas, Amy. *Traveling with Sugar: Chronicles of a Global Epidemic*. Oakland: University of California Press, 2019.

Morgan, Lewis Henry. *The American Beaver and His Works*. Philadelphia: J. B. Lippincott, 1868.

Morinville, Cynthia, and Nicole Van Lier. "On Nature, Degradation, and Life-Making in Late Capitalism." *Capitalism Nature Socialism* 32, no. 4 (2021): 43–61. https://doi.org/10.1080/10455752.2021.1900309.

Moyer, Eileen, and Vinh-Kim Nguyen. "Edgework in Medical Anthropology." *Medicine Anthropology Theory* 4, no. 5 (2017).

Moyer, Eileen, and Vinh-Kim Nguyen. "(Re)Framing and the (Medical) Anthropological Lens." *Medicine Anthropology Theory* 2, no. 3 (2015).

Mulligan, Jessica M. *Unmanageable Care: An Ethnography of Health Care Privatization in Puerto Rico*. New York: New York University Press, 2014.

Mulligan, Jessica M., and Heide Castañeda. *Unequal Coverage: The Experience of Health Care Reform in the United States*. New York: New York University Press, 2017.

Murphy, M. "Alterlife and Decolonial Chemical Relations." *Cultural Anthropology* 32, no. 4 (2017): 494–503. https://doi.org/10.14506/ca32.4.02.

Murphy, M. "Chemical Infrastructures of the St Clair River." In *Toxicants, Health and Regulation since 1945*, edited by Nathalie Jas and Soraya Boudia, 103–16. New York: Routledge, 2016.

Murphy, M. *The Economization of Life*. Durham, NC: Duke University Press, 2017.

Murphy, M. *Sick Building Syndrome and the Problem of Uncertainty: Environmental Politics, Technoscience, and Women Workers*. Durham, NC: Duke University Press, 2006.

Murphy, M. "Toward Non-innocent Reassemblies." *Engaging Science, Technology, and Society* 2 (August 2016): 128–31. https://doi.org/10.17351/ests2016.94.

Murphy, M. "Unsettling Care: Troubling Transnational Itineraries of Care in Feminist Health Practices." *Social Studies of Science* 45, no. 5 (2015): 717–37. http://www.jstor.org/stable/43829053.

Murray, Douglas L. *Cultivating Crisis: The Human Cost of Pesticides in Latin America*. Austin: University of Texas Press, 1994.

Musset, Alain. "León/Sutiaba (Nicaragua): Frontière ethnique et justice spatiale." *Annales de géographie* 665–66, no. 1–2 (2009): 116–37. https://doi.org/10.3917/ag.665.0116.

Nading, Alex M. "Disposability, Social Security, and the Facts of Work in Nicaragua's Sugarcane Zone." *Tapuya: Latin American Science, Technology, and Society*, 2024. https://doi.org/10.1080/25729861.2024.2357392.

Nading, Alex M. "Dissipation, Solidarity, and Kidney Disease in Nicaragua." In *How Nature Works: Rethinking Labor on a Troubled Planet*, edited by Sarah Besky and Alex Blanchette, 97–113. Santa Fe, NM: School for Advanced Research Press, 2019.

Nading, Alex M. "Ethnography in a Grievance." *Medicine Anthropology Theory* 6, no. 2 (2019). https://doi.org/10.17157/mat.6.2.631.

Nading, Alex M. "Filtration." *Society and Space* (blog), April 1, 2019. https://www .societyandspace.org/articles/filtration.

Nading, Alex M. "Living in a Toxic World." *Annual Review of Anthropology* 49, no. 1 (2020): 209–24. https://doi.org/10.1146/annurev-anthro-010220-074557.

Nading, Alex M. "Local Biologies, Leaky Things, and the Chemical Infrastructure of Global Health." *Medical Anthropology* 36, no. 2 (2017): 141–56. https://doi.org/10 .1080/01459740.2016.1186672.

Nading, Alex M. "'Love Isn't There in Your Stomach': A Moral Economy of Medical Citizenship among Nicaraguan Community Health Workers." *Medical Anthropology Quarterly* 27, no. 1 (2013): 84–102. https://doi.org/10.1111/maq.12017.

Nading, Alex M. *Mosquito Trails: Ecology, Health, and the Politics of Entanglement.* Oakland: University of California Press, 2014.

Nading, Alex M. "Orientation and Crafted Bureaucracy: Finding Dignity in Nicaraguan Food Safety." *American Anthropologist* 119, no. 3 (2017): 478–90. https://doi.org/10 .1111/aman.12844.

Nading, Alex M. "The Plantation as Hotspot: Capital, Science, Labour, and the Earthly Limits of Global Health." *Medicine Anthropology Theory* 10, no. 2 (2023): 1–26. https://doi.org/10.17157/mat.10.2.6928.

Nading, Alex M., and Lucy Lowe. "Social Justice as Epidemic Control: Two Latin American Case Studies." *Medical Anthropology* 37, no. 6 (2018): 458–71. https://doi.org/10 .1080/01459740.2018.1485021.

Nakassis, Constantine V. "Indexicality's Ambivalent Ground." *Signs and Society* 6, no. 1 (2018): 281–304. https://doi.org/10.1086/694753.

Nash, June. "The Devil in Bolivia's Nationalized Tin Mines." *Science and Society* 36, no. 2 (1972): 221–33.

Nash, Linda. *Inescapable Ecologies: A History of Environment, Disease, and Knowledge.* Berkeley: University of California Press, 2006.

Neely, Abigail H., and Arunsrinivasan Ponshunmugam. "A Qualitative Approach to Examining Health Care Access in Rural South Africa." *Social Science and Medicine* 230 (June 2019): 214–21. https://doi.org/10.1016/j.socscimed.2019.04.025.

Nguyen, Vinh-Kim. *The Republic of Therapy: Triage and Sovereignty in West Africa's Time of AIDS.* Durham, NC: Duke University Press, 2010.

Nixon, Rob. *Slow Violence and the Environmentalism of the Poor.* Cambridge, MA: Harvard University Press, 2011.

O'Connor, Flannery. *Mystery and Manners: Occasional Prose.* New York: Macmillan, 1969.

Olson, Valerie A. "The Ecobiopolitics of Space Biomedicine." *Medical Anthropology* 29, no. 2 (2010): 170–93. https://doi.org/10.1080/01459741003715409.

O'Neill, Kevin Lewis. *City of God: Christian Citizenship in Postwar Guatemala.* Berkeley: University of California Press, 2010.

Ottinger, Gwen. *Refining Expertise: How Responsible Engineers Subvert Environmental Justice Challenges.* New York: New York University Press, 2013.

Oyarzun, Yesmar. "Plantation Politics, Paranoia, and Public Health on the Frontlines of America's COVID-19 Response." *Medical Anthropology Quarterly* 34, no. 4 (2020): 578–90. https://doi.org/10.1111/maq.12623.

Pacheco-Zenteno, Felipe, Jason Glaser, Kristina Jakobsson, Ilana Weiss, Esteban Arias-Monge, and Kristina Gyllensten. "The Prevention of Occupational Heat Stress in Sugarcane Workers in Nicaragua—An Interpretative Phenomenological Analysis." *Frontiers in Public Health* 9: 713711 (2021). https://www.frontiersin.org/articles/10.3389/fpubh.2021.713711.

Packard, Randall M. *A History of Global Health*. Baltimore: Johns Hopkins University Press, 2016. https://doi.org/10.56021/9781421420325.

Paredes, Alyssa. "Experimental Science for the 'Bananapocalypse': Counter Politics in the Plantationocene." *Ethnos* 88, no. 4 (2023): 837–63. https://doi.org/10.1080/00141844.2021.1919172.

Patel, Raj. "The Long Green Revolution." *Journal of Peasant Studies* 40, no. 1 (2013): 1–63. https://doi.org/10.1080/03066150.2012.719224.

Pérez-Baltodano, Andrés. *Entre el Estado Conquistador y el Estado Nación: Providencialismo, pensamiento político y estructuras de poder en el desarrollo histórico de Nicaragua*. Managua: IHNCA/UCA Instituto de Historia de Nicaragua y Centroamérica, 2003.

Perry, Keisha-Khan Y. *Black Women against the Land Grab: The Fight for Racial Justice in Brazil*. Minneapolis: University of Minnesota Press, 2013.

Peters, John Durham. *The Marvelous Clouds: Toward a Philosophy of Elemental Media*. Chicago: University of Chicago Press, 2015.

Petryna, Adriana. *Life Exposed: Biological Citizens after Chernobyl*. Princeton, NJ: Princeton University Press, 2013.

Pickering, Andrew. "The Mangle of Practice: Agency and Emergence in the Sociology of Science." *American Journal of Sociology* 99, no. 3 (1993): 559–89. https://doi.org/10.1086/230316.

Polanyi, Karl. *The Great Transformation*. Boston: Beacon Press, 2001.

Povinelli, Elizabeth A. *Between Gaia and Ground: Four Axioms of Existence and the Ancestral Catastrophe of Late Liberalism*. Durham, NC: Duke University Press, 2021.

Povinelli, Elizabeth A. *Economies of Abandonment: Social Belonging and Endurance in Late Liberalism*. Durham, NC: Duke University Press, 2011.

Povinelli, Elizabeth A. *Geontologies: A Requiem to Late Liberalism*. Durham, NC: Duke University Press, 2016.

Prince, Heath. "A Measure of the Return on Ingenio San Antonio's Investment in the Adelante Initiative: An Initial Estimate of Costs and Benefits of a Water, Rest, and Shade Intervention." Technical Report. La Isla Network, 2020. https://repositories.lib.utexas.edu/handle/2152/88122.

Prince, Ruth J. "The Diseased Body and the Global Subject: The Circulation and Consumption of an Iconic AIDS Photograph in East Africa." *Visual Anthropology* 29, no. 2 (2016): 159–86. https://doi.org/10.1080/08949468.2016.1131517.

Proparco. "A Loan to Support Responsible Sugar Production in Nicaragua." March 5, 2018. https://www.proparco.fr/en/carte-des-projets/suganc.

Puar, Jasbir K. *The Right to Maim: Debility, Capacity, Disability*. Durham, NC: Duke University Press, 2017.

Pulido, Laura. "Flint, Environmental Racism, and Racial Capitalism." *Capitalism Nature Socialism* 27, no. 3 (2016): 1–16. https://doi.org/10.1080/10455752.2016.1213013.

Queiroz, Allan S., and Raf Vanderstraeten. "Unintended Consequences of Job Formalisation: Precarious Work in Brazil's Sugarcane Plantations." *International Sociology* 33, no. 1 (2018): 128–46. https://doi.org/10.1177/0268580917747776.

Quesada, James. "A Brief History of Violence in Nicaragua." In *Higher Education, State Repression, and Neoliberal Reform in Nicaragua*, edited by Wendy Bellanger, Serena Cosgrove, and Irina Carlotta Silber, 171–88. New York: Routledge, 2022.

Rabinbach, Anson. *The Human Motor: Energy, Fatigue, and the Origins of Modernity*. Berkeley: University of California Press, 1992.

Rabinow, Paul. *Essays on the Anthropology of Reason*. Princeton, NJ: Princeton University Press, 2021.

Raffles, Hugh. *The Book of Unconformities: Speculations on Lost Time*. New York: Pantheon, 2020.

Rajak, Dinah. *In Good Company: An Anatomy of Corporate Social Responsibility*. Stanford, CA: Stanford University Press, 2011.

Redfield, Peter. "Bioexpectations: Life Technologies as Humanitarian Goods." *Public Culture* 24, no. 1 (2012): 157–84. https://doi.org/10.1215/08992363-1443592.

Reichman, Daniel R. *The Broken Village: Coffee, Migration, and Globalization in Honduras*. Ithaca, NY: Cornell University Press, 2011.

Reinberger, Hans-Jörg. "Experimental Systems: Historiality, Narration, and Deconstruction." *Science in Context* 7, no. 1 (1994): 65–81. https://doi.org/10.1017/S0269889700001599.

Reno, Joshua O. *Military Waste: The Unexpected Consequences of Permanent War Readiness*. Oakland: University of California Press, 2019. https://doi.org/10.2307/j.ctvp7d49w.

Riles, Annelise. "Anthropology, Human Rights, and Legal Knowledge: Culture in the Iron Cage." *American Anthropologist* 108, no. 1 (2006): 52–65. https://doi.org/10.1525/aa.2006.108.1.52.

Riles, Annelise. *Documents: Artifacts of Modern Knowledge*. Ann Arbor: University of Michigan Press, 2006.

Ripoll, Santiago. "The Moral Economy of Labour and Resistance to Commoditisation in the Matagalpa Highlands of Nicaragua." *Journal of Peasant Studies* 49, no. 7 (2022): 1553–80. https://doi.org/10.1080/03066150.2021.1928085.

Roberts, Elizabeth F. S. "What Gets Inside: Violent Entanglements and Toxic Boundaries in Mexico City." *Cultural Anthropology* 32, no. 4 (2017): 592–619. https://doi.org/10.14506/ca32.4.07.

Romero, Adam M., Julie Guthman, Ryan E. Galt, Matt Huber, Becky Mansfield, and Suzana Sawyer. "Chemical Geographies." *GeoHumanities* 3, no. 1 (2017): 158–77. https://doi.org/10.1080/2373566X.2017.1298972.

Rosenberg, Charles E. "What Is an Epidemic? AIDS in Historical Perspective." *Daedalus* 118, no. 2 (1989): 1–17.

Rottenburg, Richard. "Social and Public Experiments and New Figurations of Science and Politics in Postcolonial Africa." *Postcolonial Studies* 12, no. 4 (2009): 423–40. https://doi.org/10.1080/13688790903350666.

Rueda Estrada, Verónica. "El Campesinado Migrante: Políticas Agrarias, Colonizaciones Internas y Movimientos de Frontera Agrícola En Nicaragua, 1960–2012." *Tzintzun,* June 2013, 155–98.

Ruiz Arias, Manuel Israel. "On Social Security the IMF Has Little to Tell Us and a Lot to Be Told." *Envío,* no. 350 (September 2010). https://www.envio.org.ni/articulo /4240.

Russ, Ann J., Janet K. Shim, and Sharon R. Kaufman. "'Is There Life on Dialysis?': Time and Aging in a Clinically Sustained Existence." *Medical Anthropology* 24, no. 4 (2005): 297–324. https://doi.org/10.1080/01459740500330639.

Russ, Ann J., Janet K. Shim, and Sharon R. Kaufman. "The Value of 'Life at Any Cost': Talk about Stopping Kidney Dialysis." *Social Science and Medicine* 64, no. 11 (2007): 2236–47. https://doi.org/10.1016/j.socscimed.2007.02.016.

Sandoval, Consuelo. "Politizan caso Nemagón." *La Prensa,* October 22, 2002. https:// www.laprensani.com/2002/10/22/politica/881095-politizan-caso-nemagn.

Sawyer, Suzana. *Crude Chronicles: Indigenous Politics, Multinational Oil, and Neoliberalism in Ecuador.* Durham, NC: Duke University Press, 2004.

Sawyer, Suzana. *The Small Matter of Suing Chevron.* Durham, NC: Duke University Press, 2022.

Saxena, Alder Keleman, Deepti Chatti, Katy Overstreet, and Michael R. Dove. "From Moral Ecology to Diverse Ontologies: Relational Values in Human Ecological Research, Past and Present." *Current Opinion in Environmental Sustainability* 35 (December 2018): 54–60. https://doi.org/10.1016/j.cosust.2018.10.021.

Saxton, Dvera I. *The Devil's Fruit: Farmworkers, Health, and Environmental Justice.* New Brunswick, NJ: Rutgers University Press, 2021.

Saxton, Dvera I. "Strawberry Fields as Extreme Environments: The Ecobiopolitics of Farmworker Health." *Medical Anthropology* 34, no. 2 (2015): 166–83. https://doi.org /10.1080/01459740.2014.959167.

Scaramelli, Caterina. "The Delta Is Dead: Moral Ecologies of Infrastructure in Turkey." *Cultural Anthropology* 34, no. 3 (2019): 388–416. https://doi.org/10.14506/ca34.3.04.

Scheper-Hughes, Nancy. *Death without Weeping: The Violence of Everyday Life in Brazil.* Berkeley: University of California Press, 1993.

Scott, James C. *The Moral Economy of the Peasant: Rebellion and Subsistence in Southeast Asia.* New Haven, CT: Yale University Press, 1977.

Scott, James C. *Weapons of the Weak: Everyday Forms of Peasant Resistance.* New Haven, CT: Yale University Press, 1987.

Scott-Smith, Tom. "Beyond the Boxes." *American Ethnologist* 46, no. 4 (2019): 509–21. https://doi.org/10.1111/amet.12833.

Sedgwick, Eve Kosofsky. "Paranoid Reading and Reparative Reading; or, You're So Paranoid, You Probably Think This Introduction Is about You." In *Novel Gazing: Queer Readings in Fiction,* edited by Eve Kosofsky Sedgwick, 1–38. Durham, NC: Duke University Press, 1997. https://doi.org/10.1215/9780822382478-001.

Senanayake, Nari. "Towards a Feminist Political Ecology of Health: Mystery Kidney Disease and the Co-production of Social, Environmental, and Bodily Difference." *Environment and Planning E: Nature and Space* 6, no. 2 (2022): 1007–29. https://doi .org/10.1177/25148486221113963.

Senanayake, Nari. "'We Are the Living Dead,' or, the Precarious Stabilisation of Liminal Life in the Presence of CKDu." *Antipode* 54, no. 6 (2022): 1965–85. https://doi.org/10 .1111/anti.12869.

Senanayake, Nari. "'We Spray So We Can Live': Agrochemical Kinship, Mystery Kidney Disease, and Struggles for Health in Dry Zone Sri Lanka." *Annals of the American Association of Geographers* 112, no. 4 (2021): 1047–64. https://doi.org/10.1080 /24694452.2021.1956295.

Seneff, Stephanie, and Laura Orlando. "Is Glyphosate a Key Factor in Mesoamerican Nephropathy?" *Journal of Environmental and Analytical Toxicology* 8, no. 1 (2018): 1-10. https://doi.org/10.4172/2161-0525.1000542.

Shapiro, Nicholas. "Attuning to the Chemosphere: Domestic Formaldehyde, Bodily Reasoning, and the Chemical Sublime." *Cultural Anthropology* 30, no. 3 (2015): 368–93. https://doi.org/10.14506/ca30.3.02.

Shapiro, Nicholas, Nasser Zakariya, and Jody Roberts. "A Wary Alliance: From Enumerating the Environment to Inviting Apprehension." *Engaging Science, Technology, and Society* 3 (2017): 575–602. https://doi.org/10.17351/ests2017.133.

Sharpe, Christina. *In the Wake: On Blackness and Being.* Durham, NC: Duke University Press, 2016.

Shook, David. "Chasing Pasos: On the Trail of Nicaragua's Lost Modernist." *Los Angeles Review of Books,* October 11, 2016. https://lareviewofbooks.org/article/chasing-pasos -trail-nicaraguas-lost-modernist/.

Shotwell, Alexis. *Against Purity: Living Ethically in Compromised Times.* Minneapolis: University of Minnesota Press, 2016.

Silva, M. W. Amarasiri de. "Drinking Water and Chronic Kidney Disease of Unknown Aetiology in Anuradhapura, Sri Lanka." *Anthropology and Medicine* 26, no. 3 (2019): 311–27. https://doi.org/10.1080/13648470.2018.1446822.

Silva, Victor Alfonso. "The History of the Nicaraguan Social Security Institute: An Analysis of Path Dependency." Master's thesis, Georgetown University, 2015. https:// www.proquest.com/docview/1725904267/abstract/B511DF89CA8D4819PQ/1.

Silver, Jake. "Tear Gas in Orbit." *American Ethnologist* 50, no. 1 (2023): 129–40. https:// doi.org/10.1111/amet.13137.

Smith, Homer William. *From Fish to Philosopher.* Boston: Little, Brown, 1953.

Solomon, Harris. "Life Support." In *Eating beside Ourselves: Thresholds of Foods and Bodies,* edited by Heather Paxson, 140–57. Durham, NC: Duke University Press, 2023.

Solomon, Harris. "Living on Borrowed Breath: Respiratory Distress, Social Breathing, and the Vital Movement of Ventilators." *Medical Anthropology Quarterly* 35, no. 1 (2021): 102–19. https://doi.org/10.1111/maq.12603.

Solomon, Harris. *Metabolic Living: Food, Fat, and the Absorption of Illness in India.* Durham, NC: Duke University Press, 2016.

Sorensen, Cecilia, and Ramon Garcia-Trabanino. "A New Era of Climate Medicine: Addressing Heat-Triggered Renal Disease." *New England Journal of Medicine* 381, no. 8 (2019): 693–96. https://doi.org/10.1056/NEJMp1907859.

Spackman, Christy. "In Smell's Shadow: Materials and Politics at the Edge of Perception." *Social Studies of Science* 50, no. 3 (2020): 418–39. https://doi.org/10.1177/0306312720918946.

Spillers, Hortense J. "Mama's Baby, Papa's Maybe: An American Grammar Book." *Diacritics* 17, no. 2 (1987): 65–81. https://doi.org/10.2307/464747.

Starosielski, Nicole. "Beyond the Sun: Embedded Solarities and Agricultural Practice." *South Atlantic Quarterly* 120, no. 1 (2021): 13–24. https://doi.org/10.1215/00382876-795668.

Steffen, Will, Jacques Grinevald, Paul Crutzen, and John McNeill. "The Anthropocene: Conceptual and Historical Perspectives." *Philosophical Transactions of the Royal Society A: Mathematical, Physical and Engineering Sciences* 369, no. 1938 (2011): 842–67. https://doi.org/10.1098/rsta.2010.0327.

Steingraber, Sandra. *Living Downstream: An Ecologist's Personal Investigation of Cancer and the Environment*. New York: Hachette, 2010.

Stengers, Isabelle. "The Cosmopolitical Proposal." In *Making Things Public*, edited by Bruno Latour and Peter Weibel, 994–1003. Cambridge, MA: MIT Press, 2005.

Strathern, Marilyn. *Property, Substance, and Effect: Anthropological Essays on Persons and Things*. Chicago: HAU, 2022.

Striffler, Steve, and Mark Moberg, eds. *Banana Wars: Power, Production, and History in the Americas*. Durham, NC: Duke University Press, 2003.

Sullivan, Matt. "Adelante Initiative Receives Major Funding." *Bonsucro* (blog). September 30, 2019. https://bonsucro.com/adelante-initiative-receives-major-funding.

Swezey, Sean, and Daniel Faber. "Disarticulated Accumulation, Agroexport, and Ecological Crisis in Nicaragua: The Case of Cotton." *Capitalism Nature Socialism* 1, no. 1 (1988): 47–68. https://doi.org/10.1080/10455758809358358.

Taussig, Michael T. *The Devil and Commodity Fetishism in South America*. Chapel Hill: University of North Carolina Press, 1980.

Taussig, Michael T. "Reification and the Consciousness of the Patient." *Social Science and Medicine. Part B: Medical Anthropology* 14, no. 1 (1980): 3–13. https://doi.org/10.1016/0160-7987(80)90035-6.

Thomas, Deborah A. "Time and the Otherwise: Plantations, Garrisons and Being Human in the Caribbean." *Anthropological Theory* 16, no. 2–3 (2016): 177–200. https://doi.org/10.1177/1463499616636269.

Thompson, E. P. "The Moral Economy of the English Crowd in the Eighteenth Century." *Past and Present*, no. 50 (1971): 76–136.

Thompson, Vikki, Dann Mitchell, Gabriele C. Hegerl, Matthew Collins, Nicholas J. Leach, and Julia M. Slingo. "The Most At-Risk Regions in the World for High-Impact Heatwaves." *Nature Communications* 14, no. 1 (2023): 2152. https://doi.org/10.1038/s41467-023-37554-1.

Tironi, Manuel. "Hypo-interventions: Intimate Activism in Toxic Environments." *Social Studies of Science* 48, no. 3 (2018): 438–55. https://doi.org/10.1177/0306312718784779.

Tittor, Anne. "The Changing Drivers of Oil Palm Cultivation and the Persistent Narrative of 'Already Degraded Land': Insights from Nicaragua." *Journal of Rural Studies* 74 (February 2020): 271–79. https://doi.org/10.1016/j.jrurstud.2020.01.003.

Torres, Sylvia. "'Mujeres que no se dejan': Resistencia étnica y género en Sutiaba, Nicaragua (1950–1960)." *Revista de Historia—IHNCA*, no. 11–12 (January 1998): 81–98.

Tousignant, Noémi. *Edges of Exposure: Toxicology and the Problem of Capacity in Postcolonial Senegal.* Durham, NC: Duke University Press, 2018.

Trouillot, Michel-Rolph. "Making Sense: The Fields in Which We Work." In *Global Transformations: Anthropology and the Modern World*, edited by Michel-Rolph Trouillot, 117–39. New York: Palgrave Macmillan, 2003. https://doi.org/10.1007/978-1-137 -04144-9_7.

Trouillot, Michel-Rolph. "North Atlantic Universals: Analytical Fictions, 1492–1945." *South Atlantic Quarterly* 101, no. 4 (2002): 839–58.

Tsing, Anna Lowenhaupt. *The Mushroom at the End of the World: On the Possibility of Life in Capitalist Ruins.* Princeton, NJ: Princeton University Press, 2015.

Tsing, Anna Lowenhaupt. "On Nonscalability: The Living World Is Not Amenable to Precision-Nested Scales." *Common Knowledge* 18, no. 3 (2012): 505–24. https://doi.org /10.1215/0961754X-1630424.

Tsing, Anna Lowenhaupt. "Supply Chains and the Human Condition." *Rethinking Marxism* 21, no. 2 (2009): 148–76. https://doi.org/10.1080/08935690902743088.

Tsing, Anna Lowenhaupt, Andrew S. Mathews, and Nils Bubandt. "Patchy Anthropocene: Landscape Structure, Multispecies History, and the Retooling of Anthropology: An Introduction to Supplement 20." *Current Anthropology* 60, supp. 20 (2010): S186–S197. https://doi.org/10.1086/703391.

Tuck, Eve. "Suspending Damage: A Letter to Communities." *Harvard Educational Review* 79, no. 3 (2009): 409–28. https://doi.org/10.17763/haer.79.3.n0016675661t3n15.

Vargas-Cetina, Gabriela. "Anthropology and Cooperatives: From the Community Paradigm to the Ephemeral Association in Chiapas, Mexico." *Critique of Anthropology* 25, no. 3 (2005): 229–51. https://doi.org/10.1177/0308275X05055210.

Vaughn, Sarah E. "The Political Economy of Regions: Climate Change and Dams in Guyana." *Radical History Review* 2018, no. 131 (2018): 105–25. https://doi.org/10.1215 /01636545-4355157.

Verisk Maplecroft. "Heat Stress Threatens to Cut Labour Productivity in SE Asia by Up to 25% within 30 Years—Verisk Maplecroft." *Verisk Maplecroft Website* (blog). October 28, 2015. https://www.maplecroft.com/insights/analysis/heat-stress-to-cut-labour -productivity-in-30-years.

Walker, Thomas W. *Nicaragua: Emerging from the Shadow of the Eagle.* New York: Routledge, 2019.

Walker, Thomas W., and Christine J. Wade. *Nicaragua: Living in the Shadow of the Eagle.* Boulder, CO: Westview, 2011.

WE-Adelante Research Team. "The Adelante Initiative: Bringing the Sugarcane Industry Forward." La Isla Network, 2018.

Wei, Clarissa. "Climate Change Is Already Killing Farm Workers around the World." *KCET* (blog). May 11, 2017. https://www.kcet.org/shows/earth-focus/climate-change -is-already-killing-farm-workers-around-the-world.

Wei, Clarissa. "The Silent Epidemic behind Nicaragua's Rum." *Vice Munchies* (blog). November 27, 2015. https://www.vice.com/en/article/qkxv7v/the-silent-epidemic -behind-nicaraguas-rum.

Weizman, Eyal. *Hollow Land: Israel's Architecture of Occupation*. London: Verso Books, 2012.

Welker, Marina. *Enacting the Corporation: An American Mining Firm in Post- authoritarian Indonesia*. Oakland: University of California Press, 2014.

Wells, E. Christian, and Linda M. Whiteford. "The Medical Anthropology of Water and Sanitation." In *A Companion to Medical Anthropology*, edited by Merrill Singer, Pamela I. Erickson, and César Abadía-Barrero, 160–79. Hoboken, NJ: Wiley Blackwell, 2022. https://doi.org/10.1002/9781119718963.ch9.

Wells, Miriam J. *Strawberry Fields: Politics, Class, and Work in California Agriculture*. Ithaca, NY: Cornell University Press, 1996.

Wesseling, Catharina. "Is an Environmental Nephrotoxin the Primary Cause of CKDu (Mesoamerican Nephropathy)? CON." *Kidney360* 1, no. 7 (2020): 596–601. https://doi .org/10.34067/KID.0002922020.

Wesseling, Catharina, Aurora Aragón, Luisa Castillo, Marianela Corriols, Fabio Chaverri, Elba De La Cruz, Matthew Keifer, et al. "Hazardous Pesticides in Central Amer- ica." *International Journal of Occupational and Environmental Health* 7, no. 4 (2001): 287–94. https://doi.org/10.1179/107735201800339236.

Wesseling, Catharina, Marianela Corriols, and Viria Bravo. "Acute Pesticide Poisoning and Pesticide Registration in Central America." *Toxicology and Applied Pharmacology* 207, no. 2, supp. (2005): 697–705. https://doi.org/10.1016/j.taap.2005.03.033.

Wesseling, Catharina, Jason Glaser, Julieta Rodríguez-Guzmán, Ilana Weiss, Rebekah Lucas, Sandra Peraza, Agnes Soares da Silva, et al. "Chronic Kidney Disease of Non- traditional Origin in Mesoamerica: A Disease Primarily Driven by Occupational Heat Stress." *Revista Panamericana de Salud Pública* 44 (January 2020): e15. https://doi.org /10.26633/RPSP.2020.15.

Weston, Kath. *Animate Planet: Making Visceral Sense of Living in a High-Tech Ecologi- cally Damaged World*. Durham, NC: Duke University Press, 2017.

Wheelock, Jaime. *Imperialismo y dictadura: Crisis de una formación social*. 3rd ed. Mexico City: Siglo Veintiuno Editores, 1978.

White, Luise. *Speaking with Vampires: Rumor and History in Colonial Africa*. Berkeley: University of California Press, 2008.

White, Richard. *The Organic Machine: The Remaking of the Columbia River*. New York: Macmillan, 1996.

Whitington, Jerome. "Fingerprint, Bellwether, Model Event: Climate Change as Specula- tive Anthropology." *Anthropological Theory* 13, no. 4 (2013): 308–28. https://doi.org/10 .1177/1463499613509992.

Whitmarsh, Ian. "Medical Schismogenics: Compliance and 'Culture' in Caribbean Biomedicine." *Anthropological Quarterly* 82, no. 2 (2009): 447–75. https://doi.org/10 .1353/anq.0.0060.

Whitmarsh, Ian, and Elizabeth F. S. Roberts. "Nonsecular Medical Anthropology." *Medical Anthropology* 35, no. 3 (2016): 203–8. https://doi.org/10.1080/01459740.2015.1118099.

Whitmee, Sarah, Andy Haines, Chris Beyrer, Frederick Boltz, Anthony G. Capon, Braulio Ferreira de Souza Dias, Alex Ezeh, et al. "Safeguarding Human Health in the

Anthropocene Epoch: Report of the Rockefeller Foundation–Lancet Commission on Planetary Health." *Lancet* 386, no. 10007 (2015): 1973–2028. https://doi.org/10.1016 /S0140-6736(15)60901-1.

Whyte, Susan Reynolds, Michael A. Whyte, Lotte Meinert, and Jenipher Twebaze. "Therapeutic Clientship: Belonging in Uganda's Projectified Landscape of AIDS Care." In *When People Come First: Critical Studies in Global Health*, edited by João Biehl and Adriana Petryna, 140–65. Princeton, NJ: Princeton University Press, 2013. https://doi .org/10.1515/9781400846801-008.

Widger, Tom. "Anti-hesitation." *Anthropology of This Century*, no. 18 (January 2017). http://aotcpress.com/articles/antihesitation/.

Wilson, Bradley R. "Breaking the Chains: Coffee, Crisis, and Farmworker Struggle in Nicaragua." *Environment and Planning A: Economy and Space* 45, no. 11 (2013): 2592–609. https://doi.org/10.1068/a46262.

Winchell, Mareike. *After Servitude: Elusive Property and the Ethics of Kinship in Bolivia*. Oakland: University of California Press, 2022.

Winchell, Mareike. "Economies of Obligation: Patronage as Relational Wealth in Bolivian Gold Mining." *HAU: Journal of Ethnographic Theory* 7, no. 3 (2017): 159–83. https://doi.org/10.14318/hau7.3.011.

Wolf, Eric R. "Specific Aspects of Plantation Systems in the New World: Community Subcultures and Social Classes." In *Pathways of Power: Building an Anthropology of the Modern World*, edited by Eric Wolf, 215–29. Berkeley: University of California Press, 2001.

Wolford, Wendy. *This Land Is Ours Now: Social Mobilization and the Meanings of Land in Brazil*. Durham, NC: Duke University Press, 2010.

Woods, Ngaire, and Amrita Narlikar. "Governance and the Limits of Accountability: The WTO, the IMF, and the World Bank." *International Social Science Journal* 53, no. 170 (2001): 569–83. https://doi.org/10.1111/1468-2451.00345.

Wool, Zoë H. "in-Durable Sociality: Precarious Life in Common and the Temporal Boundaries of the Social." *Social Text* 35, no. 1 (2017): 79–99. https://doi.org/10.1215 /01642472-3728008.

Wool, Zoë H., and Julie Livingston. "Collateral Afterworlds: An Introduction." *Social Text* 35, no. 1 (2017): 1–15. https://doi.org/10.1215/01642472-3727960.

World Bank. "Nicaragua—Climatology." Climate Change Knowledge Portal, 2023. https://climateknowledgeportal.worldbank.org/country/nicaragua/climate-data -historical.

Wylie, Sara Ann. *Fractivism: Corporate Bodies and Chemical Bonds*. Durham, NC: Duke University Press, 2018.

Wynter, Sylvia. "Novel and History, Plot and Plantation." *Savacou*, June 1971, 95–102.

Wynter, Sylvia. "Unsettling the Coloniality of Being/Power/Truth/Freedom: Towards the Human, after Man, Its Overrepresentation—an Argument." *CR: The New Centennial Review* 3, no. 3 (2003): 257–337.

Yates-Doerr, Emily. "Reworking the Social Determinants of Health: Responding to Material-Semiotic Indeterminacy in Public Health Interventions." *Medical Anthropology Quarterly* 34, no. 2 (2020): 378–97. https://doi.org/10.1111/maq.12586.

Yi Dionne, Kim. *Doomed Interventions: The Failure of Global Responses to AIDS in Africa*. New York: Cambridge University Press, 2017.

Yusoff, Kathryn. "Indeterminate Subjects, Irreducible Worlds: Two Economies of Indeterminacy." *Body and Society* 23, no. 3 (2017): 75–101. https://doi.org/10.1177/1357034X17716746.

Zelaya, Feliz. "Causas de la Enfermedad Renal Crónica en la Población Laboral del Ingenio San Antonio, Chinandega, 2000–2001." Universidad Nacional Autónoma de León, 2001.

Zigon, Jarrett. *"HIV Is God's Blessing": Rehabilitating Morality in Neoliberal Russia*. Berkeley: University of California Press, 2011.

Zubrin, Robert. "In Defense of Biofuels." *New Atlantis* (blog). 2008. https://www.thenewatlantis.com/publications/in-defense-of-biofuels.

Index

Page numbers in italic indicate figures and tables.

eGFR (glomerular filtration rate), 67, 121, 184n48

Elinoff, Eli, 60, 172n8

embankments, 68–69, 74, *75*, 78, 82, 83

end-stage renal disease (ESRD), 130–31, 136, 139, 143–44, 146

environmental health: about, 8, 104, 165n8; kidney function/disease, 66–67, 68, 82, 83, 179n32; renal health, 66–67, 68, 82, 83, 179n32; violence/structural violence, 62, 64, 78, 177n26; workers/working conditions, 68, 176n8. *See also* air quality; forest resources/deforestation; soil/soil condition; water availability/quality

environmental justice, 15, 96, 104, 154–55. *See also* AMBED (Asociación Montelimar Bendición de Dios); human rights (social justice)

epidemic, 96, 180n39, 180nn42–44. *See also* CKDnt (chronic kidney disease of nontraditional causes) and epidemic

ESRD (end-stage renal disease), 130–31, 136, 139, 143–44, 146

ethical obligations/moral economy: about, 18, 109, 156, 167n50, 181n58; dialysis treatment/bus service to clinics, 141–42, 144; ex-workers, 110, 112, 120, 121, 123, 135; haunting, 12–13; human bodies and health, 56, 57, 73, 77–78; monoculture, 12–13, 77, 166n39, 166–67n43; Montelimar Corporation, 12, 29–30, 40–41, 73, 112; NSEL, 29–30, 31–32, 112; patrons/patronage systems, 12, 13, 112, 133; plantation agriculture, 125; social security systems, 116; state agencies, 40–41; World Bank/IFC, 24, 29, 149

ethnographic collaboration, 3, 4, 24, 92–93, 168n8, 180n33

Executive Decree 42, 52

ex-workers: ASOCHIVIDA, 31; dialysis treatment/bus service to clinics, 2, 130; ethical obligations and, 110, 112, 120, 121, 123, 135; nonplantation alternatives, 107–9, 156

fair trade status, 32, 50–51, 166n36, 170n28

Farman, Abou, 168n55

farms/farmers. *See* medium/large farms/farmers; small farms/farmers

fired workers. *See* ex-workers

floods and flood control, 30, 68, 69, 71, 79–80, 81, 140. *See also* waterways and water availability/quality

forest resources/deforestation: about, 4, 5, 19; climate change, 46; heat and heat stress hypothesis, 46, 54; Ministry of Agriculture and Forestry, 16, 28, 108; monoculture, 46, 48, 49; sugarcane industry, 5, 24, 60; water availability/quality, 61

Fortun, Kim, 15, 42, 126, 167n52, 170–71n36, 177n18, 181n46

fragility: INSS, 119, 120–21, 126; waterways and water availability/quality, 71, 176n11, 177n33;

workers/working conditions, 10, 97, 127, 177n33, 180n44

Francis, Hilary, 49, 172n22

FSLN (Frente Sandinista de Liberación Nacional), 50–51, 115, 116–17

fungibility: women/women's work, 72, 177n15; workers/working conditions, 11, 18, 24, 72, 132, 141, 145, 149

futures: haunting and helicopter crop-dusting, 157–58, 166n29; imagine futures, 151, 153; nonplantation alternatives, 108, 109, 156; sugarcane industry/monoculture, 49, 81, 124, 157–58; workers/working conditions, 12, 38, 43, 67, 111, 114

garden plots. *See* subsistence gardens/plots

Gibson-Graham, J. K., 183n16

Glaser, Jason, 91

global health: CKDnt and, 7, 52, 92; critical approach, 56, 174n53; digital media and toxic mediation, 98, 181n47; genre and, 92, 179n23; health projects and, 56, 174n53; sugarcane plantations, 11, 166n36. *See also* planetary health

glomerular filtration rate (eGFR), 67, 121, 184n48

glyphosate ("ripener"): about, 9, 59, 91; helicopter crop-dusting, 9, 60–61, 91, 99–100, 102, 156, 157; temporalities, 95–96, 180n34; water availability/quality, 62, 175n78; well water, 60, 61, 76–77; workers, reduction of, 60–61, 156

Gould, Jeffrey L., 12, 182n2

grace, 33, 34, 42, 43

Graeber, David, 123, 125, 184n48

Grandin, Greg, 172n17

grievances/grief and plantation patienthood, 135, 139, 140–41, 142, 145, 148, 185n14, 186n25. *See also* corporate grievance mechanisms

Guevara Jerez, Francisco A., 152–53

Günel, Göçke, 57

Guthman, Julie, 5–6, 111, 184n52, 185n7

Han, Clara, 177n33

Haraway, Donna, 172n7

haunting: AMBED and name as, 33, 43; ethical obligations/moral economy, 12–13; helicopter crop-dusting, 8–10, 157–58, 166n29

health and human bodies. *See* human bodies and health

health care systems: about, 5, 17–18, 118; Ministry of Health, 40–41, 118–19, 121, 123, 130, 138; temporalities, 125, 144. *See also* INSS (National Institute of Social Security)

health clinics: INSS, 8–9, 35, 91, 118–19, 129, 130, 131, 134; Ministry of Health, 118–19, 121, 123, 130, 138; Montelimar Corporation, 121, 132. *See also* bus service to clinics; dialysis treatment; health care systems; hemodialysis treatment

planetary health: about, 3–5, 8; climate change, 47, 170–71n36, 172n8; critical approach, 18–20, 168n55; edges and, 19–20, 158, 168n57; futures, 153–54; human bodies and health, 4, 5, 7, 18, 66, 155–56; workers/working conditions, 5–6, 7, 18, 55, 66, 165n8. *See also* air quality; forest resources/deforestation; global health; soil/soil condition; water availability/quality

plantation agriculture: about, 7, 12, 118, 183n30; cotton production, 48, 49, 50, 115, 116, 131–32; ethical obligations/moral economy, 12–13, 125, 166–67n43; floods and flood control, 71, 81; futures, 152; human dying and death, 131, 132, 185n14; kin/kinship, 58, 114; numbers (números), 114–15, 116, 117, 118, 121; open systems, 15, 167n52; seasonal labor, 5, 12, 51, 63, 114, 115, 117; Somoza era, 11, 48, 52–53; subsistence gardens/plots, 30, 48, 63, 103–4; toxic substances/toxicity, 4, 6, 46. *See also* agrochemicals/pesticides; ethical obligations/moral economy; helicopters and crop-dusting; management practices; monoculture; nonoccupational (común) condition; occupational (laboral) condition; sugarcane plantations

plantation patienthood: about, 131, 185n4; cabra (informal laborers), 142–43, 145; fungibility, 132, 141, 145; grievances/grief, 135, 139, 140–41, 142, 145, 148, 185n14, 186n25; quality of life, 144, 145, 186n39; violence/structural violence, 141, 142. *See also* plantation agriculture

Povinelli, Elizabeth A.: embankments, 68–69, 78, 83; epidemic narratives, 180n43; exhaustion, 141, 186n32; knowledge production, 165n24, 169n12; peasant studies, 183n17; toxic mediation, 178–79n13

Puar, Jasbir, 156

Rabinbach, Anson, 54

racialized differences/inequality: heat and heat stress hypothesis, 57–58, 173–74n52, 174n64, 174n66; monoculture, 6, 10–12, 58, 166n32, 174n66. *See also* Indigenous people

renal health, 66–67, 68, 69, 82, 83, 179n32. *See also* kidney function; kidney function/disease; urine/urination

reproductive labor (laundry, washing, and cleaning): about, 78, 96; AMBED/Montelimar Corporation internal grievance mechanism, 72, 73, 74, 176n13; atmospheric fix/homework, 47, 171n5; irrigation systems, 74, 75; politics and water, 75–76, 177n22; water availability/quality, 60, 71–74, 94–95, 175n74. *See also* women/women's work

"ripener." *See* glyphosate ("ripener")

Ripoll, Santiago, 116

Roberts, Elizabeth F. S., 170–71n36

Roberts, Jody, 41–42, 104

Rockefeller Foundation–*Lancet* Commission on Planetary Health, 153

Rosenberg, Charles E., 96, 98, 103

Rottenburg, Richard, 168n55, 174n53

Ruiz Arias, Manuel Israel, 111–12, 119–20, 182n6, 182n15

Sandinista movement, 12, 23, 48, 50–51, 79, 116, 148

Sandino, Augusto César, 23–24, 48–49

Scaramelli, Caterina, 176n12

Scheper-Hughes, Nancy, 166–67n43, 177n28, 185n14

Shapiro, Nicholas, 41–42, 104

Sims, J. Marion and family, 13, 167n45–46

small farms/farmers: about, 91, 136, 182n2; chicken farms, 107–8, 111, 126; Indigenous people, 26, 48, 49–50; NSEL and grievances, 28, 30; Somoza era, 49–50, 114, 115, 116. *See also* medium/large farms/farmers

Smith, Homer William, 7

social justice (human rights), 19, 112, 118, 126–27, 141, 166n36, 187n12. *See also* environmental justice

social responsibility. *See* ethical obligations/moral economy

social security, 109, 114–15, 116, 117, 125, 184n52

social security systems, 109, 111–12. *See also* INSS (National Institute of Social Security)

soil/soil condition: about, 9, 10; CAO grievances, 31, 32–33; erosion, 3–4, 5, 51, 75, 79; toxic substances/toxicity, 16, 28, 50, 51, 59, 74, 83, 86

Solomon, Harris, 135

Somoza Debayle, Anastasio, 12, 48, 78, 113, 115

Somoza Debayle, Luis, 115

Somoza era: agrochemicals, 50; atmospheric condition, 50; cotton production, 48, 50; farms/farmers, 49–50, 114, 115, 116; forest resources/deforestation, 46, 48, 49; Green Revolution, 52–53, 59, 78, 91; industrial agriculture, 11, 48, 51, 52–53; INSS benefits, 50, 113, 114, 115, 117, 133, 182n15; irrigation dams, 78–79; modernity/development, 49, 58, 113, 115; Sandinista movement, 12, 23, 79; "smell of insecticide" as "smell of Nicaragua," 47–48, 50, 61, 172n22; subsistence gardens/plots, 48, 52; toxic substances/toxicity, 47–48, 50, 51, 58, 61, 172n22; United States and, 48, 172n17

Somoza García, Anastasio: assassination, 49, 115; cotton production, 49; INSS benefits, 50, 133; Montelimar plantation/mill, 12, 51, 79, 82, 113, 115; sociopolitical alliances, 48–49, 50. *See also* Somoza era

Special Law 364, 51–52

Starosielski, Nicole, 173n41

Stengers, Isabelle, 170–71n36

subsistence gardens/plots: about, 18, 51; Indigenous people, 26, 48; plantation agriculture, 30, 48, 63, 103–4; plot as term of use, 103, 181n56; Somoza era, 48, 49; water availability/quality, 59, 60

subsistence gardens/plots and helicopters/crop-dusting: about, 10, 103–4; crisis/epicrisis, 87–88, 178n3; digital photographs, 89, *90*, 90–91; research and presentation, 102; toxic substances/toxicity, 86, 87–88, 99–101, 178n10. *See also* subsistence gardens

sugarcane industry: diabetes, 1–2; FSLN, 51; futures, 49, 81, 124, 157–58; IFC loans, 52; industrial agriculture, 11, 28, 35, 52–53; liability limitations, 58, 110, 112, 120, 133, 146; mechanization, 149–50; profits, 10, 16, 19–20, 58, 135, 173n31; water availability/quality and waterways, 70–71. *See also* agrochemicals/pesticides; heat and heat stress hypothesis; irrigation dams; irrigation systems; monoculture; workers

sugarcane plantations: forest resources/deforestation, 5, 24, 60; global health, 11, 166n36; human bodies and health, 11, 12, 24, 109, 156; kidney function/disease, 7, 165n24; land (knowledge of the ground), 24, 168n5; management practices, 11, 57–58, 174n64; water availability/quality, 2, 5, 9, 40, 41, 42, 81, 177n33; white privilege and wealth, 13, 167n45–46. *See also* agrochemicals/pesticides; helicopters and crop-dusting; monoculture; plantation agriculture; soil/soil condition; sugarcane industry; workers

sugarcane zone (zona), 19, 20. *See also* plantation agriculture; sugarcane industry; sugarcane plantations

Taussig, Michael T., 184n48
Thomas, Deborah, 101, 103
Tironi, Manuel, 14, 74, 172n7, 175n78
toxic mediation: about, 17, 89, 178–79n13; edges and, 89; environmental health, 104; tree curtains, 85–86, 88, 89, 100, 178n10. *See also* indexicality and toxic mediation
toxic substances/toxicity: about, 2, 4, 6–7, 10, 178n4; Bolaños family, 51–52, 173n31; children and, 61, 102, 103; dehydration/rehydration, 58, 59; dying/death and, 10, 95, 96, 133; ecological systems, 93, 179n32; epidemiological research/documentation, 53, 105–6; FSLN bans, 50–51; heat and heat stress hypothesis, 54, 173n41; industrial agriculture, 46, 91, 179n17; laws/legal adjudication, 42, 50–51, 111, 112; Nemagon (dibromochloropropane [DBCP]), 51–52, 179n18; nonhumans, 94–95, 96, 97, 98–99, 100; "smell of insecticide" as "smell of Nicaragua," 47–48, 50, 61, 62, 172n22; soil/soil condition, 16, 28, 50, 51, 59, 74, 83, 86; storytelling, 88–89, 96; subsistence gardens/plots, 86, 87–88, 89,

99–101, 178n10; temporalities, 95–96, 97, 180n34, 180n37; thin description, 97, 180n44; water quality tests, 104–5, 181n61. *See also* glyphosate ("ripener"); helicopters and crop-dusting; indexicality and toxic mediation; toxic mediation

trade and economy, 32, 49, 50–51, 52, 166n36, 170n28

transportation to clinics. *See* bus service to clinics
Tropical Storm Nate, 69–70, 77, 79
Tsing, Anna, 166n36, 170–71n36, 183n30

United States: ASOCHIVIDA, 28, 30, 31–32, 41; crisis/epicrisis, 178n3; investment strategies, 58; Pacific coast and military forces, 23–24, 48, 49, 50, 115; petrochemical industry, 50, 51, 176n8; workers/migrant workers, 111, 125–26, 175n5, 176n8

urine/urination: kidney function, 65–67, 68, 82, 83, 110, 175n5; political ecology and, 82–83; renal health, 66–67, 68, 69, 82, 83, 179n32; urinalysis, 67–68, 175n5. *See also* kidney function; kidney function/disease

Van Zandt, Townes, 186n25
Vaughan, Tyson, 60, 172n8
Vaughn, Sarah, 79
violence/structural violence: bus service to clinics, 136, 185n21; cotton production, 131–32; crisis/epicrisis, 87–88, 178n3; environmental health, 62, 64, 78, 177n26; human bodies and health, 89, 96, 124–25; INSS, 112, 118, 123–24, 127, 184n48; media and toxic mediation, 92, 179n30; necropolitics, 132, 133, 135, 149; plantation patienthood, 141, 142; racial and gendered violence, 10–11, 166n32

washing. *See* reproductive labor (laundry, washing, and cleaning)
water, rest, and shade protocol, 55–58, 63, 173–74n52, 174n53, 174n64, 174n66
water availability/quality: about, 3–4, 16, 118; CAO grievances, 30, 32–33; climate change, 6, 46; dehydration, 53, 58–59, 63; ethical obligations/moral economy, 77–78; forest resources/deforestation, 61; futures, 152–53; glyphosate ("ripener"), 62, 175n78; heat and heat stress hypothesis, 53, 54, 58–59; hemodialysis treatment, 80; hydration, 60, 80–81, 83; laws, 74, 77; rehydration, 59; reproductive labor, 60, 175n74; subsistence gardens/plots, 59, 60; sugarcane plantations, 2, 5, 9, 40, 41, 42, 81, 177n33; water quality tests, 77, 104–5, 181n61; water sharing, 74–76, 177n22; women/women's work, 59, 60, 61, 62, 63, 175n74, 175n78. *See also* irrigation dams; irrigation systems; well water

www.ingramcontent.com/pod-product-compliance
Lightning Source LLC
Chambersburg PA
CBHW020702270326
41928CB00005B/223